KU-588-667

S.P.Q.R.

University of Liverpool
School of Archaeology, Classics & Egyptology
12-14 Abercromby Square
Liverpool L69 7WZ

Tel: 0151-794 2659
Fax: 0151-794 2442

S.P.Q.R. is the abbreviated form
(often found on Roman coins) of
Senatus PopulusQue Romanus,
the Senate and People of Rome.

'This day in the Duke's chamber, there being a
Roman story in the hangings, and upon the standards written these four letters S. P. Q. R., Sir G.
Carteret came to me to know what the meaning of
those four letters were ; which ignorance is not to
be borne in a Privy Counsellor, methinks, that a
schoolboy should be whipt for not knowing.'

PEPYS, *Diary*, July 4, 1663.

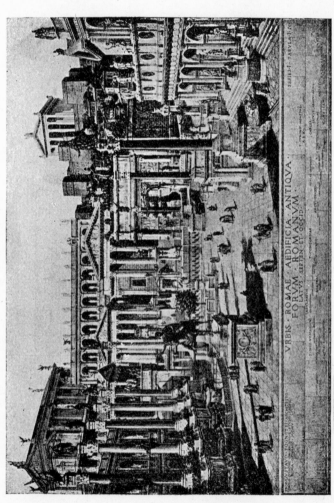

Reproduced from H. Stuart Jones' Companion to Roman History by courtesy of The Clarendon Press.

THE ROMAN FORUM

A reconstruction of the western end of the Forum in the fourth century A.D.   The buildings in
existence in the time of Publius are mentioned on pages 33 and 34.

S. P. Q. R.

THE HISTORY AND SOCIAL LIFE OF ANCIENT ROME

PARTS I, IV AND V
LIFE, LITERATURE AND MYTHOLOGY

BY

E. C. KENNEDY, M.A.

ASSISTANT MASTER AT MALVERN COLLEGE AND SOMETIME SCHOLAR OF
QUEENS' COLLEGE, CAMBRIDGE

PARTS II AND III. HISTORY

BY

G. W. WHITE, M.A.

HEAD OF THE CLASSICAL SIDE IN MALVERN COLLEGE AND SOMETIME
SCHOLAR OF ST. JOHN'S COLLEGE, OXFORD

LONDON
MACMILLAN & CO LTD
NEW YORK · ST MARTIN'S PRESS
1961

*This book is copyright in all countries which
are signatories to the Berne Convention*

First Edition 1944
Reprinted 1947, 1950, 1952, 1953, 1957, 1961

MACMILLAN AND COMPANY LIMITED
London Bombay Calcutta Madras Melbourne

THE MACMILLAN COMPANY OF CANADA LIMITED
Toronto

ST MARTIN'S PRESS INC
New York

PRINTED IN GREAT BRITAIN

PREFACE

OUR purpose in writing this book has been to provide the average boy, who ceases to learn the language when he has passed the School Certificate, with " the knowledge and understanding of such matters as are essential for the intelligent reading of Latin " (to quote the revised syllabus for School Certificate Latin issued by the Oxford and Cambridge Schools Examination Board). We have covered the same ground as we covered last year in our *Roman History, Life and Literature*, but the sections dealing with Social Life, with Mythology and with Literature have been entirely rewritten, while the Historical Sections have been either rewritten or abridged and simplified. The result should not, we think, be beyond the comprehension of the ordinary Middle School boy, and certainly we have had his special needs continually in mind in deciding what to include and what to omit. If we help him at all to gain some understanding of ' the grandeur that was Rome ', we shall be satisfied.

The only books we have consulted in addition to those mentioned in the preface of *Roman History, Life and Literature* are Mr. R. W. Moore's *Roman Commonwealth* and *The Cambridge Ancient History*. For advice and criticism we are most grateful to Professors H. M. Last and A. B. Cook, to Mr. H. W. Flewett, and to our colleague, Mr. R. T. Colthurst.

G. W. WHITE
E. C. KENNEDY

HARROW-ON-THE-HILL,
    May, 1943.

CONTENTS

ix

PART III

THE INTERNAL HISTORY OF ROME TO A.D. 96 FROM MONARCHY TO PRINCIPATE

PART IV

LATIN LITERATURE

PART V

MYTHOLOGY

LIST OF ILLUSTRATIONS

MONS CAELIUS

AGGER SERVII

AMPHITHEATRUM FLAVIUM

Via Appia

Via Latina

III

II

I

A key to the Roman numerals will be found to the right of this plan.

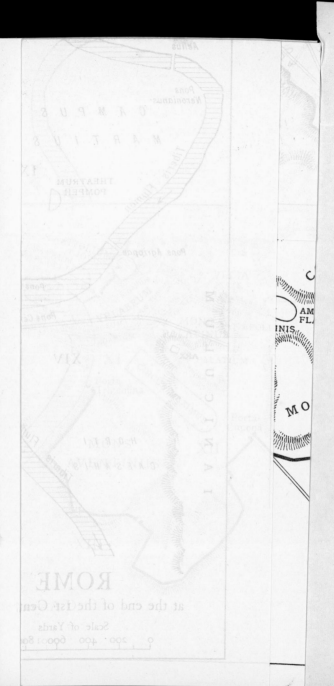

PART I

ROMAN SOCIAL LIFE

CHAPTER I

PUBLIUS CRITONIUS POLLIO

THE Colline Gate at Rome is in the extreme north of the city, and from it the Salarian Way runs north-eastwards to Ancona on the east coast of Italy. Like most of the main roads the Salarian Way is lined with tombs for a few miles from Rome, and near the first milestone on the left of this road, in what later became a vineyard, was discovered the tomb of a boy whose ashes were placed beneath a stone bearing the following inscription [1]:

> P . CRITONIVS P · F POLIO
> MATER · MEA MIHI
> MONVMENTVM
> COERAVIT QVAE
> ME DESIDERAT
> VEHEMENTER · ME
> HEICE · SITVM · IN
> MATVRE VALE SAL
> VE

The spelling of some of the words is unfamiliar, and ME has been repeated by the stone-mason in error. In the usual form the epitaph runs: *Publius Critonius, Publii filius, Pollio. Mater mea mihi monumentum curavit, quae me desiderat vehementer hic situm immature. Vale,*

[1] Corpus Inscriptionum Latinarum, (C.I.L.) I, 2, 1295.

salve. " Publius Critonius Pollio, the son of Publius. My mother, who misses me sadly, set up this monument for me, lying buried here before my time. Farewell and good health."

Nothing is known about the life of this boy, not even exactly when he lived, for these tombstones are not dated, but the character of the lettering puts it at some time in the first century B.C. The name Critōnius, which is the name of the boy's *gens*, or clan, is a ' plebeian ' one ; that is to say, his family was originally of lower birth and had fewer privileges than the aristocratic ' patricians ', though in time the plebeians obtained nearly all the rights of the patricians. It is probable that Publius' father was not a senator but a member of the wealthy middle-class ' equestrian ' order, for the Critonian family is not a well-known one ; the only two members of the family known in history were Lucius Critonius, whose name and likeness appear on a coin of about 85 B.C. when he was an official called ' plebeian aedile ', and another Lucius, perhaps his son, who was aedile in charge of the corn-supply under Julius Caesar in 44 B.C. It is possible that our Publius was the nephew of the younger Lucius.

All we know then is the name and family of Publius Critonius, and that he died young, deeply mourned by his mother. Perhaps it will be justifiable if we make this boy the centre of a sketch of everyday life at Rome, giving him an imaginary home and background which can be filled in with details common to the lives of all boys of his class and time. Remember then that Publius' family circle is fictitious, but that the general facts of life at Rome are accurate. Let us assume that he was born in 31 B.C., the year of the battle of Actium, and died at the age of 14 in 17 B.C. His life thus falls at the end of the Republic and at the beginning of the Empire, during the ' Augustan Age ' when Augustus was laying the foundation of imperial power that lasted for another five centuries; it was a time of peace and prosperity after the civil wars, and also the greatest period of Latin literature, so that it is an era which is perhaps the most interesting and profitable for beginners to study. Let us therefore follow young Publius through some typical scenes in the life of a Roman boy.

CHAPTER II

THE FAMILY—CLOTHES—NAMES—SCHOOL— THE PRIVATE HOUSE—MONEY

IF you look at the plan of Rome facing page 1 you will see a road called Alta Sēmita, or High Street, in the north-west of the city, running up towards the Colline Gate. It is in this road that we will imagine that Publius lives. The other members of the family are his father Publius, after whom the boy is named, his mother Caecilia, who belongs to an old plebeian clan, his brother Titus, who is five years younger than the fourteen-year-old Publius, and his little sister Critonia, now aged seven. There are also about twenty slaves living in the house, several of whom we shall meet later on. The elder Publius is fairly well off, though not a rich man according to the extravagant standards of wealth at Rome, and possesses a comfortable income derived from the ownership of land and from money invested in businesses at home and abroad. He has never gone into politics, being content to leave that to his elder brother, Lucius Critonius, who has held some offices of state and is now a member of the Senate as an ex-magistrate; Uncle Lucius is generally regarded as the head of the family, but he is a bachelor and has made young Publius his heir, being very fond of all his brother's children.

It is one day in June, 17 B.C., and the household, as usual, is starting to get up before dawn, for most of the day's work is done before midday and the badness of the light provided by oil lamps makes it important not to waste the hours of daylight. Publius and Titus share a bedroom and are awakened in good time by their *paeda-*

gōgus, or tutor, an old Greek slave called Daedalus, who has also been tutor to their father. Since the time when they grew too old to have a nurse Daedalus has looked after them continually and has done his best to bring them up to be like their father, though the boys sometimes grow tired of hearing him say, " Now when your father was your age he never used to behave like that ". He is not responsible for their school-education, though he knows quite a lot about Greek and Roman literature and could probably teach them as well as most schoolmasters, but he accompanies them to and from school and, like the other tutors, sits behind the class during lessons.

The boys jump out of bed as soon as they are called, both because they are used to early rising and because it is inadvisable to be late for school. Getting up does not take long, for they only clean their teeth with pow-dered pumice-stone and dip their hands and faces in cold water, knowing that they will have their daily bath before dinner, and they have few clothes to put on. First comes a linen under-garment, like a vest, then a linen or woollen tunic, short-sleeved, belted, and reaching to the knees, and finally the distinctive Roman out-door dress, the *tŏga*. Their legs are bare, and on their feet they wear sandals indoors and leather shoes out of doors ; they never wear hats except occasionally a sun-hat on a journey or when it is very hot.

This morning Daedalus brings them in a clean toga each, for the sweeping folds soon get dirty, especially on schoolboys, and he helps his charges to adjust them in the proper style. Look at the size and shape of the toga as he lays it out on Publius' bed. It is semi-circular, about twelve feet along the straight edge and five feet deep —more of course for a grown-up—and as the Critonii are free-born children they have what is called an ' em-broidered toga ', with a purple band along the straight

edge. When Publius is about sixteen he will lay that
aside and put on the plain white ' manly toga ', which he
will wear all his life unless he becomes one of the higher
magistrates, when he will once more wear the embroidered
gown. Not even Uncle Lucius has attained this honour,
but as a senator he wears a broad purple stripe down the
front of his tunic and a special crescent on his shoes,
while the elder Publius, as a member of the equestrian
order, has a narrow purple stripe on his tunic. Daedalus
has to put Titus' toga on for him, but Publius is fairly
expert at draping it round his body, under the right arm
and twice over the left shoulder, leaving a fold in front
as a pocket and a loose end at the back. " I hate wearing
this clumsy great toga," he says. " I wish we didn't
have to wear it at school all the time." " Yes, but you
must get used to it," replies Daedalus. " When you are
a man you will always have to wear it out of doors and
on official occasions. The toga is the sign of Roman
civilization and one day you will be proud of it."

Before the boys finish dressing, look at the little
circular gold box that each one wears on a string round
his neck. This is called a *bulla* and contains an amulet to
bring good luck. It was presented to them on the ninth
day after birth, when their first name was given them,
and will be worn until they put on the manly toga. Publius
has three names, of which, as is usual at Rome, the first
was given him by his parents, like our ' Christian ' name [1];

[1] There were not many of these to choose from, the most common,
with their abbreviations, being

A. Aulus.	D. Decimus.	M' Mānius.	Ser. Servius.
C. Gāius.	L. Lucius.	P. Publius.	S. or Sex. Sextus.
Cn. Gnaeus.	M. Marcus.	Q. Quintus.	Ti. or Tib. Tiberius.
		T. Titus.	

This name was called the *praenōmen*, the name of the *gens* was the
nomen, the name of the family the *cognomen*, and the fourth name, when
found, the *agnomen*.

the second name, Critonius, is the name of his clan (*gens*) and, like all such names, ends in -ius, while the third, Pollio, is his surname or family name, showing the branch of the clan to which he belongs. He may also acquire a fourth name later on, perhaps in honour of some great exploit, or because he is adopted into another family, or to show another branch of his family.

While the boys are finishing dressing a boy-slave called Giton brings in their breakfast on a tray. This is a light meal, which they sometimes have to eat on the way to school, and consists of bread, honey, cheese, and fruit, with a cup of water or a little wine. The rest of the family may have theirs a little later, but Publius and Titus will be at school till noon and must have it now. The slaves are busy cleaning and dusting the house, and the boys kiss their mother good-bye and hurry off, accompanied by Daedalus and Giton, whose task it is to be the ' satchel-slave ' and carry his young masters' school books in a circular wooden satchel.

The brothers must part when they reach school, for Titus is still at an elementary school, where he stays from the age of seven till about twelve, while Publius is now at the secondary stage of his education under the famous ' grammarian ' Orbilius, where he will remain until he is sixteen and can learn oratory from a ' rhetorician '—skill in public speaking is the chief aim of Roman education —and then perhaps finish his training abroad by studying philosophy at the university of Athens. The two schools are both in the Vīcus Longus not far apart from one another, so Giton attends Publius to Orbilius' *lūdus*, as the Romans rather ironically call it, and Daedalus takes the younger brother to Aper's school.

This is merely one large room, open to the street like a shop, on the ground floor of a tall building. The school-master, a freed slave called Aper, has not yet arrived,

Rhein. Landesmuseum, Trier

A ROMAN SCHOOL

From a funeral monument of the second century A.D. The boy carrying a satchel is explaining to the master why he is late. The other boys are holding papyrus rolls.

though his assistant, Marcus, has taken the shutters down
and is getting the thirty-odd boys into their places. When
Aper arrives there is an instant hush and the boys quickly
settle down on their backless stools, while the master sits
in an armchair on a daïs and the boys' tutors gather for
a whispered chat at the back of the room. The boys are
divided into two classes for reading, Aper himself taking
the older boys, Marcus the smaller ones, including Titus,
who is quite happy playing with a set of little wooden
letters which he puts together under Marcus' supervision
and spells out the syllables of words. Aper's class, however, gets into trouble, for after they have all chanted
some sentences together he calls upon a boy called
Tiberius to stand up and read out of his copy of the old
' Laws of the Twelve Tables '. Tiberius soon goes wrong
and gets a taste of the cane that Aper carries, until the
shouts of the master, the blows of the stick and the
cries of the boy wake up someone who is still asleep in
the house opposite ; he sends his slave in with a polite
message asking for less noise at least until dawn has
broken, for all this time the room has been lighted by
little lamps that the boys have brought with them, so
that their books and writing-tablets are blackened with
soot.

The next lesson is taken by a special teacher of arithmetic called Vindex. You can imagine how hard it is
to do sums in Roman numerals, but constant practice
makes even Titus able to add and subtract on his fingers
or on a wooden frame called an ' abacus ' which has
counters strung on wires across it. The older boys
learn to multiply and divide, and to do fractions and
decimals too, dividing the Roman pound into a hundred
parts and thus working out its fractions. " Subtract
one-twelfth from five-twelfths," orders Vindex. " Can
anyone do it ? Hurry up, Albanus, you ought to have

answered long ago." After a long pause Albanus works
out the sum. "One-third." "Good; you'll be an
excellent business man. Now add one-twelfth to the
original amount." "A half, sir," replies Albanus, and sits
down, thankful that his ordeal is over.

The third and last subject taught at Aper's is writing.
Each boy has a pair of wax tablets, which he rests on his
knee while he writes with a pointed pen called *stilus*,
erasing what he has written when necessary with the
other end, made specially smooth and flat for this purpose.
The older boys write from Aper's dictation in letters
joined together in the 'cursive' or 'running' style, as
we write nowadays, but Titus and his companions are
tracing capital letters from a 'copy' made by Marcus,
who sometimes has to sit beside a boy and guide his fingers
over the wax. He is a kindly soul, and has a stock of
sweets with which to reward the smallest boys, and they
are sorry to leave him and join the loud-voiced Aper who
is so ready with his cane and strap. They spend five years
on reading, writing and arithmetic, so progress is slow and
the work dull. Titus envies his brother at the school of
Orbilius and wishes he were there too.

Publius, however, wishes he were not there, for his
shoulders are aching from a flogging which he received
for being late. When he left Daedalus he did not go
straight to school but went towards the Esquiline Hill to
meet his friend Sextus Licinius, with the result that when
they finally arrived they got a warm welcome. Orbilius
is now an elderly man, for he taught the poet Horace
thirty years ago, and he is the most famous grammarian
in Rome, famous alike for his teaching and his flogging.
He has a better establishment than Aper's, because he
commands the highest fees, though even he is not well
paid, but he can at least teach in a building that is not
open to all the noises of the street. To-day the boys are

reading Homer, at which Publius does well, for he knows Greek perfectly from compulsory conversation in that language with Daedalus. Orbilius specializes in teaching the poets, his favourites being Homer and the early Latin poet Līvius Andronīcus. Publius stands up and recites a piece of Homer without a mistake, so he is restored to favour and is able to enjoy the next lesson, which is on the Roman poet Virgil.

Virgil's *Aeneid* has been published quite recently, and has at once become popular and famous. Orbilius first reads aloud a passage himself and then makes two or three boys repeat it in the proper way. Then he lectures for an hour on the language, mythology, and metre of the book, and finally sets the class an essay on the character of Dido, to be followed by some verses written in Virgilian style on Aeneas' lost wife Creusa. Publius likes Virgil's poems and loves writing poetry himself just as much, so he thoroughly enjoys this part of the morning's work.

During school he manages to whisper to Sextus an invitation to come back home afterwards to see his new puppy, so as soon as Orbilius announces that it is mid-day and that lessons are over, the two friends go off together, followed as usual by Giton and Sextus' tutor ; Daedalus is still at Aper's with Titus, so Sextus sends his satchel-slave there to tell him that the two older boys have gone home. Sextus is not so fond of poetry as Publius is and complains about Orbilius' strap. " I wish we had longer holidays," he says. " Don't you, Publius? " " Well, we don't do badly," replies the other. " We get every eighth day off, when it's market day, five days at the Quinquatrus in March, five days at the Saturnālia in December, besides the public holidays and the hot summer season. Still, I quite agree with you that school is too long when we do dull stuff like geometry and history, though I do like Homer and modern poets such as Virgil and Horace." You must remember that there were no novels or adventure stories in those days and that their place was taken by the legends of ancient Greece and by poetry of all kinds.

The little party has now reached the one-storeyed, whitewashed house in High Street where Publius lives. It does not look like a private house from outside, for all that there is to see is the front door, with a shop on each side, while the sides of the house are blank except for a few small windows high up. Life in a Roman house is centred on the interior and aims at complete privacy, well away from the bustle of the streets.

While the boys are waiting for the porter to open the door Sextus asks about the shops in front. "Does your father own these as well?" "Oh yes," says Publius, "he owns them, of course, but he has let them off and only gets the rent for them. The one on the left is taken by Laenas the corn-merchant, and the other by a perfume-seller called Menippus. I'm not supposed to visit them, but I sometimes slip in and help them keep shop when Daedalus isn't about. Father would be angry if he knew, but I like them and it's fun. But come in now and see Mother and Lydia."

Scaevola the door-keeper has recognized the young master's knock and quickly opens the door to usher the boys through a short vestibule into the hall of the house. Scaevola is a slave from Transalpine Gaul, not a very good-tempered person as a rule, as befits one who has to keep away unwelcome visitors, but he is spared the degradation of being chained to a ring in the wall, like a watch dog, which is how some masters treat their door-keepers. He lives in a little room just inside the inner door, and now welcomes Publius with what is almost a smile, for the boy is always kind to him and likes hearing his tales of his native land and of his adventures as a

Alinari

'BEWARE OF THE DOG'

A mosaic from the floor of the entrance to the vestibule of the ' House
of the Tragic Poet ' at Pompeii.

gladiator, when he lost his right hand in the arena and
earned the name Scaevola, ' Left-handed.'

" Hullo, is that your Lydia? " asks Sextus, pointing to
the picture of a fierce black hound in the tessellated floor
of the vestibule, with " Beware of the dog " written at its

feet. "Well, not exactly," says Publius, laughing, "but Lydia is rather like that, as you'll see in a minute." Once safely past the dog and the almost equally fierce Scaevola Sextus sees another inscription, this time *salvē*, 'welcome', on the floor of the *ātrium*. This is the chief room of a Roman house and is a large oblong hall surrounded by six or eight bedrooms, one of which is shared by Publius and Titus. There is a square opening, called the *compluvium*, in the tiled roof, to let in the rain, which is caught in a marble basin, the *impluvium*, in the middle of the floor ; four pillars support the roof, one at each corner of the *compluvium*. The floor is tessellated and partly covered with thick rugs, but the only furniture is a few chairs and stools, all made of wood inlaid with ivory or silver, with a small table, some richly decorated lamp stands and a few bronze and marble statuettes which the elder Publius has brought back from a visit to Greece. The walls are painted with gaily coloured scenes representing the four seasons, and the household gods and a serpent, the ' genius ' of the house, are also depicted on the walls ; when the sun is shining, as it usually does in Rome, the hall provides a cool and pleasant change from the noise and bustle of the streets.

Publius' mother is sitting in a high-backed chair, the recognized seat of the mistress of the house, and welcomes her son's guest. " I'm glad to see you looking so well, Sextus. Have you come to play with Publius' new puppy? She's in the peristyle, Publius, with Critonia, but don't start her barking, because Father is working in his study." " All right, Mother, I'll keep them both quiet. Come on, Sextus," and he leads his friend past a little recess in which the portrait masks of any members of the family who have been distinguished in the past are kept—in this family Publius' grandfather, Lucius, is the only ancestor of note—through a short passage beside which is the study, *tablīnum*, of the master of the house, and so into the peristyle, a delightful garden with a shady colonnade all round it and more bedrooms opening off it. On one side is the dining-room, *triclīnium*, and beyond the peristyle are the bathrooms, kitchen quarters and a side entrance, near which is the family hearth, the centre

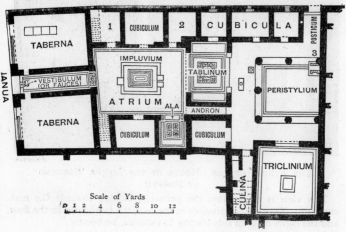

PLAN OF THE TOWN HOUSE (*domus*) OF A RICH MAN

This is the so-called 'House of the Tragic Poet' at Pompeii, which was built a few years before the destruction of the town by Vesuvius in A.D. 79. At the entrance to the *vestibulum* was the famous *Cavē Canem* mosaic, shown on page 13. The room marked 1 was the porter's room, 2 was a store-room, and at 3 was the *larārium*, or domestic shrine. The *Cubicula* were bedrooms, the *culīna* the kitchen, the *iānua* the front door, with shops (*tabernae*) on each side, and the *postīcum* was a side entrance.

of domestic worship, where the figures of the Household Gods are kept.

In the garden of the peristyle a fountain is playing in a small pool containing gold-fish, and beside it sits Publius' old nurse, Pullia, now in charge of his little sister Critonia, who is dividing her attention between a family of dolls, a

Anderson

THE ATRIUM OF THE 'HOUSE OF THE SILVER WEDDING'
AT POMPEII

This view is taken from the peristyle, looking towards the main
entrance. Note the *compluvium* in the roof, the *impluvium* in the floor,
and the doors on each side leading to *cubicula*, bedrooms.

house which she is making out of wooden bricks, and a
fat black puppy. Critonia and Lydia the puppy run to
welcome Publius, and the sound of their voices and the
barking of the dog as they play together soon bring out
the elder Publius from his study, though apparently he
is not at all unwilling to be disturbed and does not intend
to act the part of the stern 'Roman father', who in
theory has the power of life and death over his family
and used to be regarded with awe by his children. "Good-
morning, Sextus. I hope you've had a good day at
school with 'The Flogger', as we used to call old Orbilius
when I was a boy. Are you going to the Field of Mars
this afternoon with Publius for some exercise before the

Anderson

THE PERISTYLIUM OF THE ' HOUSE OF THE SILVER WEDDING '
AT POMPEII

This is an open garden surrounded by a colonnade. Between the
two pillars in the left background can be seen the entrance to the
atrium, for there does not seem to be the usual *tablinum*, study, between
the atrium and the peristyle.

baths? " " Yes, sir," answers Sextus, " and we're going
to have a game of odd-and-even before I go home to
lunch."

There are two varieties of this game, both very simple,
one consisting of guessing whether your opponent is
holding an odd or even number of nuts or pebbles in his
hand, while in the other method, which is still played in
Italy to-day under the name of ' mora ', both players have
to extend any number of fingers they like at the same
time and one of them guesses whether the total number of
fingers held out is odd or even. After they have had a
few rounds of both kinds of game Titus arrives back from
school with Daedalus and Sextus' tutor, who has come to

take his charge home to lunch, but first the boys must decide which is to come to the other's house to fetch him on his way to the Field of Mars, in the afternoon. " Let's toss up," suggests Publius. " I've got a *dēnārius* of grandfather's in my purse. You call, Sextus. Heads or ships?" Sextus calls ' ships ', but the silver coin, a little larger than a sixpence, comes down with the head of the goddess Cĕrēs uppermost and the ' tail ' side underneath, which in this case is the figures of two men seated on a bench ; one of them is Publius' grandfather, as the letters L . CRI show, and the boy is very proud of the coin and collects as many of this type as he can.

" You come here, then, and fetch me, Sextus," he says. " By the way, Father, why do we call ' ships ' when there are no ships on our coins? " His father explains that the old copper coinage of the Republic had the head of a deity on one side and the prow of a ship on the other, and the custom of calling ' heads or ships ' has persisted, although this coinage has not been issued for about seventy years. Romans were very short of small change in consequence of this, he says, until a few years before this time, when Augustus allowed the senate to issue brass and copper coins with his head on one side and S.C., standing for *senatus consulto*, ' by decree of the senate ', on the other.

The denarius that Publius has just tossed up is the chief silver coin in use. It is worth just under a shilling in modern money, but its purchasing power is much greater, and it is equal to sixteen of the copper coins called *asses*. The denarius at first had the head of the goddess Roma on one side and Castor and Pollux on horseback on the other, but types referring to the families of officials who struck the coins soon appeared on both sides, like this coin of Critonius, and portrait heads of famous people like Julius Caesar, Pompey and the emperors are of great interest. Gold coins, called *aurei*, also have these portraits. Sums of money are usually expressed in sesterces ;[1] the *sestertius* (silver in the Republic, brass under the Empire) contains 4 *asses* and is therefore equivalent to a quarter of a denarius. A sesterce is worth 2d.-2½d., and a thousand sesterces about £9.

[1] To express large amounts in sesterces is so awkward that various abbreviations are used. Thus HS VIII is 8 sesterces ; HS $\overline{VIII}$ is 8,000 sesterces ; and $\overline{HS}$ $\overline{VIII}$ is 800,000 sesterces. HS stands for IIS, i.e. 2½, because a sesterce was originally 2½ *asses* when the denarius contained 10 *asses*. Copper was first minted perhaps in 269 B.C., and silver in 187 B.C. L. s. d. stands for *librae*, pounds, *solidi*, later Roman gold coins, and *denarii*, wrongly translated as pence.

CHAPTER III

EXERCISE—THE BATHS—DINNER

SEXTUS now goes off home, and the Critonian family have their light midday meal, called *prandium*, consisting of cold meat, vegetables, bread and wine, in the garden of the peristyle. After lunch the parents have their usual siesta, or afternoon nap, while Titus and Critonia get out their white mice, harness them to a little cart that one of the slaves has made for them, and try to drive them round the atrium, though not very successfully, since the mice are frightened by the yelps of Lydia, who wants to join in the fun, and has to be held firmly by Giton. Publius is eager to be off, and keeps looking at the sun-dial which stands beside the fountain in the garden. The Roman day is divided into twelve equal ' hours ', which vary in length according to the time of sunrise and sunset, so that only the end of the sixth hour, at noon, is the same every day. Most people are content to tell the time roughly from the sun, though a question frequently heard is *quota hora est?* ' what time is it? ' It is past the seventh hour when Sextus at last arrives, full of apologies for being so late. He says that the slave boy in charge of the water-clock, which works on the same principle as an hour-glass, forgot to reverse the machine when the water had run through to the bottom compartment, so that is why he is behind time.

The two boys hurry off to the Campus Martius, or Field of Mars, the open space in the bend of the Tiber where athletic sports are held. Here there are scores of young men and boys indulging in all kinds of exercise, running, jumping, riding, wrestling, and throwing the discus or javelin. Our two friends first join a group of boys who are throwing the discus, at which Publius excels, for though he is not so tall as Sextus he is well-built and muscular. Sextus can beat him in a sprint, but does not possess enough staying power to keep up with Publius in a race to the Theatre of Pompey and back, after which both boys are ready for a plunge in the yellow Tiber. Publius is tired after his long run and is content to splash about near the bank of the swift-flowing river, but Sextus swims right across and back again without a rest, ' a regular Horatius ' as the others call him. The two boys then lie on the bank sun-bathing until Publius says that he must go off to the baths, where he has promised to meet his father in good time. Like most well-to-do families, the Critonii have their own bathrooms and hot-water system at home, but the men-folk as a rule prefer to go to the public baths.

The bath is one of the chief events in the daily routine of every Roman, and the public baths are elaborate buildings which contain gymnasia, reading-rooms, and lounges, besides the luxurious apparatus of a Turkish bath. They are the customary meeting-places for friends, and, like the barbers' shops, are the places in which to pick up the latest gossip. To-day the two boys go to their usual bathing-establishment at the foot of the Esquiline, where they find Publius' father in the gymnasium playing a game of ball with two of his friends ; they stand in a triangle and throw three balls to one another in quick succession. In another part of the room some elderly gentlemen are playing with a large, light ball, while else-where two teams of players are taking part in a game something like net-ball. The boys are invited to join in by the elder Publius, but they say that they are tired by their exercise and prefer to watch the others until they have finished.

B

The entrance fee to the baths is the nominal sum of one *quadrans*, the smallest copper coin, less than a farthing ; Publius is given his *quadrans* every day after lunch by his father or Daedalus. The boys hand over their coins to the door-keeper and follow the elder Publius into the changing-room, where they undress and give their clothes to the attendant, who knows them well and always has a cheery word for them as regular clients. The first stage of the baths is the warm room, which is heated from below by hot air circulating in the ' hypocaust ', a hollow space under the floor where it is supported on a number of short pillars. Here the boys sit on a bench and perspire, until it is time to go into the hot room, which contains a pool of hot water for them to sit in while an attendant pours cold water over them at intervals. " More cold water, please," requests Publius. " I'm dying of heat. Are you going into the very hot room, Sextus, just next to the furnace? I'm not. Let's have the cold plunge at once to get cool." So they have another swim in the swimming-bath, which is very like the big pool in the Roman baths at Bath, and then dry themselves and go to the massage-room for the most important part of the cere- mony, the ' rub-down ' with oil by an expert masseur.

There are several of these attendants in the room, each one pummelling and pounding away at his victim, who lies flat on a high couch and submits to the treatment which will leave him feeling delightfully fresh and vigorous, with all his muscles toned up for the rest of the day. Publius falls to the lot of a burly negro, a slave like all the bath attendants, who first anoints him liberally with olive oil and then rubs the oil well in for the next ten minutes. This part of the operation is quite pleasant but if you have any superfluous flesh the masseur then apparently does his best to remove it, as the groans and complaints of the portly old gentleman on the couch next to Publius seem to imply. But the rubbers ignore all protests, knowing well that their clients will come back again to-morrow for the same treatment and will give them a nice tip now and then if they do their work properly. After the massage is finished Publius is rubbed down with a metal ' scraper ' called a *strigil*, which removes any excess of oil and leaves his flesh firm and glowing with health. He then receives a final rub-down with a towel and returns to the changing-room, where he dresses again and waits in the lounge until his father is ready. Sextus has already gone home, and Publius passes the time by watching two men playing a game called *latrunculi*, which is played with counters on a board and is something like draughts.

At last his father appears and says they must go home to dinner. The time is getting on for the ninth hour, about 3 p.m. by our clocks, and though some dinners will have started more than an hour ago it is considered a sign of self-indulgence and greed to dine so early in the day. " Daedalus told me that there is a dinner party to-day, Father. Who is coming? " " Only a few of the family, to celebrate the engagement of your cousin Quinta to young Aulus Papirius. There'll be those two, of course, Aulus' parents and your Aunt Calpurnia, that's five, Uncle Lucius, Mother and I." " But that's only eight. Who is the ninth? " " A young man called Publius Critonius Pollio, provided that he behaves himself and goes off to bed as soon as the tables are cleared." " Oh, Father, can I really? " cries Publius, greatly excited at the prospect of his first real dinner party. " What fun it'll be! "

As soon as he reaches home Publius rushes in to find Caecilia. " Mother, Mother, I'm coming to the party to-night. Did you know? " " Yes, dear. I've told Daedalus to put out a nice blue dinner-tunic for you.

Go and find him and get dressed at once ; the guests will
be here soon." Publius changes as soon as he can and
hurries into the dining-room to look at the tables, where
the steward, Habinnas, is putting the finishing touches to
the flowers. " What's for dinner to-night, Habinnas? "
he demands. " Something nice, I hope." " Here's the
menu, young master," replies the steward, who has an
important position as head of the household and is
responsible for over-seeing the work of all the male slaves,
Caecilia herself looking after the women and girls. He
reads from a piece of papyrus on which the cook, a Greek
slave who cost a large sum of money, has written down the
various courses.

" *Hors d'œuvres*.	Lettuce, radishes, fish-pickle, eggs.	
Dinner.	Roast kid, meat balls, sprouts.	
	Chicken and ham, asparagus.	
Dessert.	Apples, pears, grapes, raisins.	

There, Master Publius, I hope you approve of that.
Pollux wanted to serve a much more elaborate meal, like
some of those that he used to cook for his last owner,
but the Master said that it was to be an informal family
party, and that everything must be simple but good.
Listen, there's the front door ; the guests are arriving, and
you must be in the hall to receive them."

A footman announces the names of the visitors, and
after a few minutes' conversation in the atrium the party
is ushered into the dining-room, where Habinnas shows
them to their places. Round three sides of a square
table—the fourth is left open for service—are placed the
three couches, each of which, like the dining-room itself,
is called a *triclīnium* ; each couch (*lectus*) has three places,
so that the usual number of a party is nine, though sometimes a place or two is left vacant in case the guest of
honour wishes to bring one or two uninvited guests, who

are called his 'shadows' and whose task it is to laugh at
his jokes and flatter him.

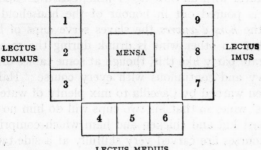

The chief guest to-day is of course Uncle Lucius, who
is given the 'consular place', no. 6 on the plan, on the
right of the middle couch; the other two places on his
couch are filled by Quinta and her fiancé, Aulus; on the
left hand or 'highest' couch are Aulus' parents, with
Publius' Aunt Calpurnia in between them, while the host,
the elder Publius, is next to his brother at no. 7, on the
right-hand couch, next to him is Publius' mother, and
Publius himself takes no. 9, the 'lowest' place on the
'lowest' couch. The couches are made of wood inlaid
with ivory, and are covered with a mattress and brightly
coloured coverlets, with a cushion on which each diner
rests his left elbow as he reclines on his side in the
fashion universal in Greece and Rome. Like everyone
else, Publius takes off his slippers for dinner, and he feels
very proud as he waits until the guests have settled
themselves and then takes his place beside his mother;
he looks very smart in his new blue dinner-tunic.

Habinnas is in general control of the meal, though each
diner has a slave to wait on him alone; the boy Giton
is allotted to serve Publius, who winks at him when no
one is looking. Conversation is general during dinner,

which is called *cēna*, though Publius is careful to remember his manners and speak only when he is spoken to. The meal starts with an offering of wine, called a ' libation ', which is poured out in honour of the household gods. After the *hors d'œuvres* the slaves serve cups of honey-wine, but no other wine is drunk during the meal at a temperate party like this, though at some tables drinking is heavy and continuous with every course ; Habinnas has been warned by Caecilia to mix plenty of water with Publius' wine, so that his two cups will do him no harm. The roast kid and chicken and ham which comprise the main courses are carved very skilfully at a side-table by a trained carver called Carpus, but once a diner has been served he has to eat with a spoon or, more often, with his fingers, so that Giton and the other waiters are kept busy handing finger-bowls and napkins all through the meal.

The last part of the meal is dessert, called the ' second tables ' because the tables are taken away and replaced by fresh ones. Publius has thoroughly enjoyed every mouthful of food and every word of the conversation ; but he feels sorry when the fruit is cleared away and a big mixing-bowl full of wine is placed on the table, for this means that the *cōmissātio*, or drinking party, is about to begin, when he will have to say good-night to the visitors and withdraw. But his pretty cousin Quinta and Uncle Lucius put in a plea that he should stay long enough to drink the healths of the betrothed pair, so to his great delight he is given half an hour longer at table.

The slaves crown each diner with a garland of roses and place a wine-cup and a silver ' dipper ' on the table before them. But first the party must appoint a ' master of ceremonies ', to decide how much wine is to be drunk and in what proportion it is to be mixed with water, for the Romans practically never drink wine ' neat '. The usual way is to throw dice and see who has the highest

throw, called 'Venus', when all four of the knuckle-bones
that serve as dice turn up with different numbers. Here
Publius has a brain-wave and quotes a line of Horace,
the author whom he likes best, and some of whose Odes
he knows by heart.

> *Quem Venus arbitrum*
> *Dicet bibendi ?* (Odes, ii. 7, 25).

"Whom will Venus appoint as master of ceremonies ?" he
enquires just as his uncle is rattling the dice. "Bravo,
Publius," cries Uncle Lucius, "so you too are an admirer
of Horace, like me. To-morrow you shall go to the shop
of the Sosii and buy the best edition of any book of his
that you like."

When they have all thrown the knuckle-bones it turns
out that Aulus and Publius have both made the highest
throw, but since Publius must soon retire he gives up his
position to Aulus, who at a hint from his father prescribes
three parts of wine to nine of water, the usual mixture
when the drinking is not going to be excessive. Aulus
now has the right to declare how many dippers of wine
each person shall put into his cup and how many cups the
party shall drink, and though it is sometimes the fashion
to drink the health of a guest in as many cups as he has
letters in his three names, Aulus does not intend to spoil
his engagement party with drunkenness, so he merely
prescribes that Quinta's health shall be drunk with five
dippers of wine. Publius' turn comes last, and after
saying *Bene tibi, Quinta*, "Good health to you, Quinta,"
he drains his cup at a draught in the approved fashion.
His mother then tells him to call for his slippers and ask
permission to retire, so after saying good-night to everyone
he leaves the table, where the drinking party will last for
perhaps an hour or so longer, though sometimes it might
continue till midnight or later.

It is now past sunset, and Daedalus, who is waiting for him in the hall, tells him that he must go to bed at once and take care not to disturb Titus, so he undresses quickly by the feeble light of an oil-lamp, blows out the lamp and is soon asleep, tired out by the many activities of the day. The sound of the guests' departure does not disturb him, but at about midnight he is woken up by the noise of a scuffle in the side-street just outside his window. It is a late reveller going home alone by the light of a candle which he carries himself, for there are no street-lamps at all at this time, when he is suddenly accosted by a footpad with a demand for his money. The man raises a shout of " Help! Police! " and is luckily rescued by a band of the firemen who have recently been appointed by Augustus to patrol the streets at night in order to help extinguish the many fires that break out in the jerry-built houses of the city and also to prevent such little incidents as these. The disturbance rouses more than one household in the neighbourhood, and some windows are thrown open to reveal the heads of curious or indignant citizens ; one of them, a woman, is so annoyed at being woken up that she empties her slop basin from the top floor of a block of flats on to the heads of the street-party below, drenching footpad, victim and police impartially. This is an unpleasant experience that may befall anyone walking the streets at night, and is generally not prefaced by any word of warning. Publius listens with great interest to the scuffle and the cries of disgust, and quickly falls asleep again as soon as the excitement has died down.

CHAPTER IV

THE SEVEN HILLS—BOOKS—THE FORUM— STREET SCENES

THE next day is one of the market days that occur at intervals of eight days, so that there is no school and Publius and Titus can do what they like. They do not get up quite so early this morning, though as usual scarcely anyone stays in bed after the sun has risen, and after breakfast Publius' father asks him if he would like to accompany him to his banker in the Forum, calling in at the booksellers on the way to buy the present that Uncle Lucius promised to give him. Publius loves walking about the town with his father, so the two set off together to see the sights and do their shopping.

First of all they climb the Quirinal Hill, where they stand for a few minutes looking southwards at the city, which extends down to the banks of the Tiber ; the area enclosed by the walls of Servius Tullius is roughly diamond shaped and is about two miles from north to south and a mile across at its broadest part. The other six hills, none of which is more than 200 feet high, are clearly visible, though all are now covered with houses except the Palatine, where Augustus has his imperial palace, and the Capitoline, where stands the great Temple of Jupiter, Juno and Minerva. In the north of Rome, besides the Quirinal, is the Viminal ; to the south are the Caelian and the Aventine ; to the east is the Esquiline ; in the centre the Palatine ; and to the west the two slopes of the Capitoline Hill, one the sacred Capitol and the other the citadel which, as Publius has often heard in legend and history lesson, the cackling of geese saved from an attack by the Gauls nearly four hundred years before. From this spot on the Quirinal Publius can get an excellent idea of what his favourite poet [1] calls " the smoke and wealth and roar of Rome ", the city which has a population of over a million and which is the capital of the empire that includes all the civilized western world.

Publius and his father then walk down the Vīcus Longus, through the rather disreputable Subūra and into the district called Argīlētum, where several booksellers have their shops, including the famous firm of the brothers Sosii. " Let's look at the names of the books advertised on the door-posts first, shall we? " suggests Publius. " Oh, good, they've got Horace as well as dozens of other authors I've never even heard of." They enter the shop and are received by a slave-assistant, but the elder Sosius recognises Publius' father, whom he has met once or twice before, and emerges from the office in which he is doing the accounts. " Good-morning, gentlemen. What can I show you to-day? " he asks. " My son here wants to buy a book of Horace. Will you show him what you've got, please? " Sosius goes to one of the pigeon-holes with which the walls of the shop are lined, each pigeon-hole containing a circular wooden bookcase, and glances at the titles written in red ink on the slips of wood or parchment attached to the projecting ends of the long narrow rolls.

Publius wants the Third Book of the Odes and is told that there are several copies of it in stock. " Here's a cheap one at three denarii, better ones at five, and an *édition de luxe* that's a bargain at seven denarii. It's a lovely little book," says Sosius; "it was specially produced to be a presentation copy. Look at the quality of the papyrus and the beautifully clear writing—one of my best copyists did that. Have a look at all of them before you

[1] HORACE, *Odes*, III, 29, 12.

decide." So Publius first of all unties the little thongs with which the ordinary books are fastened and inspects them, but his eyes keep straying to the more expensive one which is kept in a smart purple parchment jacket. Then he takes it out of its jacket and holds it in his right hand, unrolling it as he reads and rolling it up again in his left hand. It is about 8 inches wide and when unrolled would be nearly 15 feet long; the writing is in columns $3\frac{1}{2}$ to 4 inches wide, with a space at top and bottom and a margin between columns. It is all in capital letters, with very little in the way of spaces between words and punctuation, but Publius is used to reading very badly written books and this is in a particularly clear hand. He is determined to have it and asks his father if it is too expensive for Uncle Lucius to give him—seven denarii is quite a large sum for a Roman schoolboy, equivalent in silver to about six shillings, but worth far more in purchasing power—and is relieved when the elder Publius hands over the money to Sosius and gives him the book to tuck under his arm.

" Perhaps you would like to see how these books are produced," suggests Sosius. " Come and have a look round the copying-room," and he leads the way into a large room at the back where more than twenty slaves are hard at work. " The pith of the Egyptian papyrus reed is cut into thin strips, which are soaked in Nile water and put down in two layers, the upper one at right angles to the lower. They are then glued together and the sheets so formed are laid side by side and joined with glue to make a roll up to 35 feet long and up to 10 inches wide. We import various qualities of papyrus—those slaves near the door are finishing off a roll of the best quality by giving it a smooth surface with pumice stone and an ivory polisher. At this end of the room my overseer, a freedman, is dictating one of Cicero's speeches to a dozen copyists to make cheap mass-produced books, but those four men at the other end are skilled craftsmen who take great pains to write a beautiful hand ; one of them wrote out your Horace."

Publius watches the work with great interest. One of the highly trained scribes has just finished copying out the poems of Catullus ; he has been using a reed pen dipped in ink made of soot and lamp-black, and he has a pen-knife on his desk and a sponge with which to erase mistakes. He now calls another slave, who cuts off the written portion from the rest of the roll and takes it into the next room, where he treats the back of the papyrus with cedar-oil to protect it against moths. When it is dry he colours the top and bottom edges with vermilion and glues to each end of the roll an ivory stick fitted with ornamental knobs, round the right-hand one of which the papyrus is tightly rolled. He then attaches to the upper knob of this stick a slip of parchment bearing the title of the book written on it in red ink, fastens the roll with thongs, and finally inserts it into a coloured parchment case, for this one also is an expensive copy ; when opened it presents a very attractive appearance with its pale yellow papyrus. It is not easy to read these books continuously and almost impossible to refer to a particular passage, but the Romans are used to these disadvantages.[1] " I'd like to have this Catullus too," says Publius. " I'll try to save up to buy it later on," and after thanking Sosius for showing him round he follows his father along the Argiletum, past the Temple of Jānus, whose gates are kept shut only in times of peace, perhaps

---

[1] Parchment, which was heavier and more durable than papyrus, did not come into general use till the third century A.D., when the Christians in particular used it in the form of a *cōdex*, i.e. sheets folded and stitched together like a modern book.

signifying that the god has not gone out to war, and so into the Fŏrum Rōmānum.

Publius' father has business to transact with one of the bankers whose offices stand at the north side of the Forum, and he tells Publius to stroll about for half an hour and see the sights while he himself is busy. The boy has often been here before and knows all the buildings, but he always finds it interesting to watch the people who throng this place, the heart of Rome and consequently of the Empire, and the centre of administration, law and oratory. One of his favourite spots is the ' Golden Milestone ' which Augustus has recently placed in the south-west corner of the Forum ; this is a many-sided block of stone which has inscribed on it the distances in miles to all the important towns in Italy, and Publius likes to imagine himself travelling along the Roman roads to the places whose names he sees written on this stone.

What is the appearance of the Forum as Publius stands here gazing at the crowd? The Market Place proper is a rectangular open space about 100 yards long by 40 yards wide, though with its surrounding buildings it is about three times as large ; it is paved with great blocks of stone and contains statues of famous generals and statesmen, and all round it are built imposing temples, lawcourts and business offices. On the western side, close to where Publius is now standing, he sees the Temple of Saturn, which is also the public Treasury, and the Temple of Concord, while behind them rise the Public Record Office and the slope of the Capitoline Hill. Behind him, on the long southern side, is a Hall of Justice, called the Basilica Iulia after Julius Caesar, and the huge Temple of Castor and Pollux ; the Sacra Via, or Sacred Way, along which triumphal processions pass, and which is now the fashionable promenade of the city, runs along this side of the Forum, starting at the foot of the Esquiline and leading up to the Temple of Jupiter on the Capitol. On the northern side is the Cūria, or Senate House, in which Publius can see that a meeting of the Senate is taking place, next to it the Argiletum with the Temple of Janus, past which he has just come, while at the eastern end is the Temple of Julius Caesar, and behind it, outside the Forum proper, is the circular Temple of Vesta and the House of the Vestals.   Publius here has the good luck to see an interesting and unusual sight, for the chief Vestal on her way home happens to meet a criminal who is being dragged off to execution.   The man falls on his knees and begs for mercy, and the Vestal learns from the officer in charge that there is some doubt about the man's guilt, so she exercises her ancient privilege of pardoning any malefactor who meets her by chance in the city. Publius' father has missed this incident, and Publius gives him a graphic account of all that has happened when he re-appears from his banker's office.

Their next port of call is in the Forum Boārium, or Cattle Market, near the river.   This place is named after its original function, but is no longer exclusively, or even mainly, devoted to it, any more than are the other streets that take their names from the trades that used to be carried on in them, like the Street of the Sandalmakers or the Street of the Perfume-sellers.   It is now the middle of the morning and business is at its height, so that Publius has to cling firmly to his father's arm to prevent himself from being swept away in the crowd.   Romans, both free and slaves, naturally predominate in the streets, but people from every province of the Empire, Gauls, Greeks, Jews, Syrians, Egyptians and Numidians, can be seen either intent on business or gazing at the gleaming temples and rich men's houses that stand close to grimy cook-shops and ramshackle apartment houses inhabited by scores of families, while the Tiber flows foaming under the bridges on which beggars crouch asking for alms.

Publius plies his father with questions as they make their way through the narrow streets which are often thick with mud. They find it hard to remain on the footpath both because of the crowds and because shopkeepers have laid out their goods on tables in booths that project over the pavement, or even on the pavement itself, while a barber is actually shaving a man in the street, brandishing his razor in dangerous fashion. Publius has a hearty laugh at the man's discomfiture when a mad dog rushes down the street and compels the barber to skip back into his shop, leaving his customer to escape as best he can. Just then the crowd parts and leaves a way clear for one of the consuls, attended by his twelve lictors with their bundles of rods and axes, on his way from the Senate House to his home on the Aventine. Publius looks at him with awe and wonders if he will ever attain to such a position. Then the mob closes up again and eight sturdy slaves carrying on their shoulders a rich lady in a litter have to fight their way through the press of shoppers, soldiers, priests, slaves, hawkers and sellers of sulphur matches from across the Tiber. Ordinary wheeled traffic is forbidden till nightfall, Publius learns from his father, to save even more pressure in the crowded streets, which are seldom more than twenty-five feet wide in the main thoroughfares and elsewhere are merely narrow alleys, but wagons carrying stone for public buildings are allowed in the daytime; a meeting between one of these and the long train of a funeral procession causes still more delay, and Publius is gladder than ever to have his father with him to save him from being jostled too roughly by the mob.

After finishing his business in the Cattle Market Publius' father turns homewards again, but this time they go past the Circus Maximus, where many conjurors, jugglers and fortune-tellers have their ' pitches ' and deceive the credulous, and across the Sacred Way between the Esquiline and the Palatine Hills. Here a religious procession is on its way through the Forum and up to the Temple of Jupiter, and while they wait to let it pass Publius and his father gaze curiously at the Palace of Augustus on the Palatine to see if they can get a glimpse of the emperor. He is nowhere to be seen, but another of the great men of Rome, Maecēnas, Augustus' chief adviser, chooses this moment to walk from his house on the Esquiline on a visit to Augustus ; he is quite plainly dressed and is accompanied by only two friends and two footmen. Now comes Publius' great thrill. Among the dandies who are strolling down the Sacred Way his father points out to him a short, bald-headed, rather stout middle-aged man with a very charming expression on his face. " That's the poet Horace," he whispers. Publius cannot help standing still and staring at the famous poet, who notices the look of admiration on the boy's face and stops to ask him his name. " I am Publius Critonius," he says, swelling with pride, " and I have just bought a copy of the Third Book of your Odes, sir, which I think are the finest poems in the world." Horace smiles and lays his hand in a friendly way on his young admirer's shoulder before continuing on his usual saunter through the city.

While they are walking through the Subura a man darts out of a wine-shop and down the street, hotly pursued by the portly proprietor shouting " Police! stop thief! " He soon comes back empty-handed and explains to the elder Publius that another of his flagons has been stolen by a customer. " I lost one only last month," he complains, " and put up that notice in the shop-front offering a reward, but it's no good." The notice says :

VRNA AENIA PEREIT DE TABERNA
SEI EAM QVIS RETTVLERIT
DABVNTVR HS LXV.

" A bronze flagon has been stolen from a shop.   If anyone
returns it he will receive 65 sesterces." [1] Publius asks
what will happen to the thief if he is caught, and is told
that the man will probably be branded with the letters
FVR, ' thief ', on his forehead.   The shopkeeper goes on to
say that sometimes a ' man of three letters ', as these
branded thieves are called, becomes rich and wishes to
hide the proof of his early indiscretion by letting his hair
grow long over his forehead, or even by having a shield
made of wax to look like his skin to wear over the scars,
but he may be given away by an awkward accident at
the wrong moment, so that he becomes a general laughing-
stock.

At last Publius arrives home and begins to give his
mother and Titus a full account of his morning's adventures, showing them his new Horace, which rouses great
admiration.   Caecilia tells him to be sure to go and thank
his uncle after lunch, and the meal is served while he is
still describing the scene at the wine shop.

[1] 16 denarii, about 13s. 6d.   This advertisement was found at Pompeii; C.I.L. iv. 64.

CHAPTER V

SLAVES AND FREEDMEN—AN APARTMENT HOUSE—CLASSES OF SOCIETY

ONE afternoon some weeks later, while Publius is sitting alone in the peristyle reading, Scaevola the door-keeper announces that Milo, the freedman who is in charge of an apartment house belonging to the family, has come to go over the accounts with his employer. After he has finished his business Milo is invited by the two senior members of the household, Habinnas and Daedalus, formerly fellow-slaves with him, to stay for a chat about old times, and Publius suggests that they should sit in the sunny garden and make themselves comfortable, so that he can listen to their conversation. Milo obtained his freedom two years ago, and Daedalus asks him how he enjoys being a freedman after a lifetime of slavery.

" Oh, it's a splendid feeling," he replies, " even after two years of it, especially to a person like me who has longed for independence all his life. I expect you others have heard the story of my life before, but perhaps you haven't, Master Publius, and you may like to hear it." The boy says he certainly would, so Milo begins to relate his experiences.

" You two have been very lucky, because you have been with this one family for many years, but my lot before Publius' father bought me was a miserable one, and I have had eight different masters. I can't remember my parents, and don't even know if I was born free, but I had to start working hard from my earliest years, with the constant threat of the whip if I was idle. One or two of my owners treated me with some consideration, but I

was unlucky in being sold again as soon as I began to be
happy. For five years I was the slave of a butcher, the
only one he had, so I had to do nearly all the work of the
shop as well as serve the family, and when he got drunk
he used to ill-treat me brutally ; I was half starved too, but
it was no use complaining, because a slave is the chattel
of his master, who can do what he likes to him. I had
no chance of collecting any savings, *peculium* as it is called,
with which to purchase my freedom, and of course as I
was never very long with one master I was not likely to
be released for good service. The only holiday I ever got
was the few days of the festival of the Saturnalia in
December when by old tradition slaves change places
with their masters and are allowed a certain amount of
licence, but the butcher used to take it out of me afterwards, to punish what he called my presumption.

" The biggest household I was in was that of a wealthy
senator who had several hundred slaves. In a house like
that every slave has one special task to do and can generally do no other, and as I had not been trained to any
particular service I was made hall-slave, whose duties were
to sweep out the atrium and keep it tidy. The master
did not even know all his slaves by sight and the control
of them was left to the steward, himself a slave, so if he
was a humane person like you, Habinnas, the household
was happy, but if not the other slaves were very badly
off. Our steward was a bully and we all suffered under
him, but the worst thing of all was when I happened to
stumble and knock against the master while he was
walking through the hall. He lost his temper and ordered
me to be flogged to within an inch of my life and then sent
down to his country estate to work on the land. Country
slaves on big farms are often worse off than town slaves,
for we had to wear chains day and night and sleep in an
underground slave-prison called an *ergastulum*. Four or

five of us planned to escape, but before my turn came the first two were caught and punished terribly ; one of them was branded with F for *fugitīvus*, ' runaway ', and flogged unmercifully, and the other, who had tried to escape before, was crucified before our eyes. I decided not to run away then. I should probably have died from over-work and ill-treatment within a few years, but fortunately my master had some losses and was compelled to sell a hundred slaves to raise some money.

" We were taken off to Rome to the slaves' market in the Temple of Castor, and while I was passing through the streets I had the piece of good fortune that changed my whole life. Your mother, Master Publius, the lady Caecilia, was walking in the Sacred Way when a runaway horse rushed down the street towards her. I managed to catch the beast and stop it before it reached her, and she was kind enough to ask my name and all about me. Next morning your father came and purchased me—I was a miserable specimen and only worth a thousand sesterces [1] —and so I passed into the service of your family. I was very grateful and worked as hard as I could, both at Rome and in the country, and when your father offered us all three our freedom two years ago I accepted it willingly and was made bailiff of his apartment house, which I have been ever since."

" What happens when you are set free? " enquires Publius. " Well, slaves can be ' manumitted ', as it is called, in various ways," says Milo. " Sometimes they are left free in their master's will, or set free informally before friends, but more often master and slave, with several witnesses, appear before the praetor ; the slave kneels and is touched on the head by the praetor's staff, and when he gets up he is free and can wear the leather ' cap of liberty ', like this one of mine. A freedman usually

---

[1] About £9.

takes his former owner's first two names and keeps his own *cognomen*, so I am really Publius Critonius Milo, but everyone calls me just Milo. Most freedmen are grateful to their patrons and do what they can to serve them ; and I am particularly bound to your family for all the kindness I have received from your father and mother."

" Poor Milo," says Publius. " I didn't realize that slaves could be treated so badly. I hope yours was an exceptional case. What about you, Habinnas and Daedalus? Why didn't you accept your freedom when Milo did? "

Habinnas says that if he were anyone else's slave, or had been treated at all badly by his master, he would certainly have bought his freedom with his savings, which are now quite big, or have accepted it when it was offered to him, but that he is content to remain steward to the Critonian family for the rest of his life. " I was born on the estate near Baiae in your grandfather's time, young Master ", he says, " the son of the steward of those days, who as a senior slave was allowed to marry and bring up his children, so I am what is called a *verna*, or home-born slave. I started work by carrying your Uncle Lucius' satchel to school when I was seven years old, and as I grew older I became footman, then butler, and finally steward of the household. I have been very fortunate to have remained in one family all my life, and I am quite satisfied with my position, and do not long for the freedom which I have never had and which could not make me better off than I am now. I think that probably the majority of slaves are well treated and happy, though of course those who were born free usually want to regain their freedom. What do you say, Daedalus? "

" I agree with you that it depends entirely on the consideration that our masters show to us. You have been very lucky and Milo has been very unlucky, while I have had both good and bad fortune. I was born free, the son of a prosperous farmer in the island of Andros in the Aegean, where we had a comfortable farm-house near the sea and were very happy. One day some pirates landed from a neighbouring island—pirates have nearly all been cleared away by now, but forty years ago there were a good many left, in spite of Pompey's campaign [1] against them—burnt our house, which was a long way from the nearest town, killed my father and mother because they tried to resist, and carried off my twin-sister and myself, aged twelve, to be sold as slaves. A dealer bought us from the pirates and shipped us off to Delos, the chief slave market in those days, where we had to stand up on a platform, naked and with our feet whitened with chalk, to show that we were newly enslaved and not guaranteed—trained slaves had a placard round their necks, describing their qualifications. We waited there for hours, being examined and prodded like animals, until we were sold for twenty gold pieces each, because we were young and handsome and might be valuable later on.

" Unfortunately we were not bought together, and in spite of our tears and protests we had to part, and I have never seen my dear Gorgo again, and now never shall. I often wonder what became of the poor girl. One of the great tragedies of slavery is that families are broken up so cruelly.

" My new master was a rich Roman living in Syracuse, who was travelling in Greece when he picked me up. He was quite kind to me and had me trained in Greek and Latin literature to be his librarian and secretary, which is why I know so much about books, Publius. I stayed with him for ten years and was fairly happy, except that I kept worrying about Gorgo, and though my master and

[1] See page 117.

the steward treated me well the lady of the house and her son, a boy of about my own age, often went out of their way to be unkind to me and accused me of doing things that the young master had done, so that I was often punished unjustly.

" Then a terrible thing happened. My master was murdered in the night and of course the slaves were suspected. They won't accept slaves' statements in court except under torture, so we were all racked and tormented to make us confess—I still bear the marks of it to this day—until finally the real murderer, a burglar, was arrested and executed, though too late to save us all from torture and several of us from death as a result. The widow hated me and decided to sell me, so I was put up for sale, this time at five times what I had originally cost, because now I was a highly trained secretary. A friend of your grandfather's was living in Syracuse and knew that Lucius Critonius wanted a secretary, so he bought me for him and sent me to Rome, where I became librarian and after a time tutor to your father and now to you and Titus, besides doing the secretarial work of the family. I didn't accept my freedom when Milo did because I wanted to see Titus finished at school, but after that I hope to become free and perhaps start a publisher's business for your father, where my knowledge of books and literature will be useful. But first I want to go back to Andros and see my old home and perhaps make enquiries about my sister, though it is pretty certainly hopeless to try to trace her after so long."

" I do hope you find her," says Publius, " and make a success of the shop too. Don't freedmen sometimes become very rich? " " Yes, they do," replies Daedalus, " but they have to start young and be very clever business men. Some of them amass huge fortunes and become very powerful. You know, don't you, that Horace is the son of a freedman? His father was a municipal slave at Venusia, in charge of public auctions, and now Horace is the friend of Augustus, though of course the nobles at court despised him for his humble birth at first."

" I must be getting back to work," interrupts Milo. " I've enjoyed this talk very much and hope we shall have another one soon. I wonder if you would like to come and have a look at the apartment house, Master Publius? It'll be yours one day, and you ought to know all about your future property. Perhaps Daedalus will come too and I can show you both round the building."

Publius accepts the invitation eagerly, so after saying good-bye to Habinnas Milo sets off with the boy and his tutor to the district of the Subura, where the property lies. He reminds Publius on the way that the great majority of the population of Rome cannot afford to live in separate houses of their own and have to hire single rooms in one of the huge apartment houses called *insulae* that rise up like islands in the sea of streets. For every private house, he tells him, there are about twenty-five apartment houses, each containing a large number of rooms, in every one of which a single person or a family lives. Milo's *insula* is easily recognizable in the distance among the other buildings that surround it because it has recently been given a fresh coat of whitewash and presents an attractive appearance from the outside with its balconies, climbing plants, and flowers in window boxes.

" The ground floor is all let off as shops, Master Publius," he explains, " except for my own office with my bed-room opening out of it behind. But come in and look round. There are still two vacant rooms to let on the two highest storeys, in fact the workmen are now plastering up a crack that appeared in one of them last week. Your father is most insistent that I should do all repairs without delay, because he doesn't want to have

the place collapsing, like some apartment houses in this
district. I have to look after all that sort of thing for
him, of course, and collect the rents and so on."

" Are these rooms expensive? " asks Daedalus. " No,
not for Rome," replies the other, " but it takes a tidy bit
out of a working man's income, and you can probably buy
a cottage in the country for the rent of one of our better

Reproduced from Kennedy's Martial and Pliny, C.U.P
RECONSTRUCTION OF AN INSULA, OR BLOCK OF FLATS, AT OSTIA

rooms. Come upstairs and see the top-floor room. They
get smaller and less comfortable the higher you go, and
those at the very top are just attics, but they all get let
very quickly." He leads the way up the narrow, almost
perpendicular stairs to the fifth storey and ushers his
guests into a tiny room with sloping ceiling and an attic
window, though it is bright and airy and the walls are
newly whitewashed. A man living alone, or even a young
married couple with a baby, will be quite comfortable in
this little room, though Publius notices at once the two

great drawbacks to this kind of home—absence of adequate heating and water facilities. " Yes, the lodgers all have to go downstairs to fetch their water," explains Milo. " They are lucky to have a fountain laid on to the ground floor, instead of having to go out to the nearest public fountain. They have to carry the slops down too ; no emptying of pails into the street in this house, even at night! Once a tenant does that, out he goes.

" Heating is also a difficulty. You see, there are no fireplaces in these blocks of apartments, so people have to cook on portable stoves and warm themselves with open braziers, both very dangerous and the cause of many fires. I go round every room at sunset, to see that all stoves are out, because I don't want to have this place burnt down, like that *insula* opposite." He walks to the window and points to a house that is just having the finishing touches put to it by the builder. " That block was destroyed by fire last winter. Some careless person went to bed with the brazier still burning, the coals fell out, and the place went up in flames. Three unfortunates on the top floor never heard the alarm and were burnt to death. Alleius Nigidus bought up the site cheap and is now erecting that jerry-built affair opposite. I'm glad that Augustus put a limit of seventy feet on those houses or that one would collapse and perhaps bring us down too. Look, you can see the placard [1] from here. ' To let in the Arriana Polliana apartment house belonging to Gnaeus Alleius Nigidus, from the first of July next, shops with booths attached, and high-class apartment rooms and a private house. Intending tenants should apply to Primus, slave of the owner.' He's built a fine private house on the ground floor behind the shops, and I hear he's already got a good let for it, to say nothing of the forty or fifty separate rooms higher up. But it won't last long ; it'll

[1] This advertisement comes from Pompeii ; C.I.L. iv. 138.

either collapse or be burnt down again, if I know that careless wretch Primus."

That evening before bed-time Publius discusses the question of slavery with his father and asks him about the various classes of society in Rome and the occupations of the people who live in the big apartment houses like the one which he has just visited. His father tells him that a large number of the ten millions who make up the population of Italy, of whom more than a million live in Rome, are slaves or freedmen, and that the free citizens are divided into three classes, the Senatorial Order, the middle-class Equestrian Order, and the common people who form the working and lower classes.

"You know, of course, that the old division into patricians and plebeians [1] has now almost entirely disappeared. After the war against Hannibal the patrician aristocracy of high-born families gave place to an almost equally exclusive aristocracy of senators, to which a man whose family had not previously held political office found it hard to obtain admission. Well, Augustus has now re-modelled the Senatorial Order so that it includes all members of the senate and their families, and a number of others to whom he has given the senatorial privilege of wearing the broad purple stripe on their tunics ; Uncle Lucius belongs to this as a member of the senate, though he has almost retired from public life now. The property qualification is a million sesterces,[2] and senators may not take part in any foreign trade ; their wealth consists of inherited property, in land, slaves and investments. Members of this class hold political and administrative posts under the Emperor, and many of them practise in the lawcourts as barristers, because, as you know, oratory is one of the chief objects of the upper-class education. You will be going to a rhetorician to be trained

[1] See page 140.   [2] About £9,000.

in public speaking when you leave Orbilius, and we hope
that you will have a successful public career."

"Shall I be able to become a senator if you are not
one?" asks the boy. "Yes, certainly. There is nothing
to prevent it, and I very much hope you will. I myself
did not follow your grandfather and Uncle Lucius, who
were both plebeian aediles and members of the senate,
into politics and so I have remained a member of the
Equestrian Order. You have read in history that the
equites originally provided cavalry in war, but the title
has long ago been transferred to the middle classes
engaged in business and finance. We wear this narrow
purple stripe on our tunics, and must possess at least
400,000 sesterces [1] and be of free birth, so you see that
even the richest freedmen cannot become either *equites* or
senators. During the last hundred years members of the
Equestrian Order have been largely engaged in banking
and money-lending, both at home and abroad, in foreign
trade, and as tax-farmers who purchase from the state the
right to collect provincial taxes and make what profit
they can. They are therefore the chief business men
of Rome, and much of the prosperity of the empire
depends on their financial stability, so that they are very
important members of society."

"Are you a business man too, Father?" asks Publius.
"Yes, but only to a small extent," answers his father.
"Most of our income is derived from the estates in
Campania, but I have a fair amount of money invested.
When we went down to the Forum the other day I was
consulting my partner about foreign loans, which bring in
up to 40% because of the high risks they involve, whereas
the interest on money at home is only 5%. But of
course none of us could exist without the efforts of the
ordinary tradesmen and artisans, many of them freedmen,

[1] About £3,600.

who form the bulk of the population of Rome. You have seen how busy the shops are, each one managed either by its owner or by his freedman or slave, and the huge warehouses at the foot of the Aventine contain every kind of commodity ; the chief exports of Italy, most of which go through Rome, are wine, olive-oil and manufactured goods, and the imports are grain, metal, and luxury articles like silk, furs, ivory and perfumes. Besides the shopkeepers, the professions of the common people include schoolmasters, doctors, confectioners, cooks, tanners, fullers, dyers, goldsmiths, jewellers and scores of other trades and crafts.

" Then there is the idle city mob, about 200,000 of them, who live on free distributions of corn and expect a succession of public entertainments ; *pānem et circenses*,[1] " bread and games ", is their continual demand, and they have to be humoured or else there might be a rising. They are really a great problem for the government, but probably many of them really cannot get employment when there is so much slave labour on the market.

" Another feature of life at Rome that you see every day is the ' client ' system. In the old days a plebeian was usually the ' client ', or dependant, of a wealthy patrician, to whom he owed certain obligations, while he could rely on his ' patron ' for support in legal difficulties, sickness, unemployment, and so on. Nowadays this system continues in a different and less beneficial form between any man of rank and riches and his poorer acquaintances. Genuine clients go to call on their patron in the morning before he gets up, to pay their respects and offer their services in return for his assistance and an occasional invitation to dinner, but the morning *salūtātio* is beginning to become a mere formality, and poor men

---

[1] The poet Juvenal, about a century later, uses this phrase in Satires, x, 81.

attach themselves to a rich man merely for what they can get out of him. The patron is flattered by having a large number of these clients, but the relationship between them is quite different from what it used to be and must be having a bad effect on society."

"What income can a man live on in Rome, Father?"
"It depends, of course, on the style in which he lives, but a single man of the middle class would probably have to possess 20,000 sesterces [1] a year, that is, a capital of 400,000 sesterces, the property qualification of an *eques*, invested at 5%, but he would not be able to have many slaves or enjoy much comfort on that income. I know you are anxious to be a senator and perhaps even consul when you grow up, but you needn't worry about money or having to earn your living, though you will have to work hard in other ways to attain your ambition in politics. So make up your mind to do your best in everything you undertake, and I am sure you will be successful. Now say good-night to your mother and go off to bed and dream of your future career. Good-night, Publius."

[1] About £180.

CHAPTER VI

A WEDDING—TRAVEL—LETTERS—A HOLIDAY
AT BAIAE—RELIGION

THE next morning the boys wake up in great excitement,
for not only is this the first day of the holidays but it is
also their cousin Quinta's wedding-day and they have
to play quite an important part in the bridal procession.
They know exactly what to do, but after breakfast their
mother goes over the details for the last time, and tells
them once more what happened at Quinta's betrothal
ceremony, which the boys missed because they were at
school.

" There was a big party at Quinta's house," she says,
" and Aulus and Quinta had to stand up together in front
of their parents and relations. Then Aulus said, ' Do
you promise to marry me? ' to which Quinta replied, ' I
do,' and he gave her a gold engagement ring and a pearl
necklace. If they were both members of a patrician
family they could be married with the old patrician
ceremonies in the presence of the High Priest, the Priest
of Jupiter and ten witnesses, during which they would
sit side by side on two stools covered with sheepskins
and eat a cake of barley, but instead of that they will have
the more usual wedding service that Father and I had
when we were married. I expect Quinta has just laid
aside the embroidered toga of her childhood and is now
dedicating her toys to the Household Gods of the family.
She must be feeling very excited, because she's only
seventeen, not much older than you, Publius, but Aulus
is very much in love with her and I'm sure she'll be
happy. Now we must all go and dress, and try to look

your best, won't you, to be a credit to your pretty cousin."

The boys go off to find Daedalus and soon re-appear dressed in their best clothes, but they have to wait much longer while their mother gets ready, assisted by her maid Nerissa and by the old nurse Pullia. She puts on a pale green silk tunic, much the same shape as those that the boys are wearing, though made of richer material and with a finer finish, and over it a gown reaching to her ankles, short-sleeved, fastened at the shoulder with a brooch and girdled with a gold belt round the waist. Since she is going out of doors she wears a square green woollen cloak, arranged in the same style as a man's toga. Nerissa has taken great pains to dress her hair in the latest style, and she is wearing several valuable rings and jewels. It is nearly a mile to Quinta's house, where the ceremony is to take place, so Caecilia and little Critonia are going in a litter, carried by four slaves, while Publius and his father and brother are content to walk.

Quinta is standing in the atrium of her father's house, ready to receive the bridegroom and guests. She is wearing the traditional Roman wedding-dress, an old-fashioned straight white tunic, fastened round the waist with a woollen girdle. Over this she has a saffron-coloured cloak, and her shoes are also yellow ; her hair is combed into six locks, and on her head she wears a flame-coloured veil, crowned with a wreath of flowers. Soon after the arrival of the Critonian family, Aulus appears, and the ceremony starts with the sacrifice of a ewe. The boys' father here has an indispensable part to play in the rites, for it is he who inspects the victim and declares that the auspices, or omens, are favourable. Ten of the guests now sign the marriage contract as witnesses, and a married woman acts as chief bridesmaid and brings Aulus and Quinta together. They clasp hands and make

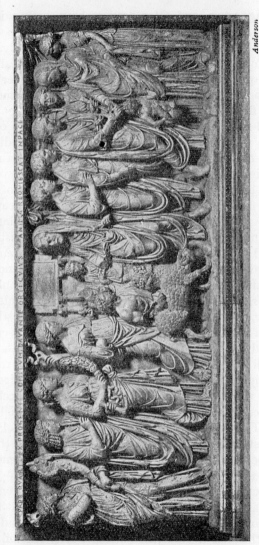

Anderson

Two Scenes at a Roman Wedding

From a sarcophagus of the second century A.D. In the centre the bridegroom is sacrificing a sheep while the bride and her attendants and two boys look on. On the right the bride and bridegroom **are** clasping hands and making their marriage-vows in the presence of their relatives.

their marriage-vows, and after prayers have been said
the religious proceedings are closed by a shout of ' good
luck ' from the guests, in which the boys join heartily.

Now follows a banquet and festivities till nightfall,
when Aulus pretends to tear his bride from her mother's
arms and leads her through the streets to their new home.
First come flute-players and torch-bearers, playing and
singing old-fashioned wedding-songs and calling on
Hymen, the god of marriage ; then Titus walks proudly
by himself, carrying a hawthorn torch and leading the
way for Quinta, who is being escorted hand in hand by
Publius and another boy, while Aulus scatters nuts among
the crowd ; finally the rest of the party brings up the rear.
When they reach Aulus' new home on the Esquiline,
Quinta anoints the door-posts and decks them with wisps
of wool, and is lifted over the threshold by her husband
to avoid making an unlucky stumble. She then stands
in the atrium, faces Aulus and repeats the old formula
ubi tu Gaius, ego Gaia, " wherever you are, I shall also
be," and he receives her with the elements of domestic
life, fire in a brazier and water in a basin. More prayers
are said, and the guests then depart, being reminded that
they are all coming to another banquet given by the
newly married pair on the next day. The boys are tired
out by the time they get home and Titus can scarcely
keep his eyes open, so they are glad to tumble straight
into bed. The banquet to-morrow is for grown-ups only,
so they must go and say good-bye to their cousin in the
morning, because they are going off for the summer
holidays on the day after.

Like most well-to-do Roman families the Critoni
generally leave the city and spend the hot and unhealthy
summer months in the country or at the sea-side.
Publius' father has a villa just outside Baiae, ten miles
from Naples and near his country estate and farms, and

he has arranged for himself, his wife and children to travel in a heavy and comfortable four-wheeled coach, called a *raeda*, which he has hired from a jobbing stable for the 150 odd miles' journey to Baiae. A party of slaves is sent on ahead under the supervision of Habinnas and Daedalus to get the villa ready, and there are three or four more acting as escort to protect the party from highwaymen. The family has to meet the coach at the Porta Capēna, in the south-east of the city, where the famous Appian Way begins, and they are carried in litters from their home to the city gate. They find plenty of room for all five of them, as well as for Pullia and the puppy, Lydia, in the conveyance, on top of which the luggage is piled.

The Appian Way is badly in want of repair, so that the coach can average only about 30 to 35 miles a day going comfortably, though travellers in light two-wheeled gigs keep passing them, and the Imperial Post just instituted by Augustus can maintain an average of over 50 miles a day, while the couriers of the Imperial Post on horseback can cover 150 miles a day with frequent changes of horses. The boys' father reminds them that the Roman roads extend all over the empire, built in a straight line when-ever possible, with milestones at intervals of a Roman mile (about 1620 yards) marking the distances to Rome and the nearest towns. At one point on their journey the Appian Way is being relaid, and he points out the five different layers that go to make up every Roman road, which the boys have plenty of time to examine as the coach crawls past the workmen at less than walking-pace. At the bottom is a solid foundation of earth, then come small stones tightly packed together, then rubble in lime, then a layer of concrete made of lime and pounded tiles, and finally the top surface of smooth blocks of stone accurately fitted together.

Publius has promised to write to his friend Sextus at Rome describing his journey, so on the day after their arrival at Baiae he sits down with a pair of wax tablets and a stilus, similar to those used at school, to compose his letter. For writing short letters and taking notes these tablets are generally used instead of papyrus, for they have the advantage that the wax can be smoothed over and written on as often as desired, and the tablets, which are hinged together, can be shut up like a modern book, tied with string and sealed up for privacy until they are delivered. Roman letters always have a formal beginning and ending, which Publius is careful to use. He begins *Publius Sexto S.D.P* (an abbreviation for *salutem dicit plurimam*), " Publius sends Sextus his very best wishes ", and ends with *cura ut valeas,* " mind you keep well ", with the date and place of dispatch at the foot of the letter. This is what he says.

" Here we are at Baiae. I wish you were with us, and I am looking forward to seeing you at Naples next month. It was rather funny when we were loading up the coach at the Porta Capena, because a lot of water from the aqueduct over the gate which is always leaking dripped down on to the driver's head and made him swear. Our first stop for the night was at Three Taverns, where we stayed at an inn called ' The Serpents ', but it was a wretched place where we all had to share the same room and the beds were full of bugs ; fortunately we had brought our own food with us, as usual. The next day we had quite an adventure, because just after we had changed horses at Forum Appii we overtook an old lady in a carriage who had been stopped and robbed by high- waymen from the Pontine Marshes, which Father says are still the haunt of such people. They had stunned her driver and cut the traces of the horses, and since her slaves had run away she was left all alone, so we took her

on with us to Tarracina. The highwaymen might have
attacked us too, but they probably didn't like the look
of our outriders. Nothing much else interesting happened on the road. We spent the next two nights at
villas belonging to Father's friends, and the last night at
' The Cock ' at Capua, which wasn't a bad place. I must
stop now, because we are going out fishing. I have
borrowed Father's signet ring to seal up these tablets
with ; he says that the head of the
boy on it is like mine. Do you see any
resemblance? Don't forget to let me
know as soon as you reach Naples."
When the letter is ready his father
gives it, together with some of his own
correspondence, to a courier whom he
has hired to take letters to Rome for
himself and his friends in the neighbourhood. State letters can go by the
Imperial Post, but private persons have to make their
own arrangements.

HEAD OF A ROMAN
BOY

From a signet gem
of the first century
B.C., kindly lent by
Professor A. B. Cook.

Baiae is one of the famous sea-side resorts of Italy, and
the family finds it a delightful change from the stuffiness
of Rome in August. The Campanian shore is studded
with villas, some of them buildings of great size and luxury,
and the boys know several of their neighbours and have
a splendid holiday bathing, boating, fishing, either from
a boat or from the villa itself, part of which is built on a
mole projecting into the sea, hunting, and visiting their
old friend Varro, the bailiff of the family estate two or
three miles inland, from whom they pick up something
about farming. Not very far from Baiae, just along the
coast, Vesuvius sends up a plume of smoke into the sky,
prophetic of an eruption nearly a hundred years later [1]
which is destined to overwhelm two whole towns, Pompeii

[1] A.D 79.

and Herculaneum, and preserve them almost intact for
centuries, buried in ashes and lava.

During one of the boys' visits to the farm, a festival
in honour of Consus, an old Italian god of agriculture, is
held to celebrate the gathering in of the harvest, the date
being August 21. There is no temple in which to worship,
and the country folk from all the district round assemble
at a simple altar made of turf and stand in a circle while
the priest offers a preliminary prayer. His assistant
then leads the victim, a sheep without blemish, to the
altar; the priest sprinkles the animal with wine and
salt meal, adorns it with garlands and ribbons, and
recites a prayer while his assistant performs the sacrifice.
Meanwhile a flute-player plays music to drown any ill-
omened sounds, and the worshippers stand in a holy
silence with their heads covered. The animal is then cut
open, its entrails are inspected by the priest, and if
declared favourable are sprinkled with wine and meal and
burnt on the altar, and the firstfruits of the harvest are
also offered to the god. After the rites are completed
the flesh of the sheep is roasted and eaten by all those
present. Varro tells the boys that great care is taken to
get every detail of the ritual correct, for if there is any
mistake an expiation has to be made to the offended deity
and the sacrifice repeated. After the ceremony the boys
say good-bye to their friend and set off back to Baiae, where
they give their parents a description of the day's proceedings and Publius at any rate has several questions to
ask his father about religion.

The elder Publius thinks that this is a good opportunity
to speak to his sons on this subject, though Titus is
probably too young to understand much of what he is
told, and this is what he says to them.

"You have both heard and read a good deal about the
gods, and you have been present at some of the big

eligious festivals at Rome, but up till now you have come
nainly in contact with the religion of home-life and the
worship of the Household Gods and the Spirits of our
ancestors. As *Paterfamilias*, or head of the household, I
myself preside over this worship and make a daily offering
o these deities, in the morning and at dinner in the
orm of a libation of wine poured out to them. You
know, of course, that the *Lărēs* are the spirits of the home ;
hey are kept in a special shrine called the *Larārium*
beside the domestic hearth and also have their images
painted on the wall. The *Penātēs* are the spirits of the
store-cupboard and are kept in the *Penetrālia* in the
innermost part of the house. Then too every person and
place has its own inner spirit, or *genius*, which is very
important in everyday life ; the ' genius ' of our family is
painted on the wall of the atrium in the shape of a serpent.
Finally the departed spirits of our ancestors, called *Mānēs*,
depend for their well-being in the Underworld on the
honour paid them by their living descendants, so we have
o be very careful to give them the worship and respect
due to them. This family worship has been in existence
from time immemorial and there are probably few people
who do not carry it out in one form or another, even
though they may not always believe in the gods of the
tate religion.

" Out here in the country the old simple belief in the
native gods of Italy, which we call the ' religion of King
Numa ', is still predominant, and the deities worshipped
and placated, so that their anger may not harm the crops
and cattle, are the spirits, *nūmina*, of the sky and the
fields, the woods and rivers, especially those connected
with any form of farming. The supreme god is Jupiter,
the father of all things, who, as you know, is worshipped
as ' Best and Greatest ' on the Capitol, together with
Juno, the goddess of womanhood, and Minerva, the goddess

of wisdom. Then there are the other native gods with whose worship you are familiar, such as Vesta, the goddess of hearth and home, and the counterpart in the state religion of our family gods, in whose circular temple in the Forum the sacred fire is always kept burning; Mars, the god of strength and war; and Italian country gods like Saturn, the god of sowing; Cĕres, the goddess of crops; Pălēs and Faunus, protectors of the flocks; Jānus, the god of beginnings; and many other deities who represent every form of human activity.

"All these gods have been worshipped since the foundation of the city, and in the country the farmers continue to hold much the same beliefs to-day that their ancestors held. But in the towns and among educated people these deities, who originally were not represented by images at all, began to be identified in appearance and legend with the Greek gods of Olympus, although in many cases they had very little in common with their Greek counterparts, and so their native Italian origin became forgotten. When Rome came into contact with the East she accepted Oriental gods as well, such as Cўbĕlē, the ' Great Mother ' of Phrygia, and Īsis, Osīris and Serāpis from Egypt; women especially became attracted to these Eastern gods. The religion of the Jews, who worship a god called Jehovah, has also made many converts lately. So you see that the dwellers in big cities, especially Rome, have such a variety of gods to choose from that they may be bewildered and neglect the ancient beliefs of their fathers, and in spite of the scores of temples at Rome and the richness of public worship and ritual performed by priests who are officials of the state, it is probable that the simple country worship at an altar made of rough stone or turf, like the one which you attended to-day, is much more genuine and devout.

"Another side of the question, which you will both

come across when you go abroad to study philosophy, is the fact that in the last hundred years many educated Romans have begun to disbelieve in the existence of the gods and have turned to philosophy instead. For example, the Epicureans believe in a material universe, in which there are no gods and no after-life for the soul, and they make mental happiness the chief end of life ; the Stoics think that the world is directed by an active and intelligent principle which they call ' god ', and so they make life according to nature and reason their chief aim. Augustus is disturbed by these and other similar atheistic tendencies and has been trying to counter them by reviving old rituals, by restoring or building many temples, and by enlisting the aid of our greatest Roman poet, Virgil, to lead the people back to the old beliefs. Let us hope that he will be successful.

" The object of the training which you are receiving is to develop in you the two best qualities in the Roman character, *gravitas*, ' steadfastness and uprightness ', and *pietas*, ' loyalty to country, gods and family '. The first is illustrated in the greatness of our empire, in the stories of our ancestors, and in the example of the leading men of the state, and the second can be acquired by your home life and everyday training in morals and religion. You, Titus, are too young to start thinking much about such things yet, but you, Publius, will soon be a man, and your mother and I, and Daedalus too, are trying to bring you up according to the ' custom of our ancestors ', so that you will be able to take your proper place in the state. So do not neglect these opportunities of sharing in the simple worship of the country gods, for the experience may be valuable to you when you are grown up."

Publius has several more talks with his father about religion, which naturally give him plenty to think about. They do not prevent him, however, from making the most

of his holidays, during which he pays more than one visit
to his friend Sextus at Naples. The time passes all too
quickly in the many attractions of sea-side, country and
farm, and the whole family, including the slaves, is sorry
when September approaches, for they usually arrange to
get back to Rome in time for the first day of the ' Great
Games ', which start early in that month.

CHAPTER VII

CHARIOT RACES—THEATRES—GLADIATORIAL SHOWS

THE 'Games' are public entertainments held at Rome in honour of the various gods, and in the time of Publius altogether 76 days in the year are devoted to them. 59 of the days are given up to plays on the stage, and the remaining 17 provide the much more popular and exciting chariot-races in the Circus; the whole period of the different Games, which occur at intervals throughout the year, is a public holiday, both for schoolboys and for the city generally. The most important and the oldest are the *lūdi magni*, or *lūdi Rōmāni*, which are a festival in honour of Jupiter, starting on September 4th and lasting for sixteen days; the enormous expense of production is met partly by the state and partly by the aediles, or sometimes entirely by Augustus.

On the morning of September 4th the elder Publius and his two sons start off together quite early, soon after dawn, for the races last all day and they want to secure good seats in the Circus. Women can go too, but Caecilia prefers to remain at home with Critonia to-day. The opening day of the chariot races at the 'Great Games' is the most important and interesting, and all Rome seems to be flocking down to the huge Circus Maximus just south of the Palatine Hill. This is a long, horseshoe-shaped building, about 650 yards long and 150 yards wide, which can hold 150,000 spectators in tiers of seats on three different levels. Admission is free, and the Critonian family joins the long queue of *equites* who are lining up to enter at the gates

leading to seats reserved for this class. As the queue
moves slowly forward Publius and Titus amuse themselves by reading the various inscriptions scribbled on
the outside wall of the Circus by idlers and racing
enthusiasts. These include the names of successful
charioteers, 'tips' for races long since run, initials of
lovers with the date of their meeting, humorous verses, in
fact the usual material that is to be found written up on
such walls in all countries. " Look, Titus," says Publius,
" there is a good couplet that just sums up all these
inscriptions in a nut-shell.

'I WONDER, O WALL'

This elegiac couplet was scratched on the wall of the amphitheatre
at Pompeii (C.I.L. 2487), and should run

admiror, paries, te non cecidisse ruinis
qui tot scriptorum taedia sustineas

but the writer was so eager to get in the *te* that he started it after the
ad of *admiror* and finally put it before instead of after *paries* ; he could
not remember the last word of the hexameter and put a dash instead.

'I wonder, O wall, that your stones do not fall,
    So scribbled upon by the nonsense of all.'

" Isn't that good, Father? I must remember to tell
Sextus about it. Ah, now we're moving forward. We'll
be inside soon."

When at last they take their seats in a good position
quite near the starting and finishing line the boys have
plenty of time to look round before the races begin.
This is Titus' first visit, so Publius explains everything
to him. " You see that low wall running the whole
length of the arena, Titus, with statues of gods and

goddesses at intervals on top of it? The chariots have
to race down one side and up the other, seven laps
altogether, about five miles in all. They start from the
western end, from those wooden barriers, called *carcěres*,
and have to be very careful when they round each
extremity of the wall in case they hit the turning-post,
or *měta*, with their wheels and have a spill. There are
four racing-stables, the Reds, the Whites, the Greens
and the Blues, the charioteer of each dressed in its own
colour, and there are ten or twelve races every day."

While they are talking the Circus has been filling up,
and everyone is discussing the runners and deciding what
colour to back in each race. The betting on the different
colours is on a huge scale, and vast sums of money will
change hands to-day. The boys' father decides that
they are too young to start betting yet, though he himself
has a few denarii on some of the races, taking his sons'
advice on which charioteer to back. After much consideration they make up their minds to put their money
on Scopas, the Green representative, for the first race,
which is for four-horse chariots, called *quadrīgae*. Like
all charioteers, Scopas, a Greek by birth, is a slave, though
he has been very successful and has earned a small fortune
already. By the time the bet has been laid with one of
the many bookmakers in the Circus the moment for the
official opening of the festival has arrived, and all eyes
are turned towards the main entrance, where Augustus
is about to make his entry, for the emperor himself is
presiding.

The ceremony started half an hour ago on the Capitol,
where Augustus made a sacrifice to Jupiter and took
his place at the head of a long procession, consisting of
his clients, bands of noble youths, the competitors, priests,
and the images of the gods carried in chariots. The
emperor is wearing the triumphal coloured tunic of

Capitoline Jupiter, and as he enters the arena a hush falls and the crowd rises to its feet. He leads the procession round the course and is then ushered to his seat in the imperial box at the western end of the circus, where the races start and finish, and quite near the row where the Critonian family is seated. At last the steward of the course announces that the competitors are ready for the first race, the emperor drops a napkin as the starting-signal, attendants fling open the barriers behind which the horses are waiting, and the four chariots leap forward, each driver eager to secure the coveted place on the inside of the wall which will make it hard for anyone to pass him.

When the first cloud of dust started by the galloping hoofs has settled, Publius sees to his disappointment that the Blue charioteer is in the lead and that Scopas is lying second, with the other two close behind him. Down the arena they all dash, round the turning-pillar at the far end and back again, to repeat the process seven times amidst the thunderous roars of encouragement from their supporters. As each lap is completed one each of the six bronze dolphins and the six wooden eggs that are placed at the turning-point are removed, so that competitors and spectators can see how many laps are left. By the end of the fourth lap the third and fourth chariots have changed places, but they are so far behind that they can be considered out of the race unless both the leaders are wrecked. Scopas is straining every nerve to overtake his rival Carbo, but though he is close behind and sometimes level with him, he cannot get far enough ahead to pass him on the straight and has to drop back again for the turn.

At last they approach the turn for the last half-lap. Carbo makes an effort to increase his lead before the final stretch, but takes the bend too fine and just grazes the stone pillar with the hub of his inner wheel. It is quite enough to smash the light two-wheeled chariot travelling at such a high speed. Carbo is thrown clear of the wreckage and is being dragged along behind his frightened horses by the reins which charioteers always wrap several times around their bodies, but he just has time to draw the knife worn specially for this purpose and cut himself clear. Meanwhile Scopas, close behind, has managed to steer his horses clear of the broken chariot, showing great skill and presence of mind in being able to swing them aside in time, and now has a free run for the last 600 yards until he passes the winning-line an easy victor, thus increasing his own fame and bringing profit to those who backed the Green stable, including of course the Critonii. So the long day wears on, with race after race run amid enormous excitement, and when the boys at last get home their father decrees that they have had enough chariot racing for this festival, though Publius at any rate can go to the plays on the stage that form a large part of the Games.

The names of the plays and other future attractions are advertised on play-bills which are set up at street-corners and other prominent places, and one morning during the same ' Great Games ' Publius comes running in to tell Daedalus that the ' Woman of Andros ', a comedy by Terence, is to be performed during the following week. " Would you like to go and see this play, Daedalus? " the boy asks ; " or perhaps it will make you unhappy to think of your old home at Andros and your sister Gorgo." Daedalus says that he knows the play well and would like to take Publius to see it, especially as he has heard that there is a good company of actors hired to perform it ; he likes to hear and read about his home, for it is so long since he left it that it no longer causes him pain.

On their way to the Theatre of Marcellus, a new stone

building just outside the city walls south of the Capitol, Daedalus reminds Publius (Titus has been left at home as being too young for these plays) that nearly all Latin tragedies and comedies are imitated from the Greek. There are a few genuine Roman plays as well as a kind ot farce called ' mimes ', and a new style of entertainment called ' pantomime ' is becoming very popular, in which one actor very skilfully plays a whole story in dance and gesture. " These old comedies of Plautus and Terence, like the ' Woman of Andros ' which we are going to see to-day, are not so popular with the common people nowadays," he says. " They prefer something more exciting and amusing as a rule, but the old plays are still revived at intervals, and I am sure you will enjoy this one. But here we are at the theatre. Have you got those bone tickets I gave you? Admission is free, but these tickets provide us with seats reserved for schoolboys and their tutors."

They enter the theatre and take their seats in their special block, but have to wait some minutes before the play begins ; Publius is very interested because it is his first visit to a comedy, though he has seen tragedies before. The building holds nearly 20,000 spectators and is built in the shape of a semi-circle ; the tiers of seats are divided into blocks by staircases that radiate from the space in front of the stage called the *orchēstra*, which contains stalls for senators and foreign ambassadors. The first fourteen rows behind them are reserved for the members of the equestrian order, among whom Publius can see his father. There are boxes to left and right of the stage for the emperor and the Vestal Virgins respectively. Coloured awnings cover the whole building on a hot day like this, for there is no roof, and the audience is sprayed between acts with jets of water and saffron scent to keep them cool.

When the play is ready to begin, curtains in front of the stage are lowered to reveal the scene, and Publius sees that the actors in the comedy are wearing ordinary clothes and slippers, though he knows that for tragedies they wear long robes and high boots. The actors are slaves or freedmen and as a rule consist of men only ; they have special wigs and masks to distinguish sex and age, and must speak very clearly to be heard in so huge a theatre. There is stage scenery, which is changed as required, and a certain proportion of the play consists of lyrics sung to music, which is more popular with the crowd than the dialogue, though Daedalus and Publius follow the course of the plot with great attention, and they are both sorry when the curtain is raised again to show that the performance is over and the leading actor comes forward and says to the audience *plaudite*, ' applaud, please '.

" I do hope you will be able to go back to Andros and find your sister," says Publius to Daedalus when they reach home. " By the way, do you think that Father will let me go to the Gladiatorial Games now that I am nearly fifteen? Several of the boys at ' The Flogger's ' go and I should like to see what they are like." " Certainly not," replies his tutor. " They are a horrible spectacle and I hope you will never go until you are quite grown up, and then only once, if at all. If you want to hear about them, ask Scaevola. He will tell you stories about the arena that will put you off going for ever."

Publius has often heard from the door-keeper how he was carried off from his home in the land of the Allobroges in Gaul when he was a young man and sold among other slaves at Rome to be a gladiator, but the Gaul has never described the darker side of the fighting in the amphitheatre.[1]

---

[1] The largest and most famous, the Amphitheātrum Flāvium, afterwards called the Colossēum, was opened a century later, in 80 A.D., and could hold at least 50,000 spectators. Much of it still stands.

" It is sheer bloody murder," says Scaevola, " and it is
a disgrace to the Roman nation that people flock to
see such degrading sights. The wild beast hunts are
bad enough, when hundreds of lions, elephants, bears
and other animals are slaughtered in the ring, but
when people make their fellow human beings kill each
other in cold blood for the amusement of the crowd
I am glad to be a barbarian Gaul instead of a civilized
Roman."

" Is it really as bad as that, Scaevola? " " Yes,
indeed it is, Master Publius," he says. " I had two or
three years in a gladiatorial ' school ' and I am lucky to
escape with the loss of my right arm. I had had several
victories and was beginning to hope for my discharge
with the wooden sword of honourable retirement when I
entered the arena for the last time and nearly met my
death.

" You know, of course, that there are several kinds of
gladiators, who are recruited from prisoners of war,
condemned criminals, or slaves. The two most common
kinds are the ' net-men ', who have no other equipment
than a trident and a net with which to entangle their
opponents—I was a net-man because I was light and
active—and their adversaries, usually big, heavy men
who are clad in full armour with a shield and a sword.
Then there are heavily armed ' Samnites ', lightly armed
' Thracians ', and various other kinds, including some men
who have to fight one another blindly because their
helmets have no eye-pieces : the crowd finds this very
amusing, of course, but the gladiators don't.

" During our training we lived very well, and some people
envied us, but it is a terrible thing to have to fight for your
life with the man who may sleep next to you, and perhaps
have to kill him as he lies prostrate. The days before
each show were a great strain on our nerves, and we liked

it more when we fought against strangers from another 'school'; gladiators armed alike seldom fight each other, and contests may be between single pairs differently armed or between two large parties. Shows are given many times in the year, either by a candidate for office, or by a victorious general to celebrate his triumph, and they are becoming more frequent, because Augustus knows that the mob likes them.

"On my last day of fighting we began the 'sport' as usual by marching round the arena and halting before the emperor's box, where we shouted, *Ave, Imperator, morituri te salutant*, 'Hail, Emperor, those about to die salute you.' Then our arms were tested, to see that the weapons were sharp, and after a sham fight, played to music, the real butchery began. My turn to go on was fifth on the programme, and it was with the usual feeling of terror that I saw the first four pairs, some of whom were my comrades, go out into the sand. One man lost his nerve and had to be driven out with red-hot irons, so his opponent had an easy time. The crowd had bets on us and shouted to encourage their choices; there was a roar of 'he's got it' whenever a man went down. The vanquished gladiator, if he was only wounded, could raise his hand in an appeal for his life to the emperor; the decision was usually left to the people, who signalled death by turning the thumb up, or mercy by waving their handkerchiefs and turning the thumb downwards [1] if the man was a favourite or had fought bravely. Slaves dressed like Charon or Mercury used to go round after a fight and prevent attempts at shamming death by striking the temples of men lying on the ground with a mallet, and corpses were dragged out of the arena on a hook.

[1] It is possible (and commonly believed nowadays, according to the popular phrase and gesture) that 'thumbs up' meant mercy.

" I had been lucky up till then, for though I had won seven or eight fights I had also been defeated twice ; but each time the crowd spared my life and allowed me to fight again.   At last my turn came and I went out to meet my opponent, fortunately not one from the same ' school ', but a triple victor from Capua.   I was the favourite, as I could tell from the shouts, and I wanted to finish the fight off quickly and perhaps get my discharge.   My adversary was very tall and strong, and though he could not run fast he could turn quickly and ward off the cast of my net.   I was the better man, I could see, and after a certain amount of sparring I managed to get my net over his head and right shoulder.   He tried to hack himself free with his sword and while doing so exposed his left side, so that I could transfix him with my trident during his struggles.   I jumped back to get out of reach, but my foot slipped in a pool of blood which the slaves had not covered over properly with sand, and I fell on one knee.   My opponent was dying, but with his last strength he lashed out at me and cut off my right arm below the elbow, and we both fell down unconscious.

" I heard afterwards that the crowd roared itself hoarse with excitement and that my backers won their bets because I was still alive, but I was carried out and would probably have been left to bleed to death—what good is a one-armed gladiator?—had it not been for your Uncle Lucius.   He had served as a military tribune when he was a young man in Julius Caesar's army in Gaul, and he took an interest in our people, so when he saw how well ' Egus the Gaul ' fought, for that is my real name, he paid my trainer a few gold pieces for my worthless body, persuaded the gladiatorial doctor to do his best for me, and when I recovered gave me to your father, who was looking out for an untrained slave to be his door-keeper. They call me ' Scaevola ' now, after some character in

Roman history who lost his right hand [1]—you know the one, I expect—and here I am, with a double grudge against the Romans, not only for conquering my country and enslaving me, but also for giving me those years as a gladiator and causing me to lose my arm. That's why I am bad-tempered sometimes and growl at people, though if I must be a slave I would rather be one here than anywhere else, because there is no ill-treatment of the slaves in your father's house." "I'm so sorry, Scaevola," says Publius. "I had no idea that you had had such terrible experiences in the arena. I certainly don't want to see the gladiatorial shows if that's the kind of thing that happens. When I grow up and inherit the property I shall set you free and let you go back to Gaul if you want to, or you can stay with us if you prefer it."

[1] Mucius Scaevola, who tried to kill Lars Porsenna and when arrested thrust his right hand in the fire to show the determination of the Romans to repel the Etruscan invaders.

CHAPTER VIII

DEATH AND BURIAL

PUBLIUS, of course, hopes that his father will live for many years yet so that he will not succeed him in the ownership of the property for a long time, but as it turns out the boy himself is not destined to live much longer. The autumn is always a sickly season in Italy, and though the Critonian family has had several weeks' holiday on the healthy Campanian coast the city is still very hot and stuffy on their return. It is possible that Publius has a touch of 'Pontine fever', a kind of malaria prevalent at this time of year, which he may have picked up while passing through the low-lying Pontine marshes on his way home from the sea-side. This makes him stay in bed for a day or two on different occasions, but he seems to have recovered fairly well and one afternoon he goes down to the Tiber for his usual exercise and swim. The sun is very hot and Publius stays in the water longer than usual, but when he returns home he has another attack of feverish shivers and is sent off to bed at once. Next morning he is much worse, and his mother sends for the family doctor, a Greek freedman called Pantagathus who was formerly one of Uncle Lucius' slaves.

Pantagathus is a clever physician for the times in which he lives, and was trained at his master's expense in Greece and Asia Minor. Most doctors at this time are foreigners, generally either freedmen or slaves, and though the best of them, like Pantagathus, have a considerable knowledge of the science of healing and can perform simple operations, without anaesthetics of course, some of them are no better than 'quacks' and

often do more harm than good. Publius knows Pantagathus well and likes him, for the Greek once very
skilfully set the boy's arm when he broke it during wrestling, and he has often prescribed for other ailments.
To-day, however, the doctor looks grave when he has
finished his examination, for the chill on top of the fever
seems likely to prove serious. He leaves some medicine
compounded of various herbs and promises to come again
next morning.

During the next few days Publius gets no better ; his
illness would probably be diagnosed to-day as a bad case of
pneumonia. Caecilia is in despair and sends to the Temple
of Aesculāpius, the god of healing, in the Island of the
Tiber, for a priest to come and pray for her son. The
priest arrives and mutters some incantations over the
invalid, for this is the usual method of averting the anger
of an offended deity, but he knows that Publius is in good
hands and that he can do no more to help him. Another
leading physician is called in to consult with Pantagathus,
but the pneumonia has taken firm hold, and in spite of
devoted nursing by Caecilia and Daedalus, Publius
gradually gets worse and finally breathes his last while his
parents sit beside his bed and wish they could give him
some of their own strength to enable him to live a little
longer. His last words are to tell his mother not to be
too sorry at his death, and to ask his father to set free the
door-keeper, Scaevola.

As soon as Pantagathus announces that the boy is
dead the whole household bursts into lamentations ; all
the slaves join in the general sorrow, for he was a great
favourite with them and always showed kindness and
interest in their affairs. His father now closes his son's
eyes and all those present call upon him by name for the
last time. The undertakers are then summoned, and a
cypress tree is planted outside the house, to warn visitors

and passers-by to avoid the pollution of a dead body. The boy's corpse is clothed in his ' embroidered toga ', for he had not yet assumed the ' manly toga ' which he was so much looking forward to putting on, a coin is placed in his mouth to pay the fee to Charon to ferry him across the Styx, and he is laid out on a bier in the atrium with his feet pointing towards the street-door.

On the day appointed for the funeral the procession is led by trumpeters and flute-players, followed by hired mourning women who sing a funeral dirge. Then comes the corpse, lying on the bier and carried in a litter, and then the relatives and other mourners, including Sextus and many others of Publius' school-friends, all wearing black clothes and carrying torches as a reminder of the time when funerals were held only at night. If Publius had been a man of rank whose family was famous in history he would have been preceded in the procession by men wearing the waxen masks of his ancestors who had held high office, and he would have been surrounded by all his marks of distinction ; the funeral train would have gone first to the Forum, where his nearest relative would have delivered a funeral laudation. If he had been a poor man or a slave he would have been buried at night in a slave's cemetery, or perhaps his ashes would have been placed in one of the big communal tombs consisting of a number of pigeon-holes intended to contain the urns holding the ashes of the dead.

As it is, however, Publius' funeral procession makes its way northwards from his house to the Colline Gate and about a mile outside the city walls along the Salarian Way, where the funeral pyre, *rogus*, has been erected. His body is laid on the pyre, garlands and last gifts are thrown on, and a torch is applied to the bottom of the pyre by his father, who keeps his eyes averted. When everything is consumed by the flames, his father finally quenches the smouldering ashes with wine, encloses them in a funeral urn, and places them in a niche in the family tomb of the Critonii, which stands beside the road. Then follows the funeral feast at home, followed by a purificatory sacrifice to the Household Gods, and finally, on the ninth day after the funeral, the elder Publius makes a sacrifice to the *Mānēs*, Departed Spirits, of his son, the family lays aside its mourning, and life goes on much as before, except that no one can forget the boy whom everybody has loved so much. His mother, Caecilia, sets up a stone at the family tomb to commemorate his name : a translation of it is given on page 1, and it is reproduced here in its proper place.

P. CRITONIVS P. F. POLIO
MATER · MEA · MIHI
MONVMENTVM
COERAVIT QVAE
ME DESIDERAT
VEHEMENTER · ME
HEICE · SITVM · IN
MATVRE VALE SAL
VE

We may repeat to Publius' remains the lines of Ovid [1] addressed to his poet-friend Tibullus, " May your bones rest quietly, I pray, in an urn for ever undisturbed, and may the earth lie lightly upon your ashes."

OSSA QVIETA PRECOR TVTA REQVIESCITE IN VRNA
ET SIT HVMVS CINERI NON ONEROSA TVO.

[1] *Amores*, III, 9. 67.

APPENDIX

THE ROMAN CALENDAR

PUBLIUS used to celebrate his birthday every year with the usual festivities. He invited all his friends to a party, at which he wore a special white robe and made an offering of cakes and incense to his ' genius ', or inner spirit, and gave and received presents from his guests. He was born on April 10, 31 B.C., or in its Latin form *ante diem quartum Īdūs Aprīles* (usually shortened to *a.d. IV Id. Apr.*), *consulibus* (shortened to *coss.*) *C. Iulio Caesare Octaviano III, M. Valerio Messalla Corvino*, which means " on the fourth day before the Ides of April in the consulship of Octavian for the third time and of Messalla." The years were thus known by the names of the two consuls in the ablative absolute, and towards the end of the reign of Augustus they were also dated " from the foundation of the city " in 753 B.C., the phrase being *ab urbe condita* or *anno urbis conditae*, in short A.U.C., so that 31 B.C. was A.U.C. 723, for the Romans used the ' inclusive ' method of reckoning and counted in an extra year.

The Roman year originally contained ten months, beginning in March and ending in December (derived from *decem*), but two extra months were added quite early in history and the year was then 355 days long, the priests adding an extra month at intervals to correct the calendar by the solar year. In 46 B.C. Julius Caesar reformed the calendar by introducing the ' Julian system ', which is almost the same as our ' Gregorian ' calendar. He added 10 days to the year and gave it an extra day to be taken a second time every fourth year, leap year, on February 24.

The names of the English months are derived directly from the Latin, though July and August were originally called *Quintīlis* and *Sextīlis* and were later changed in honour of Julius Caesar and Augustus. The Roman names are really adjectives agreeing with *mensis*.

Instead of reckoning forward from the first of each month, as we do, the Romans had three fixed dates in every month, the Kalends on the 1st, the Nones on the 5th or 7th, and the Ides on the 13th or 15th, and used to count *backwards* from the nearest of these. Try to remember this rhyme :

> " March, July, October, May
> Make Nones the 7th, Ides the 15th day ' ;

the others have the Nones on the 5th and the Ides on the 13th. If the date you want is one of these fixed dates, use the word with the name of the month agreeing with it ; thus March 15, when Caesar was murdered, was the Ides of March, *Idus Martiae*, usually in the ablative for ' time when '. The day before each fixed date was *Prīdiē* with the accusative ; e.g. December 31 is *Pridie Kalendas Iānuārias*, or *Prid. Kal. Ian.*

For the other dates work backwards according to the following rule : for days before the Nones or Ides add *one* (because of the ' inclusive ' method of reckoning) to the date on which the Nones or Ides fall, and subtract the English date, e.g. September 2 is the 4th day before the Nones, *dies quartus ante Nōnas Septembres*, but the Romans changed the order of the words and called it *ante diem quartum Nonas Septembres*, or *a.d. IV Non. Sept.* For days before the Kalends of the next month, add *two* to the number of days in the previous month and subtract the English date, e.g. January 25 is the 8th day before the Kalends of February, or *a.d. VIII Kal. Feb.* The following table gives the dates of all the months except

February, which is the same as those in the first two columns as far as the Ides: after that February 14 is *a.d. XVI Kal. Mart.*, and so on.

Day of English Month	*Ianuarius* (also *Augustus* and *December*)	*Aprilis* (also *Iunius,* *September, November*)	*Martius* (also *Maius,* *Iulius, October*)
1	Kal. Ian.	Kal. Apr.	Kal. Mart.
2	a.d. IV. Non. Ian.	a.d. IV. Non. Apr.	a.d. VI. Non. Mart.
4	Prid. Non. Ian.	Prid. Non. Apr.	a.d. IV. Non. Mart.
5	Non. Ian.	Non. Apr.	a.d. III. Non. Mart.
6	a.d. VIII. Id. Ian.	a.d. VIII. Id. Apr.	Prid. Non. Mart.
7	a.d. VII. Id. Ian.	a.d. VII. Id. Apr.	Non. Mart.
12	Prid. Id. Ian.	Prid. Id. Apr.	a.d. IV. Id. Mart.
13	Id. Ian.	Id. Apr.	a.d. III. Id. Mart.
14	a.d. XIX. Kal. Feb.	a.d. XVIII. Kal. Mai.	Prid. Id. Mart.
15	a.d. XVIII. Kal. Feb.	a.d. XVII. Kal. Mai.	Id. Mart.
20	a.d. XIII. Kal. Feb.	A.D. XII. Kal. Mai.	a.d. XIII. Kal. Apr
30	a.d. III. Kal. Feb.	Prid. Kal. Mai.	a.d. III. Kal. Apr.
31	Prid. Kal. Feb.		Prid. Kal. Apr.

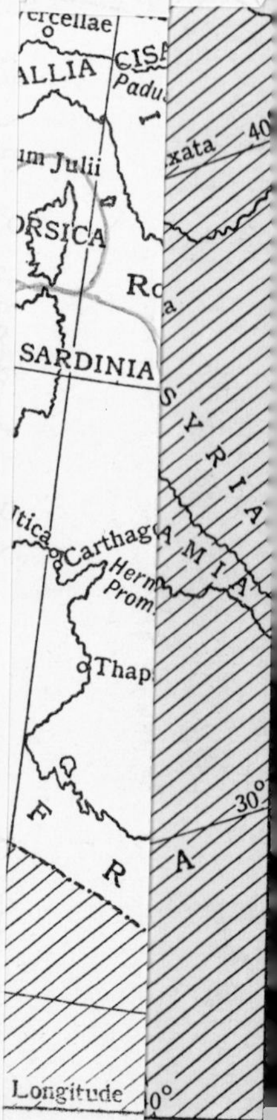

rcellae

ALLIA CISA
Padu

xata 40°

m Julii

RSICA

Ro

SARDINIA

SYRIA

MIA

tica Carthag
Herm
Prom

Thap

30°

F R A

Longitude 40°

PART II

THE EXTERNAL HISTORY OF ROME
TO A.D. 117
FROM CITY-STATE TO EMPIRE

CHAPTER I

ROMAN IMPERIALISM

IF you stand on any part of the Roman Wall which spans the wild moorland country that lies between the Tyne

E.N.A.

THE ROMAN WALL NEAR HEXHAM

and the Solway and you are fortunate enough to be alone, you can see in your mind's eye the soldiers of the Ninth Legion moving up from York in column of route to carry into Scotland the power of Roman arms and can hear the steady tramp of their feet. The road by which they are coming runs straight as an arrow over hill and down dale ; parts of it are still in use, parts of it perhaps have disappeared and become merged with the fields and the fells, but the curious thing is that from the air the track of the road can be seen over all its length, just as it was over eighteen hundred years ago.

Our Debt to Rome

Most of us know that the language these legionaries spoke, the Latin language, is the common element in the languages spoken to-day in Western Europe, in Italy, in Spain, in France and in our own country ; most of us know that the principles of Roman Law provide the common element in the legal systems of this part of the world (in our own island Scottish law, though not English, is based on the Roman system) ; but we are apt to forget that Rome's ideas of government and international relations, of citizenship and the relations between man and man, are as deeply embedded in the fabric of our society as are her roads in the soil of our land. We are apt to forget too that, although her own urge to create expressed itself in practical things, she it was who handed on to us the masterpieces of Greek thought and Greek imagination and, by adopting Christianity, the sublime conceptions of the Jewish religion ; but for the Roman Empire Christianity itself might well have perished. From Western Europe again the torch has been handed on by us to America, to Africa, to India, to Australia, to all parts of the globe where our civilization has made its way, so that amid all the differences of custom and outlook that divide race from race and nation from nation there is one common bond the true understanding of which may well do much to promote the peace of the world—the bond of Rome's legacy to mankind.

" The use of history, it may be said, is to light the present hour to its duty." However much ways of life and methods of administration may change, however striking the progress of science and of art, human nature alters no more quickly than the face of the earth and things that have happened once are likely to happen again. We no longer wear the toga : we do not recline at meals : our battles are not fought with javelin and sword. But emotion still fires the heart : there are brave men and cowards : there are self-seekers and patriots, as there were when Rome was the mistress of the Mediterranean. Admittedly not all periods of history are equally worth studying ; for some nations, like some individuals, lead uneventful, commonplace lives and from time to time the spirit of enterprise grows dim. But the story of Rome is intensely interesting, and if you find it dull the fault is either yours or mine. It is interesting because it is the story of a triumph over obstacles ; in the beginning Rome was a Cinderella among cities, and again and again in after years she found herself in the most deadly peril when her very existence was at stake, when she dangled, as it were, on the edge of a precipice and her bitterest enemy prepared to cut the rope. It is interesting also because it is the story of a successful experiment—not an experiment with chemicals consciously pursued, but an experiment with men in which instinct and luck played a bigger part than reason.

THE PAX ROMANA

What Rome discovered was the secret of giving the peoples over whom she ruled the twofold blessing of freedom and peace. It took her years to discover the wisdom of being generous and she often forgot the lessons experience had taught her. There are many instances in Roman history of cruelty, stupidity and selfishness; so there are in our own. Her way of life was based on what was legally slavery; but the condition of many men, women and even children in the England of the early nineteenth century was a serfdom equally hard and still more hopeless. Yet in the long run the provinces of Rome benefited from Roman rule, as our colonies have benefited from ours. They moved gradually closer and closer to a full partnership in the Empire, and most of them from the very moment of annexation were allowed a measure of self-government; Rome insisted only on the right to control their foreign policy in order to ensure that freedom should not mean a licence to make war, as it had done in the case of the free cities of Greece. The licence to make war has been the curse of Europe; from that curse Rome freed such parts of the continent as lay inside the boundaries of her Empire probably to a degree greater than has since been known. That her success was not complete is explained by the fact that parts of the continent, in particular Germany, were never incorporated in her territory and did not acknowledge her authority, and by the fact that her own system of government did not change sufficiently rapidly as her territory expanded, and for various reasons, which we shall examine later,[1] she never became a democracy. The *pax Romana* was, however, no idle dream. You will realize this if you will trace on the map the boundaries of the Roman Empire as they were in A.D. 69, remembering that they were still further extended by the conquest of the Black Forest region of Germany (Agri Decumates), Roumania (Dacia) and Arabia. In all that vast territory there were only about 300,000 troops (half of whom were

[1] See pages 145–6.

on-Italian auxiliaries) and nearly all of them were
ationed on or near the frontiers ; for the danger of a
ative insurrection except in newly conquered districts
as negligible. Why were the provincials ready to
ccept the sovereignty of Rome? Because Rome did not
erely refrain for the most part from interfering in their
iternal affairs ; she freely offered them the gifts of
ivilization and welcomed them in due time as fully-
edged Romans, while allowing them to remain Athenians
r Spaniards or Britons.

THE DUAL CITIZENSHIP

We take it as a matter of course that an Australian
ay remain an Australian and yet enjoy the rights of
3ritish citizenship. But until the days of imperial
Rome the idea of such a dual loyalty would have seemed
trange indeed. The Assyrians, for example, would not
ave conceived it possible that a Jew could remain a Jew
nd yet be a loyal subject of Nineveh ; their method was
o destroy national feeling by moving large sections of
he conquered race into Assyria itself and sending
Assyrian colonists to take their place ; in that way Israel
ecame Samaria. The Athenians attempted to impose
n their allies in the League of Delos their own type of
lemocratic constitution and justified their attack on the
iny island of Melos by the doctrine that right is might.
Even to-day similar methods, carried to extremes of
nhumanity, are practised by the German Reich, and it
vould not be untrue to say that very few of the great
mperial powers that have flourished since the fall of
Rome have appeared to profit from her experience and
o understand that without generosity and a large measure
f tolerance an empire cannot endure. An Englishman
specially should know something of the history of the

D   S.P.Q.R.

Roman Empire. He cannot be completely impartial i
reading of the actions of his own countrymen in thei
dealings with foreigners nor completely unbiassed by th
political prejudices of his own upbringing. To Roma
history, on the other hand, he can bring a fresh mind an
an unfettered judgment. He will notice at once tw
important differences between Rome and Britain, con
sidered as imperial powers. The British Empire consist
of countries inhabited for the most part by people o
British origin (the Dominions) or by races comparativel
uncivilized (the Colonies) or by civilized nations whos
blood and outlook are not at all similar to our own (India
the Roman Empire in like manner contained citie
inhabited for the most part by people of Roman origi
(the *coloniae civium Romanorum*) and civilized nation
whose blood and outlook were quite different (e.g. Egyp
and Judaea), but it contained also European cities mor
civilized than Rome was herself (the Greeks) and eve
the more backward tribes in Gaul and Britain wer
racially similar to their conquerors. Secondly, the Roma
Empire was not spread all over the globe, but confined t
an area limited by the Rhine, the Carpathians, th
mountain-gates of Armenia, the Sahara and the Atlanti
—for the Romans were not really a seafaring peopl
This lends, perhaps, a special significance to Roma
history at the present time when the future of Europ
and the Mediterranean area is in the melting-pot, an
certainly makes it less complicated—there simply are n
events in America or China or Australia to bother about–
so that one can more easily see ' the wood ' as well a
' the trees '.

You must not suppose that the Roman Empire wa
built in a day. No statesman solemnly sat down t
discover by a process of reasoning how to make it
success and rose up crying " Eureka! A twofold citizer

ship will of course provide the solution : all our subjects,
while retaining their own nationality, must become
citizens of Rome." In fact the solution did not come
by reasoning at all but was hammered out on the anvil
of experience. It took the best part of five hundred years
after Rome set out on her career of conquest for all
Italians south of the Po to receive the full rights of
citizenship, or *civitas*, and they had to make good their
claims by force of arms in the Social War of 90–88 B.C.
The rest of Italy between the Po and the Alps was
enfranchised by Julius Caesar in 49 B.C., but it was
another two hundred and fifty years before it could be
said that only Roman citizens lived within the boundaries
of the Empire (A.D. 212). Non-Roman cities on which
the *civitas* was conferred were called *municipia civium
Romanorum* to distinguish them from *coloniae*, which were
settlements of Romans planted by Rome in conquered
territory to ensure the loyalty of the district or to provide
a means of livelihood for her discharged soldiers. It is
important to understand that Romanization—that is the
adoption by Italians or provincials of the Latin language,
Roman law, Roman customs and Roman outlook—was a
necessary preliminary to the grant of the citizenship and
that this process, though encouraged by far-seeing
statesmen (like C. Gracchus and Julius Caesar) and
emperors (like Claudius and Vespasian) was in the main
spontaneous. The Roman army, the Roman colonists,
and the Roman merchants were the chief ambassadors of
Rome, for they taught her subjects to respect her and to
see the advantages of conforming to her usage.

THE ALLIES AND THE PROVINCES

It became the recognized practice about the second
century B.C. to grant the citizenship to non-Romans in

two stages. The first stage, called *Latinitas* from the privileges granted to Rome's Latin allies in the early days of the Republic (before the dissolution of the Latin League in 338 B.C.), conferred the *ius commercii* (the right of owning land and trading under the protection of the Roman law) but neither the *ius suffragii* (the right of voting in the Roman assembly) nor the *ius honorum* (the right of holding office in Rome) ; magistrates of ' Latin ' towns, however, automatically received the full *civitas*. *Latini* remained technically *socii*, as did all other non-citizen communities. The more privileged were called *civitates liberae* because they were exempt from the provincial governor's jurisdiction (and from direct taxation until about 100 B.C.—thereafter in certain cases only), though their relations with other cities were controlled by Rome : the less privileged were subject to the governor, though allowed a good deal of internal freedom, and were called *civitates stipendiariae* because they always paid tribute (*stipendium*).

The provinces were not particularly well governed under the Republic, the average governor regarding his one year's term of office (for which he had had no specific training and received no salary) as an opportunity for enrichment rather than as a responsibility—it is a significant fact that the first permanent court in Rome (the *quaestio repetundarum* established in 149 B.C.) tried only cases of extortion (i.e. the illegal seizure of provincials' money or property by Roman officials). But the whole system was reformed by Augustus and in 27 B.C. the frontier provinces—in other words those that contained legionary troops—were brought under the Emperor's direct supervision. A definite and coordinated policy now became possible in these provinces and the Emperor's *legati*, or viceroys, who governed them as his deputies, were no longer confined to a single year of office. The result was that they were able to learn their job properly and really to identify themselves with the interests of the inhabitants. The older provinces were still governed by proconsuls responsible to the senate and holding office for a year as under the Republic, but they also gained from Augustus' reorganization, since their governors were the same men who now earned a wider experience in the imperial provinces and officials in both types of province were no longer unpaid. The abuse of military power by army commanders, which had brought about the downfall of Republican government, became more difficult now that they were merely the subordinates of the Emperor, to whom alone the armed forces of the state took the oath of allegiance. Indeed the tightening-up of the civil administration would not have been possible if Augustus had not secured for himself command of all the armies. By so doing he was able to re-establish the *pax Romana*, which the civil wars between Marius and Sulla, Pompey and Caesar, and Antony and himself had so rudely shattered, and to win thereby an imperishable name.

THE ACQUISITION OF THE EMPIRE

Such in broad outline was the Roman Empire; such the means whereby Rome was able to keep it under her sway. But how did she acquire it? The successive stages of her advance are traced in the next four chapters, her expansion in Italy, her victory over Carthage, and her simultaneous expansion in Europe, Africa and Asia. To make it as easy as possible for you to grasp how one conquest led on to another, the narrative does not leave the West and North and switch over to the South and East until the whole tale of the Rhine and Danube frontier to the end of Trajan's reign has been told, and you will know relatively nothing of what was going on in Rome herself until the story of her adventurous journey from City-state to Empire has been completed. This should enable you to form a much clearer picture of the landmarks of the journey than you would gain from a parallel narrative of external and internal affairs, to understand more fully the connection between Rome's various wars and to grasp why things happened as they did instead of knowing merely what happened. But you must try to memorize events with their dates, not because dates are important in themselves but because without dates it is fatally easy to forget exactly when an event occurred, and use the maps provided to find out where places are.

Besides looking for the connection between apparently isolated facts you should consider the extent to which sheer luck, national character and geographical position were responsible for Rome's success. You must notice how often Rome embarked upon a war which ended in conquest not through deliberate purpose but because her help was asked for, her intervention sought ; how often too her enemies weakened one another, as the Etruscans weakened the Gauls in the early days of the Republic and the Gauls the Etruscans. You must notice how often when Rome seemed to be losing a war her foes, whether the commander in the field or the government that had appointed him, made a fatal mistake ; they did the one thing that would deprive them of victory or failed to do the one thing that would ensure it. Rome made innumerable mistakes but never a fatal one, and she had the great faculty of profiting from errors, of producing fresh strength and resolution in the face of defeat. The three great disasters of Republican days were the Allia (390 B.C.), the Caudine Forks (321 B.C.) and Cannae (216 B.C.). Probably no nation could have recovered from them as quickly as Rome did. She was lucky certainly in that the Gauls, the Samnites, the Carthaginians in turn failed to make full use of their victories, but luck by itself would not have saved her.

THE ROMAN CHARACTER

The Romans' greatest asset was their morale. They never cracked. When once they had put their hands to the plough they did not turn back. Lacking imagination, they had a genius for practical affairs. They looked for the next job to do and did it without much thought for the possible consequences. If things went badly, they grunted and redoubled their efforts. The dogged tenacity with which they refused to acknowledge defeat, the dour persistence with which they returned to the charge, their robust confidence in times of peril, their stoical common-sense are qualities which earn our admiration. It might be said of them, as it has been said of us, that they were often defeated but never lost the last battle. No other people would have chosen 'weight' as the quality they most respected, but *gravitas* was the typical Roman virtue. By 'weight' they meant the type of personality that must be taken seriously; they were serious men themselves and they demanded that they should be treated with respect. They were not a lovable people. They lacked charm, as they lacked imagination. They produced no really great thinkers or artists, and few Latin writers were born in Latium, still fewer in Rome itself. But there is a massive grandeur about them, an impressive dignity, a manliness (it is no accident that *virtus*, manliness, came to mean excellence in general) that compels respect.

When the Gauls took Rome in 390 B.C., so the story goes, they found the streets of the city completely

deserted. The younger Romans had retired to th
Capitol, there to stand siege, but provisions were in
sufficient to keep alive the old people also. These, there
fore, remained in their houses calmly awaiting death. O
panic there was none. Such of the aged as were senator
seated themselves in their ivory chairs of office in th
middle of their halls, arrayed in their robes of state. S
motionless were they, so utterly composed that the Gaul
were amazed and one of them, thinking that the impassiv
features of Marcus Papirius belonged to a statue, bega
to stroke his beard. Thereupon the statue came to lif
and smote the Gaul on the head with its ivory rod. Thi
was the signal for a general massacre, but not one of thes
old men forgot his dignity or failed to meet death proudl
and unflinchingly. Such was the stuff of which th
true-born Romans of the early Republic were made an
that is what they meant by *gravitas*.

In the second century B.C. the Roman frontier wa
pushed forward across the Adriatic and the Aegean, an
slaves from Greece and Asia Minor began to pour int
Rome. Old-fashioned senators, like Cato the Censo
were alarmed at the influence which the debased cultu
of the East began at once to exert on certain sections
the population. Idleness, luxury, frivolity and exce
became increasingly frequent, and it appeared that th
virility of the capital city would be undermined. But
was a very gradual process. The simple seriousness
the old days died, it is true, and in some cases was replac
by the attitude of the ne'er-do-well, to whom there a
only two things that matter—*panem et circenses* (fr
bread and amusements). Yet contact with the Ea
brought gain as well as loss. The old *gravitas*, fine as
was in many ways, had been rigid and narrow. The ne
gravitas was more thoughtful, broader and more tolera
and brought with it a new sense of responsibility.

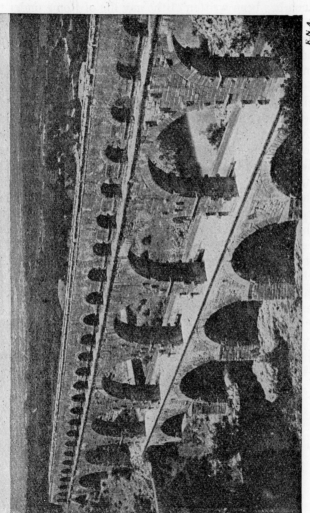

E.N.A.

THE PONT DU GARD NEAR NÎMES

This combined aqueduct and bridge is 158 feet high from the river-bed. The water flowed in a channel (*specus*) on the topmost row of arches, and was the chief water-supply of the Roman town of Nemausus (Nîmes) in S. France.

much has been written of the gay life of Rome under the
Empire, our attention is focussed so continuously on the
pleasure-seekers of the capital, that we are apt to forget
that these diverting scenes are no more typical of the
Empire as a whole than are the products of Hollywood of
the United States of America. In the first and second
centuries A.D., the provinces enjoyed far better government than they had had under the Republic and good
government means good governors. The doings of
Roman ' Society ' affected the Roman world as little as
the doings of London ' Society ' affect the British Empire
and those who followed Augustus' lead towards a more
efficient administration and a better way of life must have
been far more numerous than is often supposed. Even
when corruption in Rome itself became really widespread
the older provinces provided the *gravitas* that the mother
city had lost. Romanization had been so thorough that
the Roman virtues lived on in North Italy, in Spain and
Gaul when they became rare in Rome, and something
permanent remained in Western Europe after the Empire
finally collapsed. For the Romans were a great people
and their political structures had the enduring quality
of their aqueducts. *Si monumentum requiris, circumspice*
--if you seek Rome's memorial, look around you.

Volturr
Pr

SARDINIA

Caralis

Mt. Eryx
Drepana

Aegates
insulae

Par

o Segesta
Lilybaeum

S I

Agrigentum o

C. Ecno

ITALY

English Miles

0 ... 50 ... 100 ... 150

Principal roads ....

CHAPTER II

THE EXPANSION OF ROME IN ITALY
753-264 B.C.

THE FOUNDING OF ROME

THE Mediterranean basin even to-day is to some extent a world of its own, because it is cut off from the rest of Europe and Asia by high mountains and from the rest of Africa by the Sahara, but in the days when means of communication were slow and primitive it was still more a self-contained unit. Although little sailing took place in the winter, the almost tideless sea for most of the year was not a barrier but one of the chief highways for commerce. Commanding this highway and almost bisecting it is the peninsula of Italy with the attendant island of Sicily—the obvious strategical base for any attempt to dominate the area. Down the peninsula of Italy runs the long chain of the Apennines, the main line of communication passing through the coastal plains of the west. Almost in the centre of this line and dominating, as Italy dominates the Mediterranean, the one navigable river of Central Italy—though even the Tiber is navigable only for small boats—situated at the lowest convenient crossing from Etruria in the north to Latium and Campania in the south, and far enough alike from the mountains and the sea to be safe from sudden raids, its hills affording some protection from inundations and from hostile armies, stands the city of Rome.

It was in 753 B.C., according to tradition, that Romulus laid the foundations of the village that was destined to become the capital of the Empire of Augustus Caesar.

He is supposed to have been a son of the god Mars and
Rhea Silvia, daughter of King Numitor of Alba Longa
and a descendant through her of the Trojan prince Aeneas
whose mother was the goddess Venus. The name
Rōmulus, so evidently derived from Rōma, and the man's
doubly divine origin would be enough to make the story
suspect even if he had not been miraculously saved from
exposure with his brother Rĕmus by a she-wolf. But arch
aeological discoveries make it more than suspect. The
Romans were a Latin people and not of Trojan descent
Like the other Latin peoples, they probably came into
Italy from the Danube basin. When they first began to
settle on the slopes of the small hills that lie on the lef
bank of the Tiber, about fifteen miles from its mouth, it is
impossible to say for certain, but it was not until the
second half of the sixth century B.C. that the several
scattered communities were united into a single town—
the so-called City of the Four Regions—with a common
stronghold in the Capitol.

The details of Livy's account of Rome under the kings
are historically of very little value, and indeed it is not
until about 350 B.C. that folklore really gives place to
history ; even thereafter there is a marked tendency to
exaggerate Rome's victories and minimize her defeats
to accept uncritically different versions of the same event
and to tell a good story without bothering overmuch
whether it happens to be true. The broad outline, how
ever, of Rome's early expansion can be redrawn with
tolerable certainty.

THE NORTH—ETRURIA AND THE GAULS
600–350 B.C.

Across the Tiber lay the Etruscan cities, loosely fede-
rated but jealous of one another. These embarked upon

a career of conquest which took them as far to the north-east as Ravenna and as far south as Campania. In the course of it they overthrew the Roman monarchy, and two of the six traditional Kings of Rome, Tarquinius Priscus and Tarquinius Superbus, were certainly Etruscans. The Latin name of Servius Tullius, who comes between them, may indicate a temporary recovery of independence, but even after the expulsion of the second Tarquin and the foundation of the Republic (510 B.C.), the hated foreigner returned for a brief space in the person of Porsenna (a title rather than a name), though patriotic Roman tradition refused to acknowledge the fact. Rome's command of the lower reaches of the Tiber remained extremely precarious until Camillus after a pro-longed siege took the Etruscan town of Veii in 396. Fortunately for Rome most of the other Etruscan cities held aloof, and their rivalries, their preoccupation with money-making and the pressure exerted on them by the Gauls in the North enabled her to advance her northern frontier as far as the Ciminian Forest without much opposition.

THE GAULS had recently established themselves in the plain of Lombardy, north of the Po, which the Romans in consequence termed Cisalpine Gaul, and in 391 a large force of them under Brennus pushed south through Etruria and threatened Rome, which sent out its citizen levies, reinforced by contingents from the other Latin cities, to meet the invaders. In 390 they met on the banks of the Allia, a tributary of the Tiber, and the Roman forces were so decisively defeated that they were compelled to abandon the city and stand a blockade in the Capitol, which fell after seven months' siege. Tradition endeavoured to minimize this disaster by asserting that Camillus, the victor of Veii, returned from exile and twice defeated the Gauls on their way home. Of the truth

of this account we may be extremely doubtful, as we may
doubt the story that the apprehensive cackling of Juno's
sacred geese saved the Capitol from a surprise attack
soon after the Gauls entered the city. Fortunately for
Rome the Gauls wanted plunder rather than an empire
and were satisfied with gold. That they never again
attacked Rome was due partly to the fact that even the
crumbling power of Etruria acted as a kind of barrier—
Rome was lucky once more.

THE SOUTH—THE LATINS 496–338 B.C., THE SAMNITES 343–290 B.C., AND PYRRHUS 282–275 B.C.

In the south also her luck held, for she was able to
strengthen herself at the expense of her neighbours before
having to face her most formidable Italian opponents
the Samnites, who lived in the Apennines to the south-
east. Three years after an indecisive battle against the
other Latin cities at Lake Regillus in 496 Rome concluded
with them an alliance on equal terms to ensure their
common safety against the Aequi and Volsci, who were
periodically making descents upon the plain of Latium.
The Latin cities bore the brunt of these attacks, and by
the time the mountain tribes were finally driven out of
Latium Rome was strong enough to insist on assuming
the leadership of the Latin League (360).

THE FIRST SAMNITE WAR. Meanwhile the Samnites
had overrun Campania, from which they had dislodged
the Etruscans. When Capua, the leading city of Campania, called for Roman assistance in expelling the
invader (343), Rome answered the call but deserted her
new ally in 341 after achieving some success, when the
Samnites offered her a treaty of alliance. This was
construed by the Latin cities as a sign of weakness
and with the assistance of the Campanian cities they

revolted. Rome with Samnite help defeated the combined forces of her opponents at Suessa Aurunca (340),
and the revolt was over by 338. The Latin League was
dissolved, some of the cities being incorporated in Roman
territory and the others being bound to Rome by separate
treaties, while the towns of Campania accepted Roman
protection. Colonies were established on the coast of
Latium and on the Campanian border as military outposts ; of these Fregellae was the most important.

The Second Samnite War broke out in 327, when
the Samnites introduced an armed force into the Greek
colony of Neapolis and Rome intervened again at the
request of Capua, which regarded this as a fresh threat
to herself. For six years the Romans controlled the
plains of the west and even crossed to the Adriatic coast,
though they dared not attack the Samnites in their
mountain strongholds, but in 321, while making for
Apulia in an endeavour to take the Samnites in the rear,
their army was trapped in the Caudine Forks and compelled to capitulate. Rome was forced to make peace and
surrender Fregellae and other outposts. In 315 the war
was renewed, and Rome suffered another serious reverse
in the pass of Lautulae while trying to keep open her line
of communications with Capua. In the next year,
however, the tide turned and Rome gained a foothold in
Apulia with the capture of Luceria. From 311 onwards
her main efforts were directed against the Etruscans,
whom the Samnites induced to join in the war, and when
she finally beat them to a standstill, the Samnites, feeling
themselves isolated, sued for peace in 304.

The Third Samnite War, like the other two, opened
with an appeal for Roman help—this time from the
Lucanians (298). The Samnites enlisted the aid of the
Gauls and Etruscans, and in 296 marched north, drawing
the Roman army after them. The ensuing Roman defeat

was soon avenged at Sentinum (295), a victory which detached the Gauls and Etruscans from their allies, and in 290 the Samnites themselves capitulated.

PYRRHUS. The establishment of a strong Roman colony at Venusia alarmed the powerful Greek city of Tarentum. In 282 she attacked a Roman fleet which appeared in the Gulf and summoned help from Pyrrhus, king of Epirus in the north-west of Greece. The first engagement of the war at Heraclea (280) on the south coast was a costly victory for Pyrrhus, gained largely by his corps of elephants, and brought the remaining Greek cities, the Samnites and Lucanians onto his side. But Rome's allies nearer home remained loyal and his second victory at Asculum (279) was even more costly ; so that in later days men called such successes ' Pyrrhic ' victories. Unable to secure the terms he wanted, Pyrrhus proceeded to attack Sicily during the next three years until the hard-pressed Samnites begged him to return. But his army was by now much less formidable and suffered defeat at Beneventum (275). Pyrrhus left Italy, and Rome shortly afterwards established garrisons in Tarentum and other towns.

The little city on the Tiber was now the undisputed mistress of all Italy south of the Po. Her predominant position had been acquired not by brilliance but by hard work. Time and again she had suffered disaster ; time and again she had profited by her mistakes, reorganized her resources and kept hammering away at the enemy until he was finally defeated.

CHAPTER III

THE CARTHAGINIAN MENACE
264–202 B.C.

THE leading power of the Western Mediterranean was the great commercial city of Carthage. Founded by Phoenicians from Tyre about 800, it had obtained control by naval supremacy of the seaboards of North Africa and Southern Spain, of the islands of Corsica and Sardinia, and of the western part of Sicily, the eastern part being already in the hands of Greek colonies, of which the chief was Syracuse. The coasts of Italy Carthage had left severely alone, concluding treaties with the dominant power of the West, first Etruria and later Rome.

THE FIRST PUNIC WAR 264–241 B.C.

In 264 the independent town of Messana in the north of Sicily (which had been seized by some Campanian mercenaries, who called themselves Mamertini or sons of Mars) was attacked by Hiero, king of Syracuse, and not unnaturally appealed to Carthage, which sent a force and demanded his withdrawal. Hiero withdrew but the Carthaginian force remained in the town. Messana thereupon appealed to Rome, which sent a force and demanded the Carthaginians' withdrawal. The Carthaginians withdrew but the Romans remained; and Carthage and Hiero formed an alliance to turn them out —a curious alliance at first sight, but Sicily was not big enough to have a third Great Power meddling in its affairs. When, however, Rome made it clear, by laying siege to Syracuse, that she had come to stay, Hiero was quite prepared to come to terms on condition that his dominion in the east of the island should in the future remain undisturbed, and Rome was wise enough to offer him that condition. In this peculiar way the First Punic War began.

Rome had now to turn herself into a naval power, for only control of the sea could enable her to consolidate any success she might win on land, and she proceeded to build a fleet of 150 ships, which defeated the Carthaginians off Mylae (260) in the north of Sicily, the Romans employing a *corvus*, or grappling-hook, to prevent their opponents from breaking away. Carthage had for so long been unchallenged mistress of the seas that this amazing success on the part of a nation which had never shown any aptitude or liking for naval warfare threw the Carthaginian authorities off their balance, and they made no effort to reverse the decision of Mylae until in 256 the Romans, having gained control of central Sicily, prepared to carry the war into the territory of Carthage itself. The decision of Mylae was, however, confirmed off Cape Ecnomus in the south of Sicily, as the Carthaginian effort had been made too late and with too much counting of the cost—a failing that contributed in no small measure to the ultimate downfall of this ' nation of shop-keepers '—and Rome was free to land her invading army under Atilius Regulus in Africa. Initial successes made Regulus overconfident, and his army was annihilated in 255. To make matters worse the Roman fleet, after beating the Carthaginians for the third time off Cape Hermaeum to the north-east of Carthage, was nearly wiped out in a severe storm.

Characteristically Rome did not allow herself to be deterred by this double disaster and immediately set to work to bring the fleet up to strength again and to capture the Carthaginian stronghold of Panormus in the west of

Sicily. But this great effort was exhausting, and when in 249 part of the fleet was beaten off Drepana and most of the rest wrecked in another storm, there was talk of peace—talk which came to nothing largely owing to the pleading of Regulus, who preferred to return to captivity and even death rather than to persuade the senate to adopt a policy of appeasement.

Had the Carthaginians supplied their new general Hamilcar Barca, with enough troops, he might well have turned the Romans out of Sicily at this juncture. But they failed him, as they were later to fail Hannibal, and in 241 off the Aegates Islands the Romans won a great naval victory, which made it impossible for Carthage to maintain a force in Sicily any longer. Their success gave them their first province, and they had earned it by their superior morale and the great sacrifices in men and money they had been prepared to make. Their second soon followed with the annexation of the two islands Corsica and Sardinia in 238—an annexation which Carthage, having lost command of the sea, was unable to prevent.

THE SECOND PUNIC WAR 218–202 B.C.

The loss of revenue which Carthage thus sustained was serious, and to make this good and at the same time to secure fresh man-power for her armies, which had hitherto relied too much on mercenaries, Hamilcar determined to extend his country's hold on Spain into the interior, where there was considerable mineral wealth. By promising not to advance beyond the River Ebro the Carthaginians allayed the suspicions of Rome, which already had the preliminary conquest of Cisalpine Gaul on its hands (225–220), but they probably never intended to keep their promise. In 219 Hannibal, Hamilcar's son, who had now succeeded to the command, attacked Saguntum on the east coast. though he knew that Rome might well come to the assistance of a city with which she was allied. He realized that Carthage could have no security as long as Rome remained undefeated; if she accepted the challenge, he was ready. Rome was not ready, but when Saguntum fell she accepted the challenge and embarked on the Second Punic War in 218, without fully appreciating the difficulties with which she would be faced. Hannibal was determined to take the offensive, and before a Roman army could reach Spain he was proceeding to cross the Alps, an operation which cost him nearly half his army of 50,000 men. He was confident that this loss would easily be made good by the desertion to him of the cities Rome had recently conquered, and his great victory near the River Trebia (218) did bring the Gallic tribes over to him. But his next success at Lake Trasimene in 217, where he ambushed the Romans between the foothills and the lake, did not have any similar effect. Central Italy remained loyal and Rome reaped the fruits of her generosity; for this failure in his calculations kept Hannibal from attacking the city and was the ultimate cause of his defeat, since the Carthaginian government would not, or could not, supply his growing deficiency in man-power.

The necessity for caution after Trasimene was fully realised by Q. Fabius Maximus, now appointed dictator, and he wisely refused to meet Hannibal in pitched battle in the belief that time was on the side of the Romans and that if Hannibal was to win, he would have to win quickly. This policy, which earned him the nickname Cunctator, demanded too much patience for the average Roman and was reversed in 216, when Fabius was replaced by consuls, who gave battle to Hannibal at Cannae in Apulia with disastrous results. Hannibal employed his favourite tactics, ordering the Carthaginian centre to give ground until the Roman centre was hemmed in on three

sides and wiped out, the superior numbers of the Romans
availing them nothing.

Following the heavy defeats of the previous two years,
Cannae forced Rome to make an effort greater even than
that which was necessitated by the Allia, especially as
the loyalty of her allies began to show signs of cracking
and most of South Italy, except the colonies and the
Greek cities of the coast, changed sides. Despite their
enormous losses the Romans nearly doubled the size of
their armies, as they doubled the *tributum*, and reintroduced ' Fabian tactics ' to such good purpose that the
poet Ennius wrote of their author, " *Unus homo nobis
cunctando restituit rem* " (One man, by refusing to meet
the enemy in pitched battle, saved the state) Hannibal
was therefore unable to deliver the final blow and attack
Rome itself ; for Central Italy remained loyal to Rome,
and no reinforcements arrived either from Carthage or
from Spain. The Romans had maintained an army in
Spain from the outset in order to keep Hasdrubal and the
troops there under his command from joining his brother
in Italy. In 210 this army was assigned to P. Cornelius
Scipio (son of the commander of the original expeditionary
force who had been killed in 211), who was then only
twenty-five, and he proceeded to show that he possessed
military genius of the highest order by employing Hannibal's own tactics to defeat Hasdrubal at Baecula (208).
Feeling that the Carthaginian forces must no longer be
divided, Hasdrubal withdrew his army to Italy but was
intercepted by both consular armies and defeated at the
battle of the River Metaurus (207), the first news of which
reached Hannibal, it is said, when his brother's head was
thrown into the Carthaginian camp. Hannibal was no
longer a menace and the senate allowed him to remain in
the far south for four more years, while Scipio won Spain
for Rome by the victory of Ilipa (206) and then carried

the war into Africa. So serious had matters become in 203 that Hannibal was recalled, only to be defeated at Zama (202) by Scipio and his Numidian ally, Masinissa.

Besides the Carthaginian dominions in Spain Rome gained from the war the territory of Syracuse, which had thrown in its lot with Carthage and capitulated only after a long siege (213–211) which the mechanical skill of Archimedes had enabled it to sustain, and the surrender of almost the whole of the Carthaginian navy, of which far too little use had been made. Rome's command of the sea was almost as important a factor in her victory as her pertinacity and the steadfastness of her allies, and it remained an important factor in her future success as an imperial power.

CHAPTER IV

THE EXPANSION OF ROME IN THE WEST AND NORTH

202 B.C.–A.D. 117

THE WEST—SPAIN, GAUL, AND BRITAIN

South-east SPAIN was formed into two provinces Hispania Citerior and Hispania Ulterior (197), but owing to the difficult nature of the terrain and the skill of its tribes in guerrilla warfare, it was not until the fall of Numantia (133) that Rome really gained control of the interior, and the Cantabri in the north were not finally subdued until the reign of Augustus (26–19). To maintain their land communications with Spain the Romans, having reconquered CISALPINE GAUL (191), made Liguria (180) part of Italy and turned the lower Rhône valley from the Alps to the Pyrenees into a province ; this was called GALLIA NARBONENSIS from the colony of Narbo which the Romans established to guard the coast road (121). So quickly was this district Romanized that it was sometimes referred to simply as Provincia (hence the French Provence) ; but its safety could never be guaranteed until its frontiers had been pushed forward to the Rhine and the English Channel or even to the Cheviots and the Elbe. Thus we may truly say that Claudius' annexation of Britain in A.D. 43 was the eventual result of Rome's defeat of Hannibal nearly two hundred and fifty years before, inasmuch as the security of Spain demanded the annexation of Gaul and the security of Gaul the annexation of Britain.

MARIUS AND THE CIMBRI. The liability of the new province to attack soon became apparent when two

German tribes, the Cimbri and the Teutones, migrated southwards and in 105 inflicted a very severe defeat on the Romans at Arausio on the left bank of the Rhône. Fortunately for Rome the barbarians made no real use of their victory, but moved westwards towards the Pyrenees in search of plunder, and it was not until 102 that they began to make for Italy. Marius,[1] who was consul for five successive years (104–100), had thus time to prepare his army and heavily defeated the Teutones at Aquae Sextiae, south-east of Arausio. Meanwhile the Cimbri had succeeded in reaching the plain of Lombardy, but Marius prevented any further penetration of Italy by his victory near Vercellae on the Raudine Plain (101). The conquest of the three remaining provinces of Gaul, Aquitania, Lugdunensis and Belgica, was, however, left until C. Julius Caesar became governor of Cisalpine Gaul and Gallia Narbonensis in 58.

CAESAR'S intervention beyond the Roman frontier was precipitated—as so often in Roman history—by an appeal for help. The Celtic tribe of the Helvetii had been driven out of Southern Germany into Switzerland, and, when their way through Narbonese Gaul was barred, began to move towards the territory of the Aedui on the right bank of the Rhône in search of a new home. Caesar advanced north to assist the Aedui and pushed the Helvetii back, but was almost immediately compelled to deal with the more formidable inroads of the German Suebi under Ariovistus from across the Rhine. His success gave him control of both sides of the Rhône as far north as the neighbourhood of Vesontio. The next year saw the subjugation of the Belgae and the Nervii in the north-east of the country, and in 56, while his fleet subdued the Veneti of Brittany, his army overran Aquitania in the south-west. In three years Caesar had

[1] See pages 125 and 152-3.

succeeded in subduing the circumference of Gaul, and after securing his right flank by driving two German tribes, the Usipetes and the Tencteri, back across the northern Rhine he felt strong enough in 55 to reconnoitre south-east Britain.

BRITAIN racially and economically had very close ties with Gaul, which were cemented by a common adherence to Druidism, and it was probably rather to secure the loyalty of Gaul than because of Britain's richness in iron and tin that Caesar contemplated its annexation. But although in the next year he headed a second and larger expedition which reached the Thames valley, neither Caesar nor Augustus, who was twice prevented by revolts from completing preparations for invasion, achieved the actual conquest even of the south. This was the work of the emperor Claudius, who in A.D. 43 sent a force of four and a half legions under A. Plautius Silvanus, which in four years subdued the country as far as a line drawn from Glevum (Gloucester) to Camulodunum (Colchester). Ostorius Scapula, governor from 47 to 52, carried the advance into Wales, where he defeated and captured Caratacus [1]. *Legio* II *Augusta* was stationed first at Gloucester and then at Isca (Caerleon), *legio* XIV *Gemina Martia* at Viroconium (Wroxeter), *legio* XX *Valeria Victrix* at Deva (Chester) and *legio* IX *Hispana* at Lindum (Lincoln). In 61 while Suetonius Paulinus (59–61) was proceeding to invade Mona (Anglesey), he was recalled by the revolt of Boudicca,[1] queen of the Iceni in East Anglia, who had sacked Camulodunum and cut the Ninth Legion to pieces. Alleged to have used his ensuing victory too severely, Paulinus was recalled, and the Roman advance slowed down until the governorship of Agricola (77–84). Agricola completed the conquest of North Wales and then carried Roman arms into

---

[1] Commonly, but incorrectly, known as Caractacus and Boadicea.

Scotland, using first Deva and then Eburacum (York), to which the Ninth Legion had been recently moved, as his base. By his victory at Mons Graupius he established the Roman frontier on a line based on the valleys of the Clyde and Tay, though it was brought back to the Cheviots late in the reign of Trajan (91–117) or early in that of Hadrian (117–138) and fortified by a stone rampart, which is still called ' Hadrian's Wall '. For this withdrawal Trajan's costly victories in the East were responsible.

VERCINGETORIX. Several revolts in the north of Gaul kept Caesar from crossing the Channel again in 53 B.C., and in 52 a really serious insurrection broke out under Vercingetorix, chief of the Arverni, whose territory in the centre of the country had never been systematically subdued. The revolt spread and might have succeeded, had not Vercingetorix shut himself up in Alesia, which Caesar eventually starved out in 51. Two years later the country was sufficiently pacified for him to withdraw most of his troops to fight Pompey.

THE NORTH—THE RHINE AND THE DANUBE

THE RHINE. A German invasion of Gaul in 16 B.C. crystallized Augustus' intention to advance the Roman frontier to the River Elbe in order to prevent the German tribes from crossing the Rhine, and from 12 B.C. onwards his stepson, Drusus, overran Western Germany, his gains being gradually consolidated on Drusus' death in 9 B.C. by his brother Tiberius. But all their work was undone in A.D. 9 by the annihilation of three legions under the command of Varus ; for though in fact the disaster might very well have been retrieved, it made Augustus deter-mine—whether through the mere weariness of age or because of the scarcity of man-power—to re-establish the

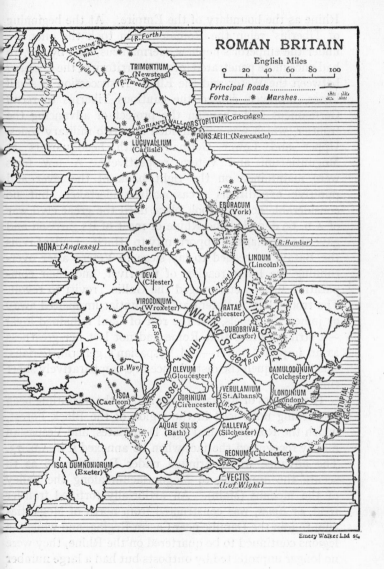

ROMAN BRITAIN

English Miles

0   20   40   60   80   100

Principal Roads ....
Forts .... *   Marshes ....

(R. Forth)

ANTONINE'S WALL

(R. Clyde)

(R. Clyde)

TRIMONTIUM
(Newstead)

(R. Tweed)

HADRIAN'S WALL   CORSTOPITUM (Corbridge)

PONS AELII (Newcastle)

LUGUVALLIUM
(Carlisle)

EBURACUM
(York)

MONA (Anglesey)   (Manchester)   (R. Humber)

LINDUM
(Lincoln)

DEVA
(Chester)

VIROCONIUM
(Wroxeter)   (R. Trent)

RATAE
(Leicester)

Ermine Street

(R. Severn)   DUROBRIVAE
(Castor)

Watling Street

(R. Ouse)

(R. Wye)   GLEVUM
(Gloucester)   CAMULODUNUM
(Colchester)

Fosse Way

ISCA
(Caerleon)   CORINIUM
(Cirencester)   VERULAMIUM
(St. Albans)   LONDINIUM
(London)

(R. Thames)   RUTUPIAE
(Richborough)

AQUAE SULIS
(Bath)   CALLEVA
(Silchester)

REGNUM (Chichester)

ISCA DUMNONIORUM
(Exeter)

VECTIS
(I. of Wight)

Emery Walker Ltd sc.

Rhine as the boundary of the Empire. At the beginning
of Tiberius' reign the Romans again took the offensive
under the emperor's nephew, Germanicus, who by A.D. 16
had once more penetrated into the territory of the Cherusci
between the Weser and the Elbe. A succession of small
losses, however, caused the cautious Tiberius to recall
Germanicus and abandon the project of advancing the
frontier, which was now divided into two military zones,
Upper and Lower Germany, with headquarters at
Moguntiacum and Vetera respectively. A few forts
were maintained on the right bank of the river and
punitive expeditions occasionally undertaken, but no
considerable activity took place until the great civil war
of A.D. 69 denuded the Rhine of most of its garrison and
gave the Germans an opportunity to attack. Under Civilis
the Batavi proceeded to lay siege to Vetera after over-
running the lower reaches of the river, and their com-
parative success encouraged the Gallic Treviri to revolt.
The troops left at Vetera and Moguntiacum melted away
or joined the rebels, but the rest of Gaul remained loyal
—a striking proof that Rome had not lost her greatness
as an imperial power—and Vespasian's general, Cerialis,
was able to quell the disturbance in a comparatively short
time.

The process of Romanization had in the meantime been
proceeding unnoticed in the region of the Black Forest,
which the Romans called Agri Decumates, and Vespasian
merely recognized the fact when he annexed it in A.D. 73.
The advance was continued under Domitian so as to
secure the approach to Moguntiacum along the valley
of the Moenus (Main). An artificially fortified frontier
road, or *limes*, was constructed from north of Moguntiacum to join the Danube near Castra Regina, and while the
legions continued to be quartered on the Rhine, they were
no longer unprotected by outposts but had a large number

of auxiliary forts in front of them on the opposite bank
of the river—an important innovation. This annexation
filled up the acute angle which had existed in the northern
frontier since Rome had secured the Alpine passes by the
subjugation of Raetia in 15 B.C. and Noricum in 16 B.C.

THE DANUBE. Further east the frontier of Illyricum
had been pushed forward to the river Savus in 35 and
34 B.C. by Octavian,[1] and from 12 to 9 B.C. it was advanced
to the Dravus by Tiberius, who penetrated as far as the
Danube. While planning a pincers movement against
the Marcomanni in Bohemia from Carnuntum on the
Danube and Moguntiacum on the Rhine simultaneously,
he was recalled in A.D. 6 by a serious revolt, which spread
from Pannonia to Dalmatia and was not subdued until
A.D. 9. Illyricum was then split up into two separate
provinces, Dalmatia and Pannonia, and by A.D. 50 the
district between the Dravus and the Danube was sufficiently Romanized for Claudius to move the Poetovio
garrison north to Carnuntum.

A similar advance was made on the lower Danube from
29 B.C. onwards, and Moesia became a province in A.D. 6.
But the Danube, like the Rhine, did not prove an altogether satisfactory frontier. Under King Decebalus the
inroads of the Dacians into Moesia became so serious
a menace in the reign of Domitian (A.D. 86) that he was
compelled to embark on a war of aggression. Circumstances, however, prevented him from carrying the war
to final victory and a peace was patched up in A.D. 89.
The offensive was resumed by Trajan in A.D. 101 and after
two considerable wars he secured the Danube line by the
annexation of Dacia (A.D. 107) as an outlying bastion
of the Empire.

[1] Great-nephew of Julius Caesar, afterwards called Augustus.

CHAPTER V

THE EXPANSION OF ROME IN THE SOUTH
AND EAST 202 B.C.–A.D. 117

THE SOUTH—AFRICA, NUMIDIA AND MAURETANIA

FOR more than fifty years after Zama CARTHAGE itself
remained unmolested by Rome. Eventually, however,
the repeated and vigorous protests of the diehard Cato—
who when asked his opinion in the senate on any matter
invariably replied " *Delenda est Carthago* " (Carthage must
be destroyed)—had their effect, and an army under
Scipio Aemilianus [1] secured her capitulation after a
desperate resistance (149–146). What remained of her
territories became the province of Africa.

MARIUS AND JUGURTHA. On the death of Micipsa,
Masinissa's successor, in 118, the kingdom of Numidia
was divided between his three sons, but one of them,
Jugurtha, killed his brothers and secured their princi-
palities for himself. Passions were aroused in Rome, as
Jugurtha had not scrupled to put certain Roman citizens
to death in his bid for power, and these were not appeased
by the dilatory methods of the generals sent out by the
senate. Finally the assembly took matters into its own
hands by entrusting the command to Marius, a *novus
homo*,[2] recently elected consul for 107. Realizing that
men who served unwillingly made poor soldiers, Marius
revolutionized the system of recruitment by calling for
volunteers,[3] with which he was sufficiently successful to

---

[1] Grandson by adoption of the victor of Zama.

[2] I.e. a man who was the first of his family to hold a high office of
state.

[3] See pages 125 and 152–3.

persuade Bocchus, ruler of the neighbouring kingdom of
Mauretania, to betray Jugurtha, who was taken to Rome
and put to death. NUMIDIA remained a native kingdom
until the reign of Augustus, when it was incorporated in
the province of Africa, while MAURETANIA was formed
into two small provinces, Caesariensis and Tingitana,
under Claudius.

THE EAST—MACEDONIA 216–146 B.C., AND
ANTIOCHUS 192–189 B.C.

On the death of Alexander the Great in 323 his empire
was split up among his generals into various independent
states, of which the kingdoms of Macedonia, Syria, and
Egypt were the chief. Just before the Second Punic War
Rome gained a foothold in Illyria on the east of the
Adriatic by destroying certain pirate bases. After Cannae
(216) Philip V of MACEDONIA, thinking that Hannibal
was on the way to complete victory, entered into alliance
with him ; but although Macedonia was technically at war
with Rome until 205, the First Macedonian War was a
very trivial affair. Philip, however, was bent on aggression, and when he began to threaten the kingdom of
Pergamum in Asia Minor and the island of Rhodes in 201,
Rome decided to intervene, war-weary as she was. Her
victory at Cynoscephalae in Thessaly (197) concluded the
Second Macedonian War and enabled her to insist on
Philip's desisting from his schemes of conquest.

The Third Macedonian War broke out in 171, though
it could easily have been avoided had the senate handled
Philip's successor, Perseus, more skilfully, and was
brought to an end by the victory of Aemilius Paullus at
Pydna (168). Perseus was deposed and his kingdom
split up into four republics, Rome still refusing to assume
the responsibilities of direct control. She had only

herself to blame, therefore, when the unsatisfactory
position encouraged a pretender, named Andriscus, to
reunite the country against her in 149, so that she had
to fight a fourth war and at long last decide on annexation.
In 146 Macedonia was constituted a regular province, and
its governor was given general control of Illyria and of
the Greek city-states, which were no longer allowed to
form themselves into leagues, although they remained
nominally independent until 81.

Between the Second and Third Macedonian Wars Rome
had had to fight (192–189) ANTIOCHUS III of SYRIA as
he had seen in Philip's discomfiture an opportunity to
turn the quarrels of the Greek cities to his own ends by invading their country. The Romans carried the war into
his territory and decisively defeated him, but refrained
from creating any provinces in Asia Minor till the Per-
gamene royal family died out in 133 ; the last king of
Pergamum, Attalus III, bequeathed them his country,
which they formed into the rich province of Asia.

THE EAST—MITHRIDATES 88–65 B.C., SYRIA AND
JUDAEA 64 B.C.–A.D. 70

A more formidable opponent, however, soon appeared.
While Rome was engaged with Jugurtha and with the
Cimbri and Teutones, the kingdom of PONTUS was extend-
ing its control under the able direction of MITHRIDATES VI
(120–63) as far north as the Crimea and over the kingdoms
of Galatia and Cappadocia in Asia Minor. In 88 he
invaded Bithynia, swept on into the province of Asia,
and sent an expeditionary force across the Aegean into
Greece.

Sulla's campaigns (88–4) compelled him to evacuate his
conquests, but the king again assumed the offensive in 74.
Lucullus was given the eastern command and in the

following year invaded Pontus, his fleet having already cleared the Aegean of Mithridates' navy. For a time Lucullus could not bring the enemy to battle, but by the end of 70 he was master of the whole of Asia Minor. Mithridates had sought refuge with his son-in-law, Tigranes, king of Armenia, and since his surrender was refused, Lucullus felt justified in undertaking the invasion of that difficult country, although he had no authority from the senate to do so. With a mere 16,000 men he won a complete victory outside Tigranocerta (69)—a convincing proof of his military genius—and pushed on towards Artaxata, the capital. His plans were checked by a mutiny among his weary troops, but had he received reinforcements, he might have resumed his march the following year. His enemies at home, however, by undermining his authority, compelled him to retire and allow Mithridates and Tigranes to regain the territory they had lost.

In 66 Lucullus was superseded by POMPEY, whose first independent command had been in Spain (77–72), where he had eventually crushed by the aid of treachery the rising of the Marian leader, Sertorius. In 67 the *lex Gabinia* had given him a special command against the pirates of the eastern Mediterranean, whose activities had become so dangerous that Rome was actually threatened with famine, and he had made the seas safe again in the space of three months, and added Crete to the Empire. Now by the *lex Manilia* (66) he was given complete command in the East. The real spade work had already been accomplished by Lucullus, and Pompey had no difficulty in defeating Mithridates or in bringing about the submission of Tigranes, who was frightened by the prospect of a war on two fronts—against Rome and against Parthia. Tigranes was left in possession of his kingdom, but Pontus was divided between the province of Bithynia, bequeathed to Rome by King Nicomedes in 74, and the kingdom of Galatia.

In 64 Pompey annexed SYRIA, which had fallen into a state of anarchy, and in the following year captured Jerusalem, when his mediation in the civil war then raging was not accepted. Most of JUDAEA remained nominally independent and in 40 was entrusted by the triumvir, Antony, to Herod the Great. On his death in 4 B.C. his kingdom was divided between his three sons, but Augustus deposed the eldest, Archelaus, for misgovernment in A.D. 6, and made his tetrarchy a minor province. The dominions of Herod the Great were temporarily (A.D. 41–44) reunited under Herod Agrippa I, a personal friend of Claudius. A serious revolt broke out in Judaea in A.D. 66. Most of the country was reduced by the future emperor Vespasian in the next two years, but the actual capture of Jerusalem in 70, after he had ascended the throne, was accomplished by his son, Titus.

THE EAST—PARTHIA AND ARMENIA
53 B.C.–A.D. 117

Pompey's conquests brought Rome face to face with the Parthians, who had succeeded to the old Persian empire, and when Crassus obtained the eastern command as his share of the first triumvirate in 56, he attempted to win military glory by attacking them. As, however, he omitted to provide himself with an adequate cavalry force, his infantry was ignominiously defeated by the mounted archers of the Parthians at Carrhae in Mesopotamia in 53, and he himself was killed. Julius Caesar made preparations to avenge this defeat but he did not live to carry his plans into action, and the initiative was actually taken by the Parthians, who overran Syria, Judaea and most of Asia Minor in 40. They were soon repelled by *legati* of Antony, who in 36 himself took the offensive, backed by the resources of Cleopatra, queen of Egypt. He invaded the Parthian territories by way of Armenia, but his lines of communication proved inadequate, and when he assumed the offensive again in 33, the attacks which Octavian began to make against him soon necessitated his withdrawal.[1]

After the battle of Actium (31), Octavian, or Augustus, as he became known, was the undisputed master of the Roman world. As such he was able to win a bloodless victory over Parthia in 20, his prestige alone enabling him to secure the return of the standards lost by Crassus and so restore Roman ' face ' in the East without a blow. But beyond annexing Egypt, which had such economic and strategic importance that he governed it by means of an equestrian *praefectus* and refused to allow any senator to set foot in it without his permission, and Galatia, Augustus did not increase Roman territory in the East; for he had no desire to undertake unnecessary commitments or to embark on a costly and dangerous campaign in that quarter, especially as he knew himself to be no military genius. He relied instead on a system of client kingdoms on the Roman side of the frontier, with Armenia as a buffer-state beyond—a system similar to that adopted by Britain on the North-West frontier of India. The absorption of the client kingdoms into the provincial system was only a matter of time, and in 72 Vespasian gave Asia Minor the strong frontier it had long needed on the upper Euphrates by enlarging Cappadocia and garrisoning it with a force of two legions.

Armenia itself presented a different kind of problem. To an emperor with military ambitions, like Trajan, its annexation—actually achieved in A.D. 114—was not a matter of any insuperable difficulty ; but its climate and

[1] See pages 175–6.

position made it exceedingly hard to hold unless the whole Parthian Empire were brought under Roman rule. The annexation of Mesopotamia as well as Armenia, however, made the Empire top-heavy and Hadrian showed wisdom in abandoning his predecessor's conquests. As a matter of fact after many years of rivalry in Armenian politics, which cost more than one Armenian king his life, since each side was naturally anxious to have its own nominee on the throne, Rome and Parthia had arrived at a reasonable compromise in A.D. 64 whereby the Parthian nominee, Tiridates, agreed to receive his crown from Nero's hands.

CHAPTER VI

THE FRONTIER POLICY OF AUGUSTUS

THE PROVINCES OF THE AUGUSTAN EMPIRE

For reference only

	Date	Means of Acquisition
Sicily	241	First Punic War (264–241).
Sardinia and Corsica	238	Conquest from Carthage.
Hispania Citerior ⎫ ,, Ulterior ⎭	197	Second Punic War (218–202). (Hispania Ulterior divided into Lusitania and Baetica by Augustus.)
Africa	146	Third Punic War (149–146). (Extended by Augustus to include Numidia.)
Macedonia (+Achaea 81)	146	Fourth Macedonian War (149–148). (Achaea formed into separate province by Augustus.)
Asia	133	Bequest of Attalus III, King of Pergamum.
Gallia Narbonensis	121	Conquest.
Cilicia (+Cyprus 58)	103	Pirate War (extended by Pompey 64; joined to Syria by Augustus, detached again by Vespasian).
Cisalpine Gaul	81	Detached from Italy by Sulla.
Bithynia	74	Bequest of Nicomedes III (extended by Pompey to include part of Pontus 63).
Cyrene ⎫ combined by Crete ⎭ Augustus	74 67	Bequest of Ptolemy Apion of Egypt 96. Pirate War of Pompey.
Syria (+Commagene A.D. 72)	63	Pompey's Eastern Settlement.
Illyricum (Dalmatia)	59	Detached from Macedonia.

Gallia Aquitania
   Lugdunensis
   Belgica
	51	Campaigns of Julius Caesar (divided into 3 provinces by Augustus).

Egypt	30	Defeat of Antony and Cleopatra.
Galatia (+Pontus Polemoniacus A.D. 64)	25	Annexation on the death of King Amyntas.
Pamphylia (+Lycia A.D. 43)	25	Separated from Galatia intermittently.

121

			Date	Means of Acquisition
Raetia	-	-	- 15	Campaigns of Tiberius and Drusus.
Alpes Maritimae		-	14	Conquest.
Noricum	-	-	- 10?	Conquest in 16.
Judaea	-	-	-A.D. 6	Deposition of Archelaus.
Moesia	-	-	-A.D. 6	Conquest (separated into Moesia Superior and Inferior by Domitian).
Pannonia	-	-	-A.D. 9	Detached from Illyricum (conquered by Tiberius 12–9 B.C.).

In order to retain under his own control all the armed forces of the state and minimize the risk of a fresh outbreak of civil war, Augustus himself became under the settlement of 27 B.C. the nominal governor of about half these provinces—roughly speaking those which lay on the frontiers or might be restive enough to require the use of military power—and administered them by means of *legati*. Africa was the only senatorial province that contained a legion. The other provinces which remained under the senate's control after the final adjustment of 11 B.C. were : Asia, Sicily, Gallia Narbonensis, Baetica, Macedonia, Achaea, Bithynia, Crete and Cyrene, and Cyprus (detached from Cilicia). Macedonia and Achaea formed an imperial province from A.D. 15 to 44, and all new provinces were imperial.

Provinces Added a.d. 14–117

	Date	Means of Acquisition
Germania Superior -	17	Military zones detached from the
,, Inferior -		provinces of Gaul (extended by acquisition of Agri Decumates and Taunus Mts. under Vespasian and Domitian).
Cappadocia (+ Armenia Minor 72)	17	Deposition of King Archelaus.
Mauretania Caesariensis Tingitana	42	Conquest.
Britain - - -	43	Invasion by A. Plautius.
Thrace - - -	46	Abolition of client kingdom.

	Date	Means of Acquisition
Dacia - - -	107	Conquest by Trajan.
Armenia - - -	114	Conquest by Trajan (abandoned by Hadrian).
Mesopotamia - -	117	Conquest by Trajan (abandoned by Hadrian).

The number of annexations in the first century A.D. is noticeably small, partly because the emperors were jealous of military successes won by anyone but themselves but more because they were following the considered advice of Augustus to his successors. Augustus was a man of remarkable common-sense and he clearly realized that his defeat of Antony at Actium in 31 B.C. must mark the end of the colossal expenditure in men and money which the civil wars and the long campaigns of Caesar in Gaul had imposed upon the state. He therefore disbanded more than half the sixty legions at his disposal, and resolved to undertake only such offensive operations as he considered really necessary to ensure the safety of the provinces. He fixed as the natural limits of the Empire the Atlantic, the Sahara and the great rivers Euphrates, Danube and Elbe. After the defeat of Varus in A.D. 9 he changed his mind about the Elbe and withdrew to THE RHINE, but his original intention to push forward makes it probable that he regarded this withdrawal as a temporary expedient. He had presumably seen that the ease with which the Chatti could approach the bridgehead at Moguntiacum along the valley of the Moenus made the line of the Rhine an unsatisfactory frontier. Domitian, therefore, in annexing the Taunus bulge and so securing the bridgehead showed a better understanding of Augustus' real policy than did the cautious Tiberius.

Although Roman armies operated beyond THE DANUBE in Augustus' reign, the river did not become the recognized frontier until Claudius established a legion permanently at Carnuntum in A.D. 50. This advance

Augustus must have anticipated, but there is no indication that he foresaw that the Danube would prove no more satisfactory a frontier than the Rhine. Nevertheless, if he had had foreknowledge of the serious Dacian inroads into Moesia which occurred under the Flavians, he would probably have approved Domitian's Dacian campaigns and Trajan's annexation of the country.

On the other hand, he would have strongly condemned Trajan's aggression in THE EAST and supported Hadrian's action in abandoning Armenia and Mesopotamia. He no doubt looked forward to the gradual absorption of the client kingdoms of Asia Minor into the provincial system and the creation of a strong frontier province on the Euphrates. But the compromise over Armenia to which Nero had assented in A.D. 64 had worked reasonably well and Trajan's offensive in that country and in Mesopotamia was not really justified by reasons of security. Augustus' own method of dealing with the Parthians was diplomacy backed by a display of force, but not the use of force.

Claudius' conquest of BRITAIN was the only considerable offensive operation undertaken between Augustus' death and Trajan's accession. At first sight it might appear to come into the same category as Trajan's Eastern wars, as being dictated by personal ambition or commercial reasons rather than by reasons of security. But the connection between Britain and Gaul was so close that Augustus himself had twice contemplated attacking the island, though circumstances had prevented his carrying out his intention, and Claudius' action was no doubt justified. If so, Trajan, as the first great general to ascend the imperial throne, was the first emperor to depart from Augustus' policy of keeping the Empire within its natural boundaries—a policy thoroughly consistent with the idea of the *pax Romana*.[1]

[1] It is recommended that Chapter I be re-read at this point.

CHAPTER VII

THE ROMAN ARMY

ORGANIZATION AND DEVELOPMENT

THE army of Rome in the regal period and the early days of the Republic was a very different body from the highly trained professional forces which guarded the frontiers of the Empire in later days. It was essentially a citizen militia, though recruited only from the patricians and their dependants and the richer peasants; every soldier was expected to provide his own armour and any man who was too poor to do this was automatically excluded from the *legio*. As in the armies of mediaeval Europe, the nobles provided the *equites* and the yeomen the *pedites* and there was no uniformity of equipment. The intro-duction of pay at the siege of Veii in 406 in course of time made virtually all citizens liable to conscription, and rendered possible the standardizations of equipment introduced as a result of the lessons learned by the Romans from their defeat at the Allia in 390 and at the Caudine Forks in 321, the *hasta*, or thrusting spear, gradually being superseded by the *pilum*, or javelin.

Further sweeping reforms were carried out by Marius,[1] when he was appointed to the command against Jugurtha in 108, in virtue of which he may be called the creator of the Roman army as we usually think of it. The increasing unpopularity of military service due to the length of the campaigns and the absence of leave, which the distance from Italy of Rome's new theatres of war rendered inevitable, decided Marius to call for volunteers, who were naturally drawn in the main from men anxious to take

[1] See pages 114 and 152–3.

up soldiering as a career. The citizen army of the early
republic was thus superseded by a professional army,
which could be trained to a much higher standard of
proficiency. The maniple, consisting of two centuries,
was displaced as the chief tactical unit by the *cohors*,
consisting of six centuries, and the full strength of the
legion, which contained ten cohorts, was raised to 6000
men, though in practice the number was often nearer
the old figure of 4000.

OFFICERS AND NON-COMMISSIONED OFFICERS

The commander of an army, who was strictly speaking
entitled to be called *imperator* only if his troops had
saluted him as such after a major engagement, had from
the beginning of the republic been assisted by a *quaestor*
in matters of finance and supply and by *tribuni militum*,
six to a legion, who commanded the legion in turn. The
military tribunate, which was normally held by young
nobles at the outset of their career, declined in importance
after the Marian reforms, and by Caesar's day the command of a legion was held by an older officer chosen by
the commander himself and called *legatus*, who employed
the tribunes as his staff. The auxiliary *cohortes* (infantry) and *ālae* (cavalry), of either 500 or 1000 men
each, which were recruited from non-citizen provincials,
were commanded by *praefecti*, usually of equestrian rank,
though sometimes veteran centurions.

The centurions were experienced soldiers who had risen
from the ranks, and there was a regular system of pro-
motion from the tenth cohort to the first. The centurions carried a *vītis*, or vine-staff, as an emblem of
rank and for disciplinary purposes. The six senior
centurions were the centurions of the first cohort, the
most senior being called *prīmus pīlus* or *prīmipīlus*

ROMAN CENTURION

From a relief at Verona of Imperial date. The ground is imaginary.

This is the gravestone of Q. Sertorius, a centurion of the Eleventh Legion, known as the ' Claudia pia fidelis '. He carries the staff (*vitis*) of office, and wears a *corona civica* of oak-leaves for saving the life of a comrade in battle (little but the tie of this crown is visible in the illustration). Over his *tunica* he wears a coat of scale-armour (*lorica squamāta*). His *phalĕrae* are fastened on the usual framework, and two *torques* hang from his neck; these are the *dona militaria*, or decorations given for valour. The circular object by his left hand is the pommel of his sword. He also wears greaves (*ocreae*) and boots (*cālĭgae*), and carries his cloak (*săgum*).

Officers of lower rank were the standard-bearers, *aquili-feri* and *signiferi*, whose duty it was to carry and guard the standards, which were of great importance to the troops, as can be seen from such phrases as *signa ferre*, to advance, *signa referre*, to retreat. The legionary standard was the *aquila*, a silver or sometimes even a gold eagle with outstretched wings, perched on a pole. The manipular *signa* were silver poles adorned with various badges, such as images of animals and metal discs. Standard-bearers often wore the skin of a wolf or some other wild animal instead of a helmet. The highest award for bravery was the *corōna cīvica*, a crown of oak-leaves, and there were also various necklets (*torques*) and badges (*phalĕrae*) given for other distinguished services.

DRESS, EQUIPMENT AND CAMPS

The dress of the legionary soldier was a long *tunica*, or shirt, reaching nearly to the knees, with a belt, a short cloak, brown for soldiers, white for officers, and heavy boots, *călĭgae*. His armour and arms were a leather jerkin, *lorīca*, strengthened with metal strips ; an iron helmet, with a plume of feathers (the helmet was not put on until just before a battle) ; a shield, made of hide rimmed with iron, about 4 × 2½ feet in size, and curved cylindrically to protect the body ; a short two-edged sword, about 2 feet long, worn on the right side, and two spears (*pīlum*), about 7 feet long with wooden shafts and long heads of fairly soft iron, which bent when they reached their mark, so that they could not be used again ; they could be thrown up to a distance of 40 yards. Legionaries on the march, in the *agmen*, were called *impedīti*, ' encumbered ,' and carried, besides their arms, a *sarcĭna*, or pack, weighing about 45 lbs. and containing two weeks' rations, cooking utensils, etc., and a spade

and two stakes, *valli*. For battle the soldiers laid aside
the packs and spades, and were *expedīti*, ready for
action. The most usual fighting-formation was the *triplex
acies*, each of the three lines being about eight men deep.

The *impedimenta* of an army were its tents, siege-
engines, etc. The siege-engines, *tormenta*, employed by
the Romans were the *ballista*, which hurled stones, and
the *catapulta*, which fired arrows or javelins. A battering
ram, *aries*, was also sometimes used, and protection for
troops advancing to the walls of a hostile town was
provided by the *testudo*, which was an ' umbrella ' of
interlocked shields.

Troops always encamped for the night in a specially
fortified encampment—a square each side of which was
about 2000 feet for an army of two legions and auxiliary
troops (about 20,000 men in all)—which was surrounded
by a ditch, *fossa*, 12 feet broad and 9 feet deep, and a
rampart, *agger*, strengthened by the stakes which each
soldier carried. The general's headquarters, *praetōrium*,
were in the centre, and the camp was divided up by
several broad intersecting roads ; each tent had a space
10 feet square allotted to it and housed 10 or 11 men. The
gate facing the enemy was called the *porta praetoria*, the
one away from the enemy the *porta decumana*, and there
were also two side gates. The ordinary day's march,
iustum iter, was about 20 miles, and a forced march,
magnum iter, was about 25 miles.

PAY AND CONDITIONS OF SERVICE

The pay of the legionaries was originally ⅓ *denarius* or
3⅓ *asses* a day. In 217 B.C. it was increased to 5⅓ *asses*
a day, and it remained at this figure until Julius Caesar
raised it to 10, practically double what it had been
before. Even then, however, it amounted to a mere

225 *denarii* a year, or less than £12, a sum which created a good deal of dissatisfaction in time of peace when there was no *praeda* to be shared, and was one of the chief causes of the mutiny which broke out among the troops stationed in Pannonia in A.D. 14, the first year of Tiberius' reign. The other principal grievances were the length of service with the colours, which had been raised to 20 years with the legions and 5 in the reserve, and the poor quality of the land which the soldiers generally received in lieu of pensions on their discharge. These grievances remained largely unremedied and the soldiers often engaged in private trading to the detriment of military discipline—particularly in the eastern provinces.

All legionaries had to possess Roman citizenship, which in some cases was specially granted them on enlistment ; under the Empire they were drawn in the main from northern Italy and the more Romanized provinces. Auxiliary troops, on the other hand, were recruited from the less civilized provinces, such as Gaul, or the less civilized parts of Romanized provinces, such as the hillier districts of Spain ; they received the citizenship only on discharge after 25 years' service.

THE FRONTIER ARMY OF THE EMPIRE

The normal number of legions under the Julio-Claudians was 25 and under the Flavians 29. In the later Empire the auxiliaries outnumbered the legionary troops, but in the first century A.D. their numbers were roughly equal, about 150,000 each. Of these practically all were stationed on the frontier, the legions in *castra*, or fortresses, of about 50 acres, the auxiliaries in *castella* of from 2 to 7 acres ; the senatorial provinces other than Africa, where one legion was stationed, contained a mere handful of troops, and in Italy there was only the praetorian guard of 9000 men. Thus the defensive foreign policy of Augustus, which the exhausted state of the treasury and the general desire for peace necessitated, turned the field armies of Pompey and Caesar into a garrison army, which could not easily take the offensive without endangering the security of the Empire, or rather into several isolated garrison armies, since legions tended to remain in one station for years on end. As a result, when the Julio-Claudian dynasty collapsed with the flight and suicide of Nero in A.D. 68, four emperors, Galba, Otho, Vitellius and Vespasian succeeded one another in the course of a year, as the nominees respectively of the Spanish army, the praetorian guard, the Rhine army and the eastern army, who were ready to fight one another in their cause.

THE FLEET

The Romans were not a seafaring people, and though they secured the command of the central Mediterranean in the First Punic War as a means of defeating Carthage, they never maintained a permanent fleet under the Republic—with the result that the pirates of the eastern Mediterranean more than once got out of hand. Augustus with his usual thoroughness established naval bases at Misenum on the south-west coast of Italy and Ravenna on the north-east, at Forum Julii in Gallia Narbonensis and at Alexandria, and piracy was kept down. The office of *praefectus classis* established by him was one of the more important posts open to equestrians, while the rowers, like the auxiliary troops, were recruited from non-citizen provincials, particularly Thracians and Dalmatians.

Table of the Principal Dates mentioned
in Part II

B.C.

753 (traditional)	Foundation of Rome.
510	Foundation of the Republic.
496	Battle of Lake Regillus.
493	Treaty with the Latin League.
c. 430–380	Aequi and Volsci pushed back from Latium.
396	Fall of Veii.
390	Battle of the Allia.
360	Latin League reconstituted under Roman leadership.
343–1	First Samnite War.
340	Battle of Suessa Aurunca.
338	Dissolution of the Latin League.
327–04	Second Samnite War [Caudine Forks 321 : Lautulae 315].
298–290	Third Samnite War [Sentinum 295].
282–75	War against Pyrrhus [Heraclea 280 : Asculum 279 : Beneventum 275].
264–41	First Punic War [Mylae 260 : Ecnomus 256 : Drepana 249 : Aegates Islands 241].
238	Annexation of Corsica and Sardinia.
225–0	Preliminary Conquest of Cisalpine Gaul.
219	Hannibal's attack on Saguntum.
218–202	Second Punic War [Trebia 218 : Trasimene 217 : Cannae 216 : Syracuse 213–11 : Baecula 208 : Metaurus 207 : Ilipa 206 : Zama 202.]
216–205	First Macedonian War.
200–196	Second Macedonian War [Cynoscephalae 197].
192–189	War against Antiochus of Syria.
171–167	Third Macedonian War (Pydna 168).
149–146	Fourth Macedonian War.
149–146	Third Punic War.
141–133	Siege of Numantia.
133	Pergamum bequeathed to Rome.
121	Colony established at Narbo.
112–105	War against Jugurtha [Marius' first consulship 107].
113–101	Wars against Cimbri and Teutones [Arausio 105 : Aquae Sextiae 102 : Vercellae 101].
90–88	Social War.
88–84	First Mithridatic War.
77–72	Pompey's campaign against Sertorius.
74–65	Third Mithridatic War.
67	Lex Gabinia.

B.C.

66	Lex Manilia.
64	Annexation of Syria.
63	Capture of Jerusalem by Pompey.
58–49	Caesar's Gallic Wars.
55 & 54	Expeditions to Britain.
53	Defeat of Crassus at Carrhae.
52	Revolt of Vercingetorix.
36 & 33	Antony invades Parthia.
35–34	Octavian advances to the Savus.
31	Battle of Actium.
26–19	Wars with Cantabri.
16–15	Conquest of Noricum and Raetia.
12–9	Drusus in Germany.
	Tiberius in Pannonia.

A.D.

6	Pannonian Revolt.
9	Defeat of Varus.
14	Mutiny in Pannonia.
14–16	Germanicus in Germany.
43	Invasion of Britain.
61	Revolt of Boudicca.
64	Tiridates crowned by Nero.
69	Revolt of Civilis.
70	Capture of Jerusalem by Titus.
72	Cappadocia becomes a major province.
73	Annexation of Agri Decumates.
77–84	Agricola in Britain.
83 & 89	Domitian's campaigns against Chatti.
86–9	Domitian's Dacian War.
107	Annexation of Dacia.
114	Annexation of Armenia.

PART III

THE INTERNAL HISTORY OF ROME TO A.D. 96.

FROM MONARCHY TO PRINCIPATE

CHAPTER I

THE ROMAN CONSTITUTION

LIKE most primitive communities, Rome was a monarchy in the days beyond which human memory cannot reach. The supreme power of the king was called *imperium* and was limited only by custom. Although he was expected to consult the *senatus*, an advisory council of elderly men, he need not follow the course it recommended. He was expected also to put before the assembly of the whole people proposals of real importance, but there was no means of compelling him to do so. The assembly could not vote on any matter that was not laid before it by the king and could not discuss a measure that he did introduce; it could only say 'Yes' or 'No' to such questions as he chose to ask it. The monarchy was not hereditary. When the king died, the *imperium* was conferred by the assembly on the man he had nominated as his successor provided that his choice was confirmed by the senate.

THE CONSULSHIP

In 510 B.C. the monarchy was overthrown by a national rising under Junius Brutus; the motive for the insurrection was partly a patriotic dislike of being ruled by

in Etruscan, partly a hatred of the despotic cruelty which
had marked the reign of the house of Tarquin. The
powers of the king, as administrator, as judge, as com-
mander-in-chief, were transferred intact to two co-equal
magistrates, at first called *praetores* [1] and later *consules*.[2]
To make certain that there should never again be a despot
ruling in Rome the liberators not only divided the *imperium* between two men, each of whom could veto the
acts of the other except on the field of battle, but decreed
that they and their successors should hold office for one
year only. These precautions were in many ways a
drag on Rome's development. In a single year the
consuls had hardly sufficient time in which to learn their
job and the administration of the Republic was in consequence not remarkably efficient. Secondly, it was
extremely difficult for either of them to gain enough
confidence during their brief term of office to oppose the
senate or give a real lead to the people—hence in part the
fact that Rome never became a democracy. Thirdly,
the power of *intercessio*, or veto, might certainly prevent
tyranny and oppression, since it could be used to stop
not merely the despotic actions of a magistrate (e.g.
unlawful arrest) but also any harsh measure he might introduce in the assembly, although it should be remembered
that the vetoing magistrate had to be present in person;
but it also could, and not infrequently did, prevent
progressive legislation really necessary for the welfare
of the state. It says much for the Romans' common-
sense that any legislation was passed at all, when with
the creation of the tribunate [3] and of new magistracies
the power of veto became widespread. Fourthly, the
divided control of the state might be a real menace to

[1] i.e. leaders (*praetor*=*praeitor*, or one who goes in front: so
raetorium was the name of the general's headquarters).

[2] i.e. colleagues.   [3] See page 141.

its safety in time of war. The Romans themselve
recognized this and about 430 B.C. resolved that in tim
of grave national emergency the consulship might b
temporarily suspended and its powers transferred to
single *dictator*. He and his assistant, the *magister equitur*
(originally appointed to command the cavalry) were
however, in no circumstances to hold office for more tha
six months—a provision that was not observed in late
days, e.g. by Sulla and by Caesar.

THE SENATE

The *patres*, or members of the senate, held office fo
life. They were originally appointed by the king, whos
power of nomination passed in 510 B.C. to the consul
In 366 the duty of revising the list of members was trans
ferred to the censors,[1] and the custom gradually aros
that they should appoint only ex-magistrates. In 81 B.C
Sulla decreed that the lowest magistracy, the quaestorship
should automatically entitle a man to a seat in th
senate. At the same time he created three hundre
senators additional to the existing membership of rathe
less than two hundred. There was a further increase t
about one thousand members under Julius Caesar, bu
Augustus stabilized the number at six hundred.

THE POPULAR ASSEMBLIES

There were at Rome from the fourth century B.C. or
wards three distinct assemblies of the whole people, th
comitia curiata, the *comitia centuriata* and the *comiti*
tributa. Each received its name from the voting unit
into which it was divided, *curiae*, *centuriae* and *tribu*
and the decision of each was determined by the majorit

[1] See page 186.

of group-votes and not by the majority of all the votes
cast in the assembly ; for each unit voted separately in
much the same way as that in which our constituencies
elect members of Parliament, and its vote counted as one
vote in deciding the issue, whatever the size of the majority
for or against might be. In the *comitia curiata* the units
were family-groups, which were under the influence of their
most powerful nobles. In the *comitia centuriata* the units
were sub-divisions of classes graded according to wealth,
each unit being considered capable of equipping one
hundred soldiers. Obviously there were many fewer
voters in the rich *centuriae* than in the poor ones ; yet
the group-vote of each *centuria* counted the same, so that
in this assembly the influence of wealth was predominant
at any rate until towards the close of the third century
B.C., when the voting-strength of the five classes was
made more or less equal). The organization of the
comitia centuriata was based on that of the army and it
therefore always met in the *Campus Martius* outside the
pomerium, or sacred boundary of the city, within which
troops were not allowed ; the other assemblies met in or
near the Forum. In the *comitia tributa* the units were
local divisions of the city, originally created to facilitate
enlistment and the payment of taxation (hence called
tributum) ; this was the most democratic of the assemblies, since it was based neither on birth nor on wealth.
It is important that you should understand clearly the
main differences between these three assemblies, and
between them and the *concilium plebis*, which was an
assembly confined originally to the *plebs*, as the depressed
class of early Rome was called. You will see from the
table on page 144 that the *comitia curiata* was the original
assembly of the city, that it was superseded soon after
the beginning of the Republic by the *comitia centuriata*
in all important matters, and that the *comitia centuriata*,

while retaining the right of electing the important
magistrates, gave place, in its turn, as the chief legislative
assembly to the *comitia tributa* and the *concilium plebis*
the origin and importance of which are explained in the
next chapter.

ROMAN CONSERVATISM

As the Roman Constitution was, like our own and unlike
that of the United States of America, unwritten, there
was no real difficulty in adapting it to suit changing cir
cumstances. Yet the Roman people was so conservative
by nature, so averse to sudden changes, that in fact the
old machinery of government tended to remain in being
long after it ought to have been scrapped. There were
always traditionalists in Rome who opposed any change
and in the power of *intercessio* they had an admirable
instrument of obstruction ready to hand [1] ; one diehard
tribune, for example, could prevent any of his nine
colleagues, even if they were absolutely unanimous, from
carrying a proposal for reform. The result was that long
after Rome became an Empire, her method of Govern
ment remained essentially that of a city-state, and
when the Principate was established by Augustus he had
very carefully to disguise the fact that the Republic wa
no more. Julius Caesar had tried to make too clean a
break with the past and had paid with his life for hi
impatience.

It took a foreign despotism to cause the only cata
strophic change in Roman Constitutional History, the
overthrow of the monarchy. But you should notice tha
even then the *imperium* itself remained unaltered and the

[1] There were other means of obstructing legislation, e.g. by seeing
or pretending to see, unfavourable omens and so preventing the *comiti*
from meeting. Cf. page 165.

method of appointing the consuls was substantially
the same as that of appointing the king had been, since
the assembly could vote only for such names as the out-
going consuls chose to bring before it and the senate had
to ratify its choice by the *patrum auctoritas*. You
should notice also that although the normal method of
assembling the people changed twice, the older methods
remained legal and could still be used under the Empire
and for certain purposes were used; to have three
different systems of assembling the people existing side
by side was typically Roman. But it is in the position
of the senate that the force of custom in the Roman
constitution is most clearly marked. Even when it
virtually ruled the state, as it did during the Punic Wars
and the century that followed, it remained in theory a
purely advisory body and its decrees (*senatus consulta*)
were binding on the people by the force of custom alone.
So strong was that force, however, that it was one of the
reasons why Rome never became a democracy.

CHAPTER II

THE OVERTHROW OF PATRICIAN GOVERNMENT 510–287 B.C.

AT the outset of Roman history the citizens were divided
into a privileged and an unprivileged class, *patricii* and
plebs. Clearly the *patricii* were the class from whom
the *patres* were chosen, and that is possibly how the name
arose ; but their privileged position was not due to this
—to say so would be putting the cart before the horse—
but rather to their greater success in dealing with the
problems of life. The plebeians were in no sense serfs,
for many of them owned land and all had the *ius suffragii*
or right of voting, but they could not hold office nor
intermarry with patricians and there was no written law
to which they could appeal. In the period of economic
difficulty which succeeded the expulsion of the kings,
when trade was almost non-existent and Rome was not
increasing her territory but rather was having her territory
overrun, many got into debt and some thereby lost their
liberty, while none enjoyed the security from hardship
and oppression which alone makes men contented with
their lot.

In consequence the internal history of the early
republic, no less than the external, is in the main the
record of a protracted struggle ; and the increasing need
of the state to call upon plebeian man-power was not
without influence in determining the patricians to grant
concessions in the face of threats to leave the city for ever
—threats which tradition alleges were made on five
separate occasions.

THE TRIBUNATE AND THE CONCILIUM PLEBIS

These threats indicate a definite organization on trades union lines, and until that organization was created (probably in 449 and not 494, as Livy asserts) the *tribuni plebis*, or leaders of the depressed classes, succeeded only in securing the codification and publication of the existing law in 451 by a patrician board of ten men, appointed for that purpose. This was, however, by no means an unimportant achievement ; for until the laws are written down where all may read them, men have no safeguard against a purely arbitrary administration of justice, and the law of the Twelve Tables did give the plebeians the first thing that the oppressed always demand—they now knew where they stood. Furthermore, although it did nothing to remove the conditions which produced poverty and debt, although it affirmed the plebeians' inability to marry into a patrician family, although it bore traces of the barbarous legal system of the days of the blood feud, yet it did grant debtors unable to meet their obligations some time in which to find the money, it did grant all individuals certain liberties in trade and family life, it did concede the right of appeal to the Comitia, and it was much more humane in outlook than most primitive legal codes drawn up to satisfy similar demands for the publication of the laws.

The *plebs*, however, was not satisfied with it, and two years later (449) constituted itself into a definite body called the *concilium plebis*,[1] which met and voted by tribes under a board consisting of two plebeian *aediles* [2] and ten *tribuni*. Very quickly the tribunes, to whom the task of dealing with the patrician authorities was entrusted, became more important than the aediles, and

[1] See Table on page 144.　　　[2] See page 186.

they proceeded to claim the *ius auxilii*, or right to protect any plebeian by personal intervention against the unlawful action of a patrician magistrate. The patricians at first attempted to ignore the new plebeian body but were eventually compelled to accord it recognition ; in 339 its resolutions, called *plebiscita*, became binding on the whole community provided that they received the *patrum auctoritas*, and the *lex Hortensia* of 287 made them binding on the whole community without such sanction. Henceforward the *concilium plebis* and the *comitia tributa* were regarded as one body, for the distinction between patrician and plebeian had ceased to have any real significance, and this body became the chief legislative assembly in Rome. Similarly the power of the tribunes, which had gradually increased from a mere *ius auxilii* to an *intercessio*, or power of veto, which could be used against any magistrate or any bill proposed in any of the assemblies, ceased to be employed purely for the redress of popular grievances, and the tribunate became a two-edged weapon, which the reactionaries could, and often did, turn against the progressives. Only exceptional tribunes after 287 resumed the old practices of political agitation : the majority of them worked with the senate, and though they were not strictly magistrates since they did not wield the *imperium*, they received in 216 the right of summoning it and presiding over its deliberations.

SOCIAL, ECONOMIC AND POLITICAL EQUALITY

While the *concilium* and the tribunes were winning their way to complete recognition, social, economic and political equality was gradually acquired for individual plebeians. According to Livy the *ius connubii*, or right of intermarriage, was conceded by the patricians under the *lex Canuleia* of 445, but it is extremely improbable,

n the face of it, that this important concession was made
t so early a date, and if it had been, the numbers of the
patricians would not have continued so seriously to
decline—a fact which compelled them in the end to come
o terms with the plebeians more readily than they might
otherwise have done. A series of enactments drastically
reducing the rate of interest and forbidding unauthorized
enslavement for debt, combined with the distribution of
newly conquered territory in allotments, gave the
plebeians the economic security for which they had so
long craved. Simultaneously the ambitions of the
plebeian leaders were satisfied by the throwing open to
them of all the patrician magistracies in turn and their
consequent admission into the senate, the very citadel
of patrician exclusiveness.

The ultimate victory of the plebeians was inevitable
from the beginning, and if we consider the remarkable
tenacity of vested interests in other periods of history,
we may say that it was quickly achieved. It says much
for the good sense of both sides in the struggle that it was
a comparatively bloodless victory, won without recourse
to revolution, and that in consequence it left no rancour
behind it. Hard as they may have been, the early
Romans were a disciplined people, and through the
united front which they presented to their common
enemies their patient self-control had its reward.

TABLE OF ROMAN ASSEMBLIES

	Instituted.	Nature.	Units.	Function in La Republic.
Comitia Curiata	Pre-historical	Assembly of the whole people by family - groups with common *sacra* and common habitat.	30 *curiae*	Purely form wills, adoptic etc.
Comitia Centuriata	c. 450 B.C. (traditionally Servius Tullius)	Originally military, later assembly of the whole people in which the influence of wealth predominated. Towards the end of the third century B.C., the voting-strength of the 5 classes was made more or less equal.	193 *centuriae*	Election of ma trates (exc quaestors a curule aedil Its legislat functions gra ally passed *comitia tribut.*
Concilium Plebis	449 B.C. (traditionally 494)	Assembly of the *plebs* only, presided over by tribunes.	4 urban and 16 rural *tribus*, increased to 35 by 241 B.C.	Election of bunes and beian aed Legislative.
Comitia Tributa	c. 366 B.C.	Assembly of the whole people by *tribus* (originally taxation districts).	Do.	Election of qua tors and cu aediles. Le lative.

With the passing of the *lex Hortensia* (287 B.C.), *plebiscita* (resolutions of the *plebs*) became binding on the whole people without the *patrum auctoritas* (sanction of the senate), and the distinction between *concilium plebis* and *comitia tributa* ceased to be observed.

CHAPTER III

THE ASCENDENCY OF THE SENATE AND THE CHALLENGE OF DEMOCRACY
287–82 B.C.

IT might be supposed that Rome was now heading for democracy, but during the next hundred years the senate in fact succeeded in tightening its hold on the helm of state, and the new plebeian members quickly acquired the exclusive attitude of the old nobility. Composed, as it now was, almost entirely of magistrates and ex-magistrates, the senate enjoyed a prestige which no ordinary official dared to assail, and that prestige was enhanced by the sagacity and dour resolution with which it steered the state through the troubled waters of the long struggle with Carthage. Had the Roman magistrates wielded the *imperium* for more than a single year, had men of experience united to form political parties in the modern sense, the ascendency of the senate might have come to an end sooner than it did. But as it was, men were on the whole satisfied with its conduct of affairs, and no single individual had the opportunity of enjoying real authority long enough to enable him to fight the senate (often backed by the *intercessio* of his colleagues) with any prospect of success, until Marius' army reforms [1] (107 B.C.) gave the great generals of the state a power which they had hitherto lacked. Without leaders the people could do nothing, and in any case the *comitia* and the *concilium plebis* provided no alternative system of government. They had no power except the power of saying ' Yes ' or ' No ' to proposals put before them by a

[1] See pages 125 and 152–3.

magistrate : no citizen might speak unless he was asked
to do so : and no amendment to the original proposal
could be put to the meeting. Furthermore, these bodies
were far too unwieldy to deal with intricate questions of
diplomacy and finance and—large as they were—could
not with justice any longer claim to speak for the citizens
of Rome, many of whom were now scattered up and down
Italy, too far away to come to the capital to record their
votes. And so, while remaining in theory a purely
advisory body, the senate in fact became by the force
of custom the real government of Rome.

When the need for sustained effort became less urgent
with the final defeat of Hannibal (202 B.C.), the senate
relaxed, and its conduct of affairs became more and more
complacent and less and less unselfish. Contact with
the degenerate Greek culture which now pervaded the
eastern coasts of the Mediterranean began to sap the old
Roman rectitude which Cato tried so hard to keep alive
and the holding of office—particularly in the provinces—
came to be regarded not as a public duty but as a means
of personal enrichment, in which *novi homines* (i.e. men
belonging to families which had never been represented
in the senate) must not be allowed to share. It was not
however, from men thus refused admission to the senate
that the inevitable attack finally came but from two
men of high rank, the brothers Tiberius and Gaius
Gracchus : in the case of Tiberius the attack was in the
main accidental, in the case of Gaius deliberate.

TIBERIUS GRACCHUS 133 B.C.

Tiberius Gracchus, elected tribune of the people in
133 B.C., was not really interested in constitutional
questions, and he came into collision with the senate
solely because his ardent desire to solve the unemploy

ment problem with which Rome was faced carried him forward without a thought for the toes he might be treading on in the process. Tiberius was appalled by the number of men, born and bred on the land, who had drifted to Rome and were living there on charity, as there were no large industries to absorb them and no possibility of creating them by building up a flourishing export trade, since Ostia, the port of Rome, could not be used by large ships. The soil of Italy, except in the plain of Campania and the valley of the Po, was not rich enough to retain its fertility under the intensive and unscientific cultivation to which it had been subjected or under the depredations of Hannibal's army, which had lived on the country for more than ten years. Furthermore, the increasing distance of Rome's campaigns from their homes made it no longer possible for the farmers conscripted into her armies to manage their farms properly, while those of them who lived in the neighbourhood of Rome had also to compete with the corn-tithes which the province of Sicily paid instead of taxes, and which the government sold well below the current rate in the Roman market. As it happened, the conquests in the East had made available for investment a large amount of capital which senators had been forbidden by a law of 218 B.C. (passed in the hope of keeping Roman foreign policy disinterested) to sink in overseas trade, and they were therefore ready to buy the land which the farmers were anxious to sell. Some they still used for corn-growing or turned into vineyards and oliveyards, but they realized that it was far more suited to sheep-rearing for the most part ; this could be made to pay handsomely if they used slave-labour, which was not liable to the interruption of military service and was now very cheap, as the Eastern conquests had produced a glut of slaves in the markets. Not content with these purchases, the

wealthy nobles had encroached on sections of *ag.*
publicus, or land belonging to the state, which had neve
been allotted to individual applicants (as it normall
was in early days, when Rome was still annexing territor
in Italy), and had come to regard what they occupie
as their own.

Tiberius believed that he saw an opportunity of curin
unemployment and at the same time restoring Italia
agriculture to its former prosperity, if he could secur
the ejection of these *possessores*, as they were called ; h
would break up the great estates, or *latifundia*, and pu
the out-of-work peasants back on the land where the
belonged. A bill to this effect was introduced in th
concilium plebis and it not unnaturally aroused consider
able opposition : among the great landowners, whos
private interests were affected : among the clear-sighted
who asked what guarantee there was that the farmer
would now succeed where previously they had failed
and among the sticklers for constitutional usage, wh
pointed out that the commission proposed for carryin
the scheme into practice consisted of Tiberius, his brothe
Gaius, and his father-in-law Appius Claudius—a famil
clique that looked ominous. This opposition was voice
by a certain Octavius, one of Tiberius' nine colleagues i
the tribunate, who interposed his veto, and it seemed tha
the measure was doomed. But Tiberius cared nothin
for constitutional usage where he believed his principle
to be right, and succeeded in carrying a measure deposin
the vetoing tribune and then in piloting his agricultura
bill through the assembly. Opposition, however, re
mained merely vocal until Tiberius went a step furthe
and announced his intention—contrary to Roman custon
—of seeking re-election. His opponents felt that ther
was now no alternative to force, and Tiberius met hi
death at their hands. He had, it is true, shown remark

bly little patience and common-sense, but this did not
ustify a resort to violence, especially as his object was
.udable even if the means he employed were undesirable ;
nd the conservatives of later days (or *optimates*, as they
alled themselves in contradistinction to the *populares*,
r anti-senatorial party) must sometimes have cursed their
predecessors for setting this fateful precedent, which
heir opponents in due course proceeded to follow.

GAIUS GRACCHUS 123–122 B.C.

The senate had largely itself to thank that ten years
ater it had to face an attack far more formidable, because
premeditated, from Tiberius' brother, Gaius, who was
:lected tribune for 123 at the age of thirty-one and re-
:lected for 122—the democrats having since Tiberius'
leath succeeded in passing a measure to legalize re-
:lection. Both brothers were pre-eminently social re-
ormers, but whereas Tiberius had had what might be
:alled nowadays a single-track mind, Gaius was also a
politician ; he deliberately set himself to undermine the
senate's position by using his great eloquence to assist
1ot only the *plebs urbana*, which needed help, not only
:he *socii*, who had legitimate grievances of their own,
put also the *equites*—the bourgeois capitalists of Rome
—who aroused his interest chiefly because they were
jealous of the senate. There can be little doubt that his
idealism was in the main as sincere as his brother's, but
he added to it a kind of craftiness, which is apparent
at any rate in his legislation on behalf of the *equites*, and
which might have made him virtual dictator of Rome if
the three classes whose cause he espoused had cared for
anything except their own selfish interests.

To help the poor of the city Gaius was not content
merely to re-enact his brother's legislation and to set

F   S.P.Q.R.

in motion again the work of the land-commission, whic
the senate had reduced almost to a standstill in respons
to the protests of certain Italian towns which complaine
that their fields were being seized ; he also assisted th
settlers to market their produce by building new roads
and founded colonies for them at Tarentum and Capua
Secondly, for the first time in Roman history, he planne
a colony overseas—at Junonia on the territory of Carthag
—and offered land to Romans and Italians alike. Thirdly
in the knowledge that all the necessitous citizens coul
not be absorbed by his ' back to the land ' campaign, h
arranged for the state to buy up all the corn enterin
Rome from overseas and to sell it at a fixed price all th
year round—a price below the previous average. As
measure of temporary relief this was perhaps necessary
but public charity is always a dangerous expedient, eve
when introduced out of compassion and not to catc
votes. Gracchus might have foreseen that others woul
find in similar devices a means to bribe the electors unt
in the end the population of Rome clamoured only fo
panem et circenses, free bread and entertainment, an
the treasury's resources were seriously strained.

The *equites* were the wealthy men of Rome who ha
not attained to membership of the senate. They ha
ceased to provide the cavalry, which the allies nov
supplied, but the old name was still applied to thos
whose property exceeded 400,000 sesterces, althoug
their interests as a class were now financial and com
mercial rather than military, When Rome annexed nev
provinces, her practice was to auction the right of collect
ing the taxes to business syndicates. In this way
breach had been created between the *equites* and th
senate, since the less scrupulous members of each orde
were bent on squeezing out of the provincials for them
selves as much money as they could, while the mor

scrupulous governors naturally endeavoured to put a
stop to illegal exactions whenever they occurred. It is
very significant that the first court established in Rome to
try special cases was the *quaestio repetundarum*, set up in
149 to deal with extortion in the provinces. As the
juries in this court were composed entirely of senators,
there had been a growing tendency for them to acquit
governors who appeared before them, whether they were
guilty or not, in the hope that they would be treated as
leniently when their turn came. In transferring to the
equestrian order the right to compose the juries Gracchus
was attacking a very real abuse ; yet he must have been
well aware that his measure would not secure justice, but
merely a bias in favour of condemnation in place of a
bias in favour of acquittal ; for the new juries were no
more disinterested than the old—guilty governors were
their rivals, innocent governors their enemies.

When Attalus III bequeathed his kingdom of Pergamum to Rome in 133 and the province of Asia was formed,
the cities were exempted from taxation in accordance
with the king's request. Gracchus in seeking for fresh
revenues to offset his colonial and corn-distribution
expenditure could not overlook one of the wealthiest
districts in the Mediterranean basin ; he passed a measure
providing that nearly all the new province should pay
tithes and that the annual auctioning of the right to
collect these should be held in Rome and not in the
province, thus making it virtually impossible for provincial syndicates to bid. The measure was a curious
one for a professed champion of the 'underdog' to
introduce, and makes it impossible for us to acquit
him entirely of hypocrisy or to sympathize with him
when the *equites* failed to support him in his hour of
need.

In his second year as tribune he brought forward a

measure granting *civitas* [1] to all Latin communities in
Italy and *Latinitas* [1] to the remainder—a measure long
overdue. Unfortunately for Gracchus' hopes, the *plebs*
was as exclusive in outlook as the senate and equally
loth to share its privileges, and the *optimates*, relying
on its support, vetoed the bill through a tribune named
Drusus. This was the beginning of the end : Gaius was
not re-elected for 121, his proposed colony at Junonia
was abandoned by law, and in the rioting against the
annulment, which his supporters started, he escaped his
brother's fate only by ordering a slave to stab him.

Gracchus for all his virtues did a disservice to the state.
The senate, it is true, was doomed, but as his attacks only
weakened it still further without overthrowing it, the
Roman republic was destined to endure a lingering death.
Henceforward, although the struggle between *populares*
and *optimates* continued, autocracy was really inevitable
and the only live issue was who the autocrat was to be
and what kind of government he would establish.

Marius, Saturninus and Glaucia 108–100 b.c.

The Gracchi had shaken the senate, but only the army
could overthrow it, and when Gaius died the army was
still the senate's servant. The failure of the senate's
generals (112–108) against Jugurtha, king of Numidia,
however, so exasperated the population of Rome that it
not merely elected a *novus homo*, named Marius, consul
for 107, but assigned him the African command,[2] though
such appointments had long been regarded as the senate's
prerogative. Marius had no use for conscripts, who had
in recent years been increasingly loth to serve, and
revolutionized the whole army system by calling for
volunteers. His main concern was to get an efficient

[1] See page 88.   [2] See pages 114 and 125.

professional army, composed of men who wanted to fight rather than to farm, and more than any other man, he was the creator of the Roman army as we think of it. But that was by no means all : the new volunteers took the oath of allegiance to their general and looked to him and not to the narrow-minded senate for their pensions —in the shape of grants of land—when their campaigning days were over. As a result generals had to take an interest in politics whether they wanted to or not, and since the senate often foolishly opposed their requests, they were naturally inclined to point to their soldiers and, if necessary, to use them. Rome had more than once met with disaster on the battlefield because her system often resulted in armies being commanded by politicians : she was now to suffer in the field of politics through her generals assuming the role of statesmen.

By holding the consulship for five successive years from 104 to 100 Marius and the *populares*, who secured his election, infringed not merely the custom of the constitution, as had been the case when the assembly appointed him to the African command and again to the command against the Cimbri [1] over the head of the senate, but the law of the land, and Marius' prestige after his victories was such that the downfall of senatorial government seemed at hand. But his ability as a general was only equalled by his weakness as a politician, and he allowed himself to become a mere tool in the hands of an unscrupulous demagogue named Saturninus, tribune in 103 and 100, who had established himself as virtual dictator of the assembly by employing gangs of ruffians to attack anyone who opposed him. In his legislation Saturninus was assisted by another unscrupulous politician, the praetor Glaucia, and now proceeded to repay his debt by arranging for the assassination of Glaucia's

[1] See page 108.

chief rival for the consulship of 99. Marius had connived
at mob rule, but murder was too much even for him, and
sure of his support, the senate was emboldened to pass
the *senatusconsultum ultimum*, which it had used against
C. Gracchus, a decree empowering the consuls to secure
by any means the safety of the state (*uti viderent consules
ne quid detrimenti respublica caperet*). Thereupon Marius
rounded up Saturninus and Glaucia, who were seized by
the mob and lynched. The senate, knowing Marius'
weakness as a politician, proceeded to annul Saturninus'
recent legislation which it had not had the courage to
oppose while Saturninus lived. Nor did it give Marius
a command, as he had hoped, and he left the country
rather than remain in obscurity in Rome.

THE SOCIAL WAR 90–88 B.C.

Ten years' stagnation followed, during which the
resentment of the allies grew at the repeated failure of
the measures designed to give them the franchise. They
felt with justice that they had contributed their fair
share to Marius' victories and saw no reason why they
should not receive a due reward, especially as they were
so often called upon to bear the brunt of service in
Rome's less lucrative campaigns. When therefore in 91 a
further attempt to give them the franchise—this time
by one of the *optimates*, the tribune Drusus whose father
had vetoed C. Gracchus' franchise bill—was foiled by the
selfish opposition of people and senate combined, the
Italians were already under arms, and Drusus' violent
death only added fuel to the flames.

With their headquarters at Corfinium the rebels had
the better of the campaign of 90 ; but Marius did something to redress the balance in the north. The *lex Iulia*
conferring the franchise on all Italians who had remained

yal, was passed in that winter as a timely means of
eventing the revolt spreading further. An additional
ncession was made in the following year by the *lex
lautia Papiria*, which granted the *civitas* to any Italian
ho applied for it in person within sixty days, and after
uch hard fighting most of the resistance was crushed
the beginning of 88.

SULLA, MARIUS AND CINNA 88–82 B.C.

Meantime Marius, who had again been passed over by
e senate, had been intriguing for the command against
ithridates, king of Pontus,[1] which the senate had
signed to Sulla, one of the consuls for 88, who had first
on distinction as a cavalry commander in the Jugurthine
ar and was now operating against the rebels in the
uth.   Once again Marius secured a military appoint-
ent over the head of the senate by a measure passed
rough the assembly. But the devil-may-care Sulla
as not the type of man to brook such treatment, and
lling upon his army, which was still besieging the town
Nola in Campania, he occupied the capital with an
ganized military force for the first time in Roman
story—a fateful precedent.

Sulla's departure for the East left the senate without
y military backing, and when it deposed Cinna, one of
e consuls for 87, he had little difficulty in collecting an
my in Campania and joining forces with Marius, who
ad sought refuge in Africa and collected an army from
s veterans there.   With these troops Marius and Cinna
peated Sulla's action of the previous year, and on the
rrender of the city proceeded to indulge in the organized
urder of their political opponents. They declared
emselves without election consuls for 86, but a few days

[1] See page 116.

after his seventh consulship had begun Marius died an
left Cinna virtual dictator of Rome. Cinna nominat
himself consul again for 85 and 84 with Carbo as h
colleague, and although he put an end to the orgies
bloodletting in which Marius had indulged and Rom
remained outwardly calm, it was obvious that Sulla
return must mean a further outbreak of civil war.

CHAPTER IV

THE SULLAN REACTION AND THE CHALLENGE OF THE GREAT COMMANDERS 82–31 B.C.

SULLA DICTATOR 82–79 B.C.

FRESH from his triumph over Mithridates, Sulla landed in Italy in 83. As he had been the first Roman to cross the *pomerium* with an armed force, so he was the first Roman to return from his province with an army at his back to enforce his will. For both these actions Marius and his followers were in large measure to blame, and both the *populares* in Rome and the Italian allies who had supported them now paid dearly for what they had done. Not content with a series of victories on the field of battle, Sulla proceeded to order the massacre of nine thousand of his opponents in cold blood and at the same time confiscated their property and debarred their sons from holding public office. But ruthless as he was, he was not merely out for vengeance. He believed that the democrats had come near to overthrowing the senate, and he saw no alternative to senatorial government except anarchy. The work of the Gracchi, Saturninus, Glaucia, Marius, Cinna and Carbo must be undone and the senate's position strengthened.

Sulla was not blind and he realized that the senate itself must be reformed. In an endeavour to give it new life, to restore the sense of public duty which had marked its deliberations during the Punic War and to destroy the narrow exclusiveness and selfishness that made it an easy target for the *populares*, he introduced three hundred new members from the equestrian order into the existing body of two hundred. He decreed also that henceforth the normal practice of filling vacancies by nominating ex-quaestors should become automatic, and to ensure a sufficient supply of these he increased the number of quaestors [1] to twenty. The juries once more were to be provided by the senate, and its customary right, twice challenged by Marius, to assign provinces and grant commands was confirmed by statute. It is very doubtful whether this statute made the senate's right any more secure, so strong in Roman eyes, as we have seen, was the force of custom, but nobody would have objected to it if Sulla had succeeded in his main intention of revitalizing the senate. In fact he failed. The new members, although a majority, assimilated the character of the old and were soon just as selfish and just as jealously opposed to the admission of *novi homines*.

Besides endeavouring to strengthen it from within, Sulla tried to protect the senate from attack from without. He abolished the tribunes' unlimited right of veto, and tried to secure that they should be nonentities through the provision that the tribunate was to debar a man from holding further office and through the repeal of the law of 129 permitting re-election. From Sulla's point of view this act was a mistake. The anti-senatorial behaviour of the Gracchi and Saturninus had led him to forget that the tribunes' right of veto had become a weapon of even greater use to conservatives than it was to progressives; these men were in no sense typical holders of the tribunate. More sensible—if somewhat harsh—was his discouragement of idleness by the repeal of the Gracchan corn law, and the fixing of a minimum age for the various magistracies made the election of hot-headed reformers less likely (the *lex Villia annalis* of 180, still in force, had not apparently been strictly observed).

[1] See page 185.

But the real danger to the senate, as Sulla's own career had shown, lay in the power of the great generals on whose established reputation the senate was forced to depend in times of crisis to raise an army; Sulla had perhaps this danger in mind when he passed his law *de maiestate*, declaring it treasonable for a provincial governor to make war or leave his province without the sanction of the senate and people. The weakness of the measure was that it was quite impossible to enforce it, and actually Sulla unintentionally increased the senate's danger by making Cisalpine Gaul a separate province instead of an appendage of Italy. This was certainly desirable from the point of view of the defence of Italy's northern frontier, but it was from this province that Julius Caesar was destined to move south against Pompey.

In 79 Sulla resigned his dictatorship and retired to his estates in Campania, to die there the following year. His character was full of contradictions : brutal, luxurious, and even vicious, he was yet capable of great self-denial ; the most autocratic of Roman statesmen with the possible exception of Julius Caesar, he did his best to put new life into the republican constitution and then voluntarily sought the obscurity of a private citizen. All his re-actionary legislation was short-lived, being swept away within ten years, because he failed to transform the character of the senate and to safeguard it against the danger of military usurpation. The Sullan constitution might have worked—had there been men both able and willing to work it.

THE " PRINCIPATE " OF POMPEY

Hardly was Sulla in his grave when a political adven-turer named Lepidus, one of the consuls for 78, raised the standard of revolt, with the restoration of the powers of the tribunate, the renewal of the corn-distribution, and the return of their estates to the proscribed as his programme. The revolt was suppressed by the senate, with the assistance of the young and ambitious Pompey, who had already gained military distinction under Sulla by defeating the Marians in Sicily and Africa. Pompey thereupon demanded to be sent to deal with the Marian general, Sertorius, who had been turned out of Spain by a Sullan army but had returned in 80 and was still in revolt. Although he had held no high office and his age made him ineligible under Sulla's legislation for a pro-consular command, the senate—significantly—granted his request. During Pompey's absence from 77 to 72, the tribunate was declared no longer a bar to higher office, and the corn-distributions were reintroduced.

A rising of slaves, led by a Thracian gladiator named Spartacus, assumed such serious proportions in 73 that the senate was forced to call upon another of Sulla's *legati*, the financier Crassus, to raise an army in his capacity as praetor. Crassus was no soldier but he had organizing ability, and by 71, when Pompey returned from Spain, the rebellion was nearly over. Pompey, however, used it as an excuse for keeping his army in being, so that he might enforce his demand for a consulship, for which he was entirely unqualified in point of age. Had Crassus been a little less cautious, he might have stood by the senate and become the leading figure in Rome, but he thought it more prudent to come to terms with his young rival for this position and demand the other consulship himself. In face of this combination the senate inevitably yielded. Pompey and Crassus were elected consuls for 70, and what remained of Sulla's reactionary legislation was systematically reversed. Once more the senate was deprived of the sole right to compose the juries, which were handed over by the *lex Aurelia*, sponsored by Pompey, to the senate, *equites* and *tribuni aerarii*—the next class in point of wealth—in equal proportions. The senatorial juries had certainly done little to justify Sulla's confidence in them, but the new panels were equally corrupt, and it is not at all likely that Pompey was actuated by entirely disinterested motives in creating them ; the importance to him of middle-class votes is a far more probable explanation. Pompey and Crassus in person carried a law restoring to the tribunate all its old powers, and by means of puppet censors (the first to hold office since 86) expelled sixty-four members of the senate, most of them nominees of Sulla. It must not be supposed that Pompey's sympathies were with the *populares*, for his outlook was essentially conservative and he had no desire to overthrow the constitution or make himself dictator—he was not made of dictatorial stuff, being in many ways the least impressive of all the great figures of the later Republic. Certainly he was an able general, though not, we think, worthy to be ranked with Marius, Sulla and Lucullus, still less with Caesar— it must be remembered that Mithridates was a spent force when Pompey defeated him—but he was at bottom a weak and selfish character, who valued above everything his own military glory. He had not done very well against Sertorius in Spain and in consequence tried to shoulder the blame for his defeats onto the senate, with whom, like a spoilt child, he was prepared to co-operate only if it gave him exactly what he wanted.

It was mainly because he did not trust the senate, after his cavalier treatment of it, to give him a fresh command that he restored the powers of the tribunate. In 67 he had his reward. The tribune Gabinius, in the teeth of senatorial opposition, passed a law conferring upon him an *imperium* in the Mediterranean and over

its coasts for fifty miles inland for a period of three years
to crush the pirates, who had recently become so bold
as seriously to endanger Rome's overseas corn supply.
Within three months the campaign was finished.   While
Pompey of set purpose dallied in the East, by the *lex
Manilia* of 66 the command against Mithridates was transferred to him from Lucullus, who had earned the enmity
of the *equites* by scaling down debts in the province of
Asia.   Their spokesman in favour of the bill was M.
Tullius Cicero, a *novus homo* from Marius' birthplace,
Arpinum, who had first made his mark in politics in 70
by his damning indictment of Verres for extortion during
his term of office in Sicily.   Cicero as a politician had two
supreme merits, his magnificent eloquence and his sincere
patriotism in an age when patriotism was rare, but they
were vitiated by his lack of real determination, his
excessive vanity and above all his inability to look facts
in the face.   The *concordia ordinum*, or alliance of the
various classes, which he advocated as a means of saving
the state, was nothing but an idle dream, for the breach
between senate and *equites* had not appreciably narrowed
since C. Gracchus' days, the majority of both groups were
destitute of statesmanlike qualities, as Cicero knew very
well in his heart, and the few really honest senators, like
the younger Cato,[1] were narrow-minded Conservatives,
incapable of co-operating with more progressive elements.

During Pompey's absence from Rome various moves
were made by Crassus in an endeavour to establish for
himself a position from which he could challenge him on
his return from the East, moves which Cicero, who was
beginning to pin a pathetic and almost childlike faith in
Pompey as a possible leader of the centre party of his
dreams, was largely responsible in checking.   In par-

[1] Great-grandson of Cato the Censor, the implacable enemy of
Carthage (see page 114).

ticular Crassus sought to secure the consulship of 63
for a man who had actually plotted to murder the consuls
for 65, the depraved and reckless Catiline, whom he
hoped to use for the defence of Italy against Pompey
if Pompey returned with an army as Sulla had done.
Cicero, however, made full use of his eloquence to show
that the return of Catiline would mean the introduction
of a species of mob rule, and was himself elected. When
his candidature for the consulship of 62 was equally
unsuccessful, Catiline, who no longer enjoyed Crassus'
backing, once more turned his attention to the possibility
of using force. Cicero learned enough of his schemes to
take precautionary measures but not enough to put him
under arrest with the certainty that his action would be
endorsed by the senate, and he accordingly allowed him
to leave Rome to join a force of discontented Sullan
veterans in Etruria. After Catiline's departure his
associates in Rome acted with singular stupidity by
making overtures for help to some ambassadors of the
Allobroges, a Gallic tribe, who happened to be in the city.
Thereby they played into the consul's hands. On
receiving information from the ambassadors he at last
felt justified not merely in arresting the conspirators but
in persuading the senate to sanction their execution.
Outside Rome Catiline secured comparatively little
support, and he was easily defeated by the armies Cicero
had mobilised.

THE FIRST TRIUMVIRATE 60–49 B.C.

Cicero's action in crushing the conspiracy had deprived
Pompey of an excellent excuse for keeping his army in
being when he returned to Italy in 62, but nearly everyone
was surprised when he disbanded his forces and merely
asked the senate to ratify his settlement of the East and

grant his veterans the usual land-allotments. Narrow-minded and shortsighted as ever, the senate kept on postponing its decision and so drove Pompey, who had been prepared to be reconciled with the *optimates*, into the arms of Caesar and Crassus, both of whom it chose to annoy at this precise juncture. Caesar, a young noble-man who had espoused the democratic cause as the best means of obtaining political advancement and had borrowed considerable sums of money from Crassus to satisfy his extravagant tastes, returned in 61 from governing Spain as propraetor and asked for a triumph for his victories over the tribes of Lusitania. On purely personal grounds the senate refused, and added insult to injury by assigning to the consuls for 59, because it anticipated Caesar would be one of them, the oversight of the forests of Italy as their sphere of proconsular duty in the following year instead of the usual province : by a law of C. Gracchus the senate had to assign proconsular commands before the result of the consular elections was known, but if they could forecast the electors' decision, the *patres* were able to defeat the obvious intention of the measure. Caesar was not the man to lie down under such treatment, and in 60 he engineered an alliance with the disgruntled Pompey, offering him his daughter Julia in marriage as a pledge of good faith. Crassus also was approached because of his influence with the *equites*, and being piqued by the senate's refusal to lower the contract price for the collection of the Asia taxes (the *equites* having overestimated the yield) and afraid of being left out in the cold, he had no hesitation in joining the alliance and forming the First Triumvirate. Not so Cicero, whose influence also would have been extremely valuable, for he viewed with dismay the disregard of constitutional usage which he saw to be imminent.

As consul for 59 Caesar duly passed the two measures

which Pompey desired, but only by using Pompey's veterans to overcome the opposition of his diehard colleague, Bibulus, and a number of senatorial tribunes. Bibulus, unable to persist in the personal intervention which the use of *intercessio* necessitated, had recourse to the device of watching the sky and declaring the omens unfavourable, and so rendered Caesar's calling of the *comitia* technically invalid. Caesar, however, was more concerned with his own future than Pompey's past, and secured the military command he wanted through the *lex Vatinia* ; this conferred on him for five years from the date on which it was carried, March 1st, 59, the governorship of Cisalpine Gaul and Illyria, to which the senate added Narbonese Gaul when it fell vacant later in the year, seeing that Caesar would take it in any case.

Caesar did not altogether trust Pompey and Crassus, and left behind in Rome as watchdog an able and dissolute aristocrat named Clodius, whose adoption into a plebeian family he secured to enable him to stand for a tribunate. Elected for 58, Clodius proceeded to surround himself with a gang of ruffians to terrorise any possible opposition, procured Cicero's banishment on the ground that in his handling of the Catilinarian conspiracy he had put citizens to death without trial, got rid of Cato, the trium-virate's other principal enemy, by sending him to annex Cyprus and incorporate it in the province of Cilicia, and abolished altogether the low price of the Gracchan corn grant. Pompey was the next object of his attack, but Pompey was not yet powerless. He thwarted Clodius' terrorism by engaging a rival terrorist of his own, named Milo, whose activities enabled him to procure Cicero's recall. Cicero began to hope again that he might wean Pompey away from Caesar, whose recall was actually suggested in certain quarters, but Crassus informed Caesar of what was afoot and Pompey was persuaded to join them for a conference at Luca on the border of Caesar's province, which he was not allowed under Sulla's *lex de maiestate* to leave without the senate's permission. Thus in March, 56, the triumvirate was renewed. Pompey and Crassus were to hold the consulship for 55 and bring forward a law prolonging Caesar's command for five years to enable him to complete the conquest of Gaul. They themselves in return were given Spain and Syria respectively—also for five years—by the *lex Trebonia*, passed during their year of office, and Pompey received special permission to govern his province through *legati*, so that he could remain in Rome. He had been the first to use *legati* extensively under the *leges Gabinia* and *Manilia*, and he was now the first to discover the full possibilities of the system—a discovery of which Augustus made good use in constituting the Principate.

The death of Julia in 54 removed the only real tie between Caesar and Pompey, the death of Crassus at Carrhae in 53[1] the only influence powerful enough to maintain a semblance of peace, for Pompey would hardly have dared to defy Caesar and Crassus combined. Thereafter the clouds of civil war loomed nearer and nearer. The street fighting of Clodius and Milo and their gangs, which neither Pompey nor the senate had done anything to check, assumed such proportions that after Clodius' death at the hands of Milo in 52 Pompey was nominated sole consul, *consul sine collega*, to restore order. While holding that office he kept the promise he had given Caesar at Luca to secure for him the exceptional privilege of standing for the consulship of 48 *in absentia*. Circumstances, however, were driving him into the arms of those senators who hated Caesar most and were determined to prosecute him for the illegalities of his first consulship. This they would be unable to do if Caesar remained commander in

[1] See page 118.

Gaul until his second consulship began on 1st January, 48,
or it was a cardinal principle of the constitution that no
Roman could be prosecuted while holding office. Fore-
seeing this, Caesar had had a special clause inserted in
the *lex Licinia Pompeia* of 55 which had prolonged his
command, stating that the question of his successor was
not to be raised till 1st March, 50, thereby making it
impossible for the consuls of 50 to succeed him ; for
under C. Gracchus' law their proconsular provinces would
have to be assigned before they were elected consuls.
Pompey, now under the senate's influence, accordingly
passed a law prescribing a five years' interval between
consulship and proconsulship, in order to make it possible
for Caesar to be relieved of his command in 49. In 51,
therefore, Caesar requested the extension of his command
to the end of 49, but this the senate refused, and early
in that year successors to his provinces were nominated.
Caesar had now no alternative and in January, 49, entered
Italy by crossing the Rubicon. Although the illegalities
of his consulship in 59 and his consequent unconstitutional
demands were the ultimate reason for the civil war, it
was the diehard element in the senate which forced the
issue when Caesar was prepared to negotiate, and almost
bullied the vacillating Pompey into accepting the challenge which they compelled Caesar to make.

PHARSALUS, ZELA, THAPSUS AND MUNDA
48–45 B.C.

For the campaign in a military sense Pompey and the
senate were almost completely unprepared, while Caesar
had at his disposal a compact and veteran army, so that
Pompey was forced to evacuate Italy without himself
fighting, and established himself in Western Macedonia.
Instead of pursuing him immediately, Caesar was careful

to secure his rear by a vigorous and completely successf
campaign against Pompey's lieutenants in Spain. Earl
in 48 he evaded the Pompeian fleet and crossed th
Adriatic, and with seven legions endeavoured to blockad
Pompey's eleven near Dyrrachium. Pompey, howeve
although afraid to risk his troops in open combat again:
Caesar's seasoned warriors, had the command of the se:
and it was Caesar who was compelled to retire first—t
the cornlands of Thessaly. Near Pharsalus the armi
eventually engaged, and Caesar won a smashing victor
Pompey himself fled with a small retinue to Egyp
where he was murdered, as he stepped ashore, by th
orders of the government of the country. The rest of h
army either surrendered or made their way to Afric
Caesar preferred to follow Pompey and foolishly remaine
in Egypt bargaining with the king, with the result th:
his small force was besieged in Alexandria and rescue
only by the intervention of native troops raised in Cilici
Syria and Judaea. With the death of the king the re
power in Egypt passed to his sister, Cleopatra, who:
charms had made a considerable impression on Caesa
During the campaign of Dyrrachium Pontus had bee
reoccupied by Mithridates' son, Pharnaces; in th
summer of 47 Caesar moved from Egypt against hi
and beat him in a stubborn engagement near Zel
describing his victory in the simple but hardly justifiab
terms *veni, vidi, vici*. On his return to Rome he foun
that a mutiny had broken out among the troops he ha
sent home after Pharsalus, but he quelled it with th
single word *Quirites* (i.e. ' Civilians ') and proceeded
attack the Pompeians in Africa. After initial difficulti
he won a great victory at Thapsus in 46, on hearing th
news of which Cato, in command of the Pompei:
garrison at Utica, committed suicide. Meanwhile Spa
had been re-won for the Pompeian cause by Pompey

sons, and before he could turn his attention to the reorganization of the empire Caesar had to fight there once more. His victory at Munda in 45 left him master of the Roman world.

THE " MONARCHY " OF CAESAR 48-44 B.C.

C. Julius Caesar was one of the few men of real genius produced by Rome. His truly remarkable versatility enabled him to win distinction of the highest order as general, military historian, administrator and statesman. The secret of his success lay in his masterful personality, which even his bitterest enemies could not deny : therein also lay the secret of his failure. Like most men who set great store by efficiency, he could not suffer fools gladly nor see the advantage of " hastening slowly ". The senate's failure to set its house in order, despite the efforts of Sulla, had made it plain that the only solution of Rome's difficulties lay in the centralization of authority in the hands of one man, but the strong conservative element in the Roman character could not stomach such a violent change, unless republican forms and institutions were outwardly preserved. Caesar had no use for sham : he would not gild the pill nor stoop to a little tactful hypocrisy in order to smooth over the transition from republic to monarchy ; he would not allow the senate even the shadow of independence, so that it might per- suade itself that it still ruled Rome. This refusal to make any concessions to conservative sentiment, more than anything else, cost him his life, for most of the senators who stabbed him to death on 15th March, 44, genuinely believed that their blows were being struck in the sacred name of liberty.

It is true that Caesar never actually adopted the hated title of *rex* in Italy and publicly refused the crown offered

him by Antony, but no one could fail to see that he was
in reality sole ruler of the Empire. Edicts were often
substituted for laws. The temporary dictatorships
which he held in the first stage of the civil war became a
ten years' office after Thapsus and a perpetual office a
month before he died. He received the *sacrosanctitas*
or inviolability, of a tribune and allowed his statue to be
set up in the temples and Antony to be made the *flamen*
or special priest, of his divinity. All the magistrates
were virtually appointed by himself, and when he appointed none in 47, 46, and 45 till half the year was over
none held office, and their work was carried on by Caesar
himself, Lepidus, his *magister equitum*,[1] and their staff
In 45 when one of the consuls died on the last day of the
year, Caesar deeply shocked republican feeling by
appointing a successor to hold office for a few hours only
as though the consulship had become merely a compli
mentary title.

In admitting 300 new members to the senate, some
of them men of low birth, some of them Gauls, he showed
a breadth of outlook and understanding of the unity of
the empire far ahead of his time. Salutary as this
measure was, however, Caesar would have been wiser to
prepare public opinion for it by effecting the change
gradually. Equally far-seeing, and less objectionable in
the eyes of the *optimates*, were his lavish grants of *civita*
to provincial troops and of *civitas* and *Latinitas* to
provincial towns in addition to the *civitas* he bestowed
on the whole of Cisalpine Gaul and the *Latinitas* he gave
to all Sicily. For the provinces to him were not merely
the *praedia populi Romani*, or estates of Rome; they
were potentially part of a great commonwealth, and the
Romanization of the West in particular was encouraged
by the foundation of a considerable number of oversea

[1] See page 136.

lonies, of which as yet there had been very few—colonies
hich not merely provided land for the veterans and the
oor of Rome at a cheaper price than it could be bought
Italy, but hastened the spread of Roman law and
lture and the feeling of imperial unity. Indeed
esar's generous and statesmanlike attitude to the
ovinces was not even approached by any of the first-
ntury emperors except Claudius and Vespasian.

Caesar planned to improve the administration of Italy,
it he did not live to complete his work nor to carry out
s schemes for land reclamation. He began the urgent
sk of rebuilding the overcrowded centre of Rome and
ore than halved the number of citizens in receipt of free
rn.[1] He doubled the legionaries' pay, removed the
buni aerarii from the jury panels, and reformed the
lendar, besides passing various necessary laws of purely
mporary significance. His premature death cut short
e first comprehensive attempt since the foundation of
e republic to establish a new system of government,
it it is amazing, when we consider how little time he
.d had to give to civil affairs, how far that attempt
.d been carried.

THE SECOND TRIUMVIRATE 43-31 B.C.

The conspirators, led by Brutus and Cassius, had failed
mpletely to envisage the situation which would arise when
e tyrant was removed. They had forgotten that many of
eir fellow-senators owed their position to the murdered
an : they had forgotten that he had kept the people
used by lavish entertainments which meant far more
them than abstract political ideals ; they had forgotten
at the army was almost solidly behind the régime they
shed to overthrow. They had neither prepared any

[1] See page 165.

policy with which to win popular approval nor any force
to back them until that approval should be won. The
initiative therefore passed at once to Antony, Caesar's
colleague in the consulship, who obtained possession of
his private papers and secured the support of the weaker
Lepidus, Caesar's *magister equitum*, who had under his
command the only armed force in the vicinity. On the
motion of Cicero the senate passed a decree of pardon
in favour of the conspirators, but it also voted Caesar a
public funeral, at which Antony so worked upon the
emotions of the mob that Brutus and Cassius were forced
for their own safety to leave the city.

Antony at first adopted a conciliatory attitude to the
senate and carried a resolution abolishing the dictatorship.
But he was probably determined from the outset to
succeed Caesar and was careful to secure from the senate
as his proconsular command for the following year the
province of Macedonia, where six legions had been
collected in readiness for Caesar's projected campaign
against the Parthians. Antony's influence did not,
however, go unchallenged, for Octavian, Caesar's great
nephew and adopted son and heir, returned to Italy from
Epirus, where he had been undergoing military training.
Being refused by Antony the money wherewith to pay
Caesar's legacy to the citizens, he determined to win
over the allegiance of the veterans as Caesar's rightful
successor by giving the legacy himself, and so gain a
position which would force Antony to come to terms.
For a time there was no open breach between them, but
Antony was sufficiently perturbed by Octavian's growing
influence to secure from the senate permission to exchange
Macedonia for Cisalpine and Narbonese Gaul, while
retaining the Macedonian legions ; for he felt, as Caesar
had done in 59, that possession of these provinces would
give him the military control of Italy.

By the time Antony left Rome in December to take over Cisalpine Gaul from D. Brutus, one of the conspirators, and Narbonese Gaul from Lepidus, Octavian was actively engaged in raising an army from among the veterans with the connivance of the senate, which was becoming alarmed at Antony's high-handed actions and under Cicero's guidance was perfectly prepared to make use of Octavian's influence, although it intended to drop him as soon as he had served its purpose. Of this he was perfectly well aware, and when in April, 43, the senate's forces succeeded in raising the siege of Mutina, where Antony had penned in Brutus on his refusing with the senate's backing to hand over his province, Octavian, on whom the command had devolved with the death of both the consuls, made no move either to cut off Antony's retreat or to make contact with Brutus. Octavian indeed completely outwitted the senate, which might have known that one who had attacked Antony for not avenging Caesar could hardly have made common cause with one of his murderers, even had the senate treated him with greater respect than it actually did. While Antony joined forces with Lepidus and the other governors of the western provinces until he had twenty-two legions under his command and had no difficulty in ousting D. Brutus from Cisalpine Gaul, Octavian bided his time and then, when the senate refused him one of the vacant consulships, marched on Rome to enforce his demand.

His first act as consul was to annul the pardon granted the conspirators, of whom the chief, M. Brutus and Cassius, were now collecting armies in Macedonia and Syria, which they had seized instead of the minor provinces of Crete and Cyrene allotted to them. His next was to rescind the sentence of outlawry which had been passed against Antony, with whom he now felt strong enough to come to terms. Through the mediation

of Lepidus a meeting was held at Bononia, where it was
agreed that the three of them should divide the western
provinces between them, Octavian as a young man of
only twenty having to content himself with third place,
and secure their appointment as *tresviri reipublicae
constituendae* for five years. Thus in less than two years
after Caesar's death Rome found herself saddled with
three dictators instead of one, dictators moreover who
did not observe Caesar's policy of clemency but instituted
proscriptions on a Sullan scale. Among their victims
was Cicero, who had publicly attacked Antony in the
orationes Philippicae with a virulence that is probably
unsurpassed in the annals of oratory.

By the time Antony and Octavian crossed the Adriatic
in 42, Brutus and Cassius had gained control of all the
East except Egypt and had entrenched themselves in a
strong position at Philippi in Macedonia. By cutting
them off from their naval base Antony forced them to
give battle, but his own victory over Cassius, who committed suicide, was nullified by Brutus' defeat of Octavian.
Three weeks later a second battle gave the triumvirs a
complete victory, and Octavian was now strong enough
to advance to second place ; for Lepidus had remained
in Italy, and by handing over his troops to fight against
Brutus and Cassius had lost the only asset which had
caused Antony and Octavian to treat him with respect.
But the position of Antony as the real victor of Philippi
was predominant, and Octavian had to be content with
the governorship of Spain and the unpleasant job of
confiscating a considerable amount of land in Italy for
soldiers whose services were no longer required, while
Antony arrogated to himself the far more congenial task
of reorganizing the East, while nominally governing the
whole of Gaul beyond the Alps in the West. In 41 Octavian
further strengthened his position, and was able, when

Antony returned to Italy in 40 and a fresh agreement was concluded at Brundisium, to secure control of all the West, while Antony held the East and Lepidus Africa. The treaty of alliance was confirmed by the marriage of Antony to Octavian's sister, Octavia.

Octavian's position was made extremely uncomfortable by Sextus Pompeius, Pompey's sole surviving son, who had maintained a precarious existence in Spain after Caesar's victory at Munda, had been put in command of the navy by the senate during the campaign of Mutina, and when placed on the list of the proscribed by the triumvirate had proceeded to seize Sicily for himself. As early as 42 Octavian had tried to dislodge him, but it was not until 36 following a naval victory off Naulochus, near the Straits of Messina, that Sicily passed into Octavian's control. Lepidus, who had assisted in the occupation of the island, made a feeble attempt to claim it for himself but was deserted by his troops. Octavian at last felt himself strong enough to display clemency and wisely spared Lepidus' life. His victory over Sextus had greatly enhanced his prestige, and while people began to look to him as the only man who could free them from the scourge of civil war, he in his turn began to cultivate their good opinion and solemnly promised in due time to restore the republic.

The alliance between Octavian and Antony had survived various crises, but it could not survive Antony's marriage to Cleopatra in 33. Octavian had no objection to divorce, having himself put away his first wife, Scribonia, in favour of a divorcée named Livia, but when a foreign queen was put in the place of his own sister, his pride was hurt. After his failure against the Parthians in 36,[1] Antony had become more and more infatuated with Cleopatra and had assigned to her and to her children

[1] See page 119.

not merely the lands of neighbouring kings but even the
Roman provinces of Syria, Cilicia, Crete and Cyrene
yet it was not until 31 that Octavian felt that he had
aroused public opinion sufficiently to ask for a formal
declaration of war against Cleopatra.

As he was consul for 31 Octavian's authority could not
be challenged, and he strengthened his position by allow
ing an oath of allegiance to be taken to him up and down
Italy ; but Antony had no longer any official status in
Roman law since the triumvirate, renewed in 37 at
Tarentum for a further five years, had expired at the
end of 33. The armies of the two sides were fairly evenly
matched, but Antony's navy was much inferior ; and
Octavian's command of the sea enabled his admiral
Agrippa, to make the position which Antony had taken
up at Actium on the west coast of Greece almost unten-
able. Antony therefore in 31 ordered a general retreat
but while he and Cleopatra succeeded in breaking out
the rest of his fleet, 300 strong, put back into harbour
practically without fighting and capitulated. In due
course Octavian invaded Egypt, whither Antony and
Cleopatra had fled, and annexed the country without any
serious opposition, as they anticipated capture by taking
their own lives. Thus it fell to a rather ordinary man
whose chief virtue was his astute common sense, to
constitute a new form of government which Rome had
been awaiting since the days of the Gracchi.

CHAPTER V

THE AUGUSTAN COMPROMISE 31 B.C.–A.D. 14

WHEN Octavian returned to Rome in 29 after annexing Egypt and reorganizing the affairs of the East, men felt for the first time since the middle of the second century a real sense of security. Octavian possessed no brilliant qualities either as soldier or as politician : he was no creative genius : he did not tower above his contemporaries ; yet the vast majority of the Empire's inhabitants allowed his ascendency to pass unquestioned —the three conspiracies of his reign were all comparatively trivial affairs—and he succeeded in accomplishing what all the great figures of the later Republic had failed to achieve—a stable and effective form of autocratic government. The true explanation of his success is to be found in his character, which owed more to his father's Italian middle-class stock than to his mother's aristocratic lineage, for he was the living embodiment of the national character which had made the Roman Empire, and men trusted him because they felt they knew him as they knew themselves. Octavian had defeated Antony by the same means as those which Rome had employed against Carthage, by determination and tenacity of purpose, by caution and patience, by making full use of his opponent's mistakes and learning from his own, and he did not discard these means when victory was won. His shrewd, practical common-sense saved him from the fatal errors which Caesar had committed, and the Principate which he constituted solved the problem of the Empire's form of government, precisely because it was not the product of ruthless logic as Caesar's constitution would have been.

THE SETTLEMENT OF 27 B.C.

In 36 Octavian had promised to restore the Republic and in a sense he did restore it. In 27 B.C. he solemnly gave back to the senate and people the direction of public affairs, because his conservative instinct told him that there must be no clean break with the past and that the outward forms of government to which the Roman nation had for so long been accustomed must at all costs be preserved. His own words in the *Res Gestae*, in which he recorded the achievements of his reign, " *Rem publicam ex mea potestate in senatus populique Romani arbitrium transtuli*," represent truly enough one aspect of his settlement. For in theory the Principate was a republican form of government. Octavian accepted the name of Augustus, by which he is generally known, as an indication that a new golden age had dawned and that the horrors of civil war had been swept away, but he preferred to be spoken of simply as the *princeps*, or first citizen. He persistently refused to accept any exceptional office and administered the state from 27 to 23 B.C. as he had done from the beginning of 31, in virtue of the consulship—an essentially republican institution. It is true that he received an abnormally wide *provincia* (all the provinces of the Empire, except Africa, that demanded the presence of legionary troops [1]), that he administered these provinces from Rome by means of *legati*, and that he received the *imperium* for ten years and not merely for one. But for the extended use of the normal *imperium* there were republican precedents in the case of Pompey (under the *lex Gabinia* of 67, the *lex Manilia* of 66 and the *lex Trebonia* of 55), and such an extension was a very different matter in conservative eyes from the acceptance

---

[1] See page 122.   [2] See pages 161–2 and 166.

of the abnormal powers of the dictatorship or the acceptance of any form of office for life. Julius Caesar had
made the mistake of supposing that a strong government
may safely ignore the prejudices of public opinion and
had paid with his life for the mistake. To Augustus it was
as clear as it had been to Caesar that any attempt to
restore the predominance of the senate would meet with
failure (otherwise Sulla[1] would have succeeded), and that
the armed forces of the state must owe their allegiance
to one man and the administration of the Empire be by
him reorganized if Rome was to continue mistress of the
Mediterranean. But he realized the importance of
placating the traditionalists. The trappings of monarchy
were to him of no moment at all provided that in fact he
ruled the Empire. The great thing was to be tactful
and to allow the senate to believe, if it wanted to, that
the Republic was not yet dead.

THE PRESTIGE OF THE PRINCEPS

Of course Augustus was in a peculiarly happy position.
He knew that by re-establishing the *pax Romana* he
enjoyed a prestige (*auctoritas*) so great that he was
perfectly safe in restoring the Republic. The senate
would insist on his continuing to administer the state
and if he refused office for life, as he must, would renew
his powers when they lapsed. They were, in fact, renewed
for periods of ten or five years at a time and there never
was, as Augustus had foreseen, any real opposition to the
proposal that they should be renewed. If the establishment of the Principate was accepted by the senate with
relief, it was acclaimed by the mass of the people both
in Italy and the provinces with an enthusiasm that
bordered on the idolatrous, and Augustus was fairly

[1] See pages 157-8.

generally regarded with the same kind of uncritical veneration the modern dictator receives from his own people. This enthusiasm the *princeps* turned to good account. Hitherto the Empire had lacked a symbol of unity such as the British Commonwealth of Nations has in the British Crown. What better symbol could there be than the person of the *princeps*? In Rome and Italy it would be enough to allow men to worship his *genius*, or spirit. But in the provinces—not only the Eastern provinces, where already kings like Alexander the Great had received semi-divine honours during their lifetime, but in the Western provinces also—the worship of Augustus must be coupled with that of Rome and leading provincials should act as high-priests of the new cult. Thus in practically every province a central *ara* was built to Rome and Augustus which became a focus of Romanization. The provincials had no love for the Republic and would accept the Principate gladly if it meant an improvement in their position, but the people of Rome and Italy looked back on the old days with pride. For them, as for the senate, the connection between the past and the present must be made clear. And so the achievements of the new régime were extolled by Virgil and other members of Maecenas' literary circle as the revival of ancient glories, and Augustus was depicted as the god who had brought back to the Roman world not only the blessings of peace but also the old faith in Rome's destiny and in the Roman virtues. When Augustus died he was solemnly deified by decree of the senate, and a body of twenty-five distinguished senators, four of them members of the imperial family, called the *Sodales Augustales* was constituted to conduct his worship.

THE SETTLEMENT OF 23 B.C.

Augustus had made a mistake in deciding to hold the consulship year after year. The arrangement taxed his own physical strength, which was not great, with unnecessary routine duties, automatically reduced the number of ex-consuls available for important government posts, and halved a senator's chances of holding the supreme office in the state, while it made too obvious the fundamentally autocratic nature of the new régime. From 23 onwards, therefore, Augustus never held the consulship except to introduce his grandsons into public life, and made use instead of the *tribunicia potestas*, or powers of a tribune, which had been conferred on him in 30, to convene the senate, introduce measures in the assembly and exercise judicial functions, receiving in addition the specific right to make war and conclude treaties. In fact the basis of his power remained the *imperium*, which was made *maius*, in order that he might continue to intervene if he chose in the affairs of senatorial provinces. But henceforward it was kept in the background and the *tribunicia potestas* was purposely stressed as being in no sense military, but essentially democratic.

REORGANIZATION OF THE CIVIL SERVICE

Satisfactory as Augustus' final solution of his own position proved to be, it is doubtful whether the Principate would have endured, had it not been for his reorganization of the Civil Service. By paying his officials and keeping them employed in the same or similar tasks for several years on end, he secured for his provinces a government both more efficient and more disinterested than they had ever known under the Republic ; the senatorial pro-

G S.P.Q.R.

vinces also were affected by the change, inasmuch as there
was no hard and fast dividing line between those who took
service with the *princeps* and those who took service with
the senate, and the same men generally gained experience
in both types of province. Despite his insistence on
efficient government, however, Augustus did not give the
provincials the encouragement they had received from
Julius Caesar. He was not lavish in his grants of *civitas*
and he did not admit representatives of the provinces into
the senate. This was no doubt due rather to a prudent
regard for senatorial prejudice (public opinion was not
yet ready to allow the provinces a fair share in the
administration of the Empire) than to conviction. But
while allowing the senate to remain almost exclusively
Italian and reducing its numbers from over a thousand to
six hundred, so that senators felt once more that their
position was one worth having, he no longer allowed it to
provide all the officials needed for government business
which had grown too complicated to be dealt with by so
small a group of men. Instead he called upon the *ordo
equester* [1] to supply him with officials for a large number
of new administrative posts, thereby giving the middle
classes responsibilities which they had not previously
possessed as well as making it possible for senatorial
officials to do their work properly. Behind the scenes
were Augustus' own private secretaries and accountants
who coordinated the work of different departments and
the policy to be pursued by different officials in a way
in which they had never been coordinated under the
Republic. In accordance with Roman practice these
secretaries were freedmen, generally of Greek origin—for
the Greeks had a flair for this kind of work—and although
they really became state officials when Augustus became
princeps, he was careful to keep them in the background

[1] See pages 48, 150–1 and 190–1.

and give them no status which might offend aristocratic susceptibilities.

It was not only the provinces that benefited from Augustus' reorganization. The administration of Rome itself was much improved. The *annona*, or corn-supply system, was completely overhauled. A fire-brigade of seven cohorts of five hundred men each, called the *vigiles*, was enrolled to protect the city, and three *cohortes urbanae*, each one thousand strong, to police it. New indirect taxes were introduced to meet rising expenditure and the finances of the Empire put on a sound basis, a special treasury called the *aerarium militare* being established in A.D. 6 to provide allotments for discharged legionaries. The juries for the *quaestiones* were now drawn from the *equites*, *tribuni aerarii* and *ducenarii* (those possessing over 400,000 sesterces, between 300,000 and 400,000 and between 200,000 and 300,000 respectively).

CHAPTER VI

STATE OFFICIALS AND THEIR DUTIES

The Imperium

As we saw in Chapter I, the supreme power in the state
which was valid alike in the city and on the field of battle
in the making of laws and in the administration of justice
passed in 510 B.C. from the King to two Praetors (late
called Consuls). It was conferred on all praetors subse
quently appointed, although they ranked as inferior t
the consuls, but on none of the other regular magistrates
Its tenure could be prolonged (*prorogatum*) beyond th
year for which it had been originally conferred and me
exercising a prolonged *imperium* were called proconsul
or propraetors, as were *privati* (ordinary citizens) grante
the *imperium* in special circumstances.[1] In times c
crisis during the early Republic the consulship was sus
pended and the *imperium* conferred instead on a *dictator*
and his *magister equitum*.[2] The outward symbol of th
imperium was the *fasces*, bundles of rods with an ax
head protruding, which signified that the magistra
before whom they were carried by public servants, calle
lictors,[3] possessed the power to flog or execute citizen
They were of Etruscan origin, like the lictors, and intr
duced into Rome by the Tarquins. Magistrates wieldin
the *imperium*, together with the censors and the curu
aediles, were further distinguished by the *sella curuli*
a judgment-seat inlaid with ivory (also of Etrusca

---

[1] See page 188.   [2] See page 136.

[3] Twelve lictors accompanied a consul or the *princeps*, twenty-fo
a dictator.

rigin), and a purple-bordered robe called the *toga
raetexta.*

THE MAGISTRATES

THE CONSULS were first elected in 509 B.C. as executive
eads of the state in place of the kings. To ensure that
n oppressive despotism should never occur again they
ere given equal power, each having the right to veto
ntercedere) the actions of the other, and their tenure of
ffice was to last only for a year : other magistracies also,
xcept the dictatorship and the censorship, were made
nnual when created. The consuls were originally called
raetores, because they commanded the armies of the
tate besides exercising administrative and judicial
unctions, but in the later Republic they rarely left the
ity and generals were nearly always pro-magistrates.
he consuls regularly presided over the senate and the
omitia centuriata, and their judicial functions, which had
apsed after the creation of the praetorship, were revived
nder the Empire when trials of senatorial officials and
ppeals from the senatorial provinces were sometimes heard
a the senate. The first plebeian to hold the consulship
as L. Sextius, elected 367 B.C. The office was usually
eld only for six months under the Julio-Claudians and
or four under the Flavians.

THE QUAESTORSHIP was the only other magistracy
hich had existed since the foundation of the Republic.
riginally there were two quaestors to assist the consuls
a judicial work (hence the name—cf. *quaestio*) and
nance, but their work soon became entirely financial
nd additional quaestors were appointed to supervise the
ollection of *tributum* in Italy (until it was abolished in
67 B.C.) and to act as financial officials in the provinces
s they were created. There were 20 quaestors under

Sulla, 40 under Julius Caesar, and 20 under the Empire.
They were elected by the *comitia tributa*, and after 31
generally, and after Sulla automatically, received a seat
in the senate.

THE AEDILESHIP dated from 449 B.C., when the
concilium plebis was constituted. Originally priests of the
temple (*aedes*) of Ceres on the Aventine who encouraged
and helped the *tribuni*,[1] or unofficial leaders of the *plebs*
in their struggle against the patricians, the two plebeian
aediles (like the ten tribunes) were not strictly magistrates
at all, even after they acquired police-court jurisdiction
with a general control over the streets and markets of the
city and the supervision of the public games. Their
colleagues, however, the two curule aediles, first appointed
366 B.C. and originally patrician and then alternately
patrician and plebeian, were strictly officials of the state
and not of the *plebs*. Julius Caesar in 44 B.C. added two
plebeian cereal aediles to deal with the corn-supply, but
Augustus[2] made other arrangements.

THE CENSORSHIP dated from the army reforms of
443 B.C. The censors were elected (for eighteen months
at first at irregular intervals and later at intervals of
five years, and they were generally ex-consuls. Their
primary function was to draw up the lists of those liable
to military service and to the payment of *tributum*, but
they acquired from the consuls the duties of letting out
public contracts for buildings and roads and of revising
the list of the senate (with the power to expel a member
by affixing the censor's brand, *censoria nota*, to his name).
Their original functions disappeared with the abolition
of *tributum* in Italy 167 B.C., and of conscription
following the army reforms of Marius in 107. We seldom
hear of censors being elected in the last fifty years of the
Republic, though the office was revived by Claudius

---

[1] See pages 141–2.   [2] See page 191.

..D. 47 and Vespasian A.D. 73, and Domitian was *censor
erpetuus* from A.D. 85.

THE PRAETOR URBANUS was first elected 366 B.C. to
elieve the consuls of judicial work and called *praetor* as
•eing their junior colleague, like them wielding the
mperium : he was called *praetor urbanus* only after the
lection of the first PRAETOR PEREGRINUS in 242 to try
ases involving citizens and non-citizens, which had
•ecome increasingly numerous with the expansion of
Rome.

Additional PRAETORS were created to govern provinces
ntil 146 B.C., when they were replaced by pro-magis-
rates and became entirely confined to judicial work in
Rome ; this increased considerably after the establishment
f the first standing court, the *quaestio perpetua de rebus
epetundis* (extortion in the provinces) in 149. Under
ulla there were seven *quaestiones*, or criminal courts, and
ight praetors, two of whom, the *praetor urbanus* and the
raetor *peregrinus*, normally tried civil cases. Under
ulius Caesar the number of praetors was raised to
6, and under the Julio-Claudians varied from 8 at the
eginning of Augustus' reign to 12 or even 16.

Criminal cases in the *quaestiones* were tried with a jury,
ften 51 in number ; civil cases without a jury in two
arts, the first part before a praetor when the legal
osition was determined, the second before a *iudex*, or
rbitrator, when the facts were investigated. Since
ere was no public prosecutor in Rome, the accusation of
notorious offender became a recognized means of
ntering public life (so Cicero first became prominent by
is successful prosecution of Verres, the corrupt governor
f Sicily, in 70 B.C.). Under the Empire important cases
ere tried with increasing frequency before the consuls
nd senate or before the *princeps*, and *delatores*,[1] or in-

[1] See page 194.

formers, became a real menace to distinguished men unles
the reigning *princeps* discouraged their activities.

THE PRO-MAGISTRATES

In 327 B.C., during the Second Samnite War, th
imperium of Q. Publilius Philo was prolonged after hi
year of office came to an end, to enable him to conclud
the siege of Palaeopolis. This expedient was subse
quently adopted from time to time under the stress c
war, sometimes even in the case of young men who wer
privati and had not held a magistracy at all (e.g. Scipi
Africanus in 210 B.C.[1]). In 146 B.C., in order to avoi
the creation of additional praetors as fresh provinces wer
added to the empire and to leave all existing praetors fre
to conduct the increasing judicial business of the stat
the senate had recourse to the pro-magistracy to provid
governors for the provinces. Immediately after their yea
of office in Rome ex-consuls and ex-praetors now too
over provinces allotted to them by the senate as pro
consuls and propraetors (i.e. substitutes for, and nc
deputies of, consuls and praetors), until the *lex Pompei*
of 52 [2] decreed a five years' interval between magistrac
and pro-magistracy.

The system was retained unchanged for the senatori
provinces [3] under the Empire. The governors, wh
normally held office for one year only, were called pro
consuls as being responsible directly to the senat
although none of them had held the consulship excep
the governors of Asia and Africa : these provinces wer
always governed by ex-consuls under the Empire as bein
the most important senatorial provinces. As Augustu
was himself proconsul of all imperial provinces,[3] h

---

[1] See pages 105 and 160.   [2] See page 167.
[3] See page 122.

viceroys were termed *legati Augusti pro praetore*, whether
they were ex-consuls or ex-praetors. The normal period
of office was from three to five years, and in some cases
exceeded ten. These viceroys were themselves assisted
by *legati* generally of praetorian rank, and the finances
of the provinces were managed by equestrian *procuratores*,
who were generally far more experienced and efficient
than the young quaestors who did the corresponding
work in the senatorial provinces.

THE CURSUS HONORUM

Under the *lex Genucia* of 342 B.C. no two magistracies
might be held simultaneously nor might the same magis-
racy be held again except after an interval of ten years.
The *lex Villia annalis* of 180 B.C. and Sulla's enactment [1]
of 81 by laying down minimum ages for each office
ended to fix the order in which they were held, but the
so-called *cursus honorum* was not finally stabilized until
he reign of Augustus. The qualifications were the possession of a million sesterces and either senatorial birth or
in the case of *novi homines* [2]) a special grant of the *latus
clavus* (a broad stripe of purple on the *tunica*, which de-
noted senatorial rank) from the *princeps*.[3] Before proceed-
ng to the quaestorship, a man was expected to hold one
of the *vigintiviratus*, or lesser magistracies, and to gain
some military experience as a *tribunus militum*.[4] After
he quaestorship a plebeian held either the tribunate or the
aedileship, whereas a patrician might pass straight to the
praetorship. After the praetorship came some provincial

[1] See page 158.   [2] See page 146.

[3] By refusing to grant the *latus clavus* the *princeps* could prevent
unsuitable persons from standing for office : by ' nominating ' or
commending ' those he favoured, he could make their election practically certain.

[4] See page 126.

appointment, such as the governorship of one of the less important provinces, either senatorial or imperial, or the command of a legion. Ten years or so after holding the praetorship, a man proceeded to the consulship and then usually went abroad again to govern one of the bigger provinces. The office of *praefectus urbi* was the crown of the senatorial career and became permanent towards the end of Augustus' reign ; the *praefectus* controlled the three *cohortes urbanae*, each 1000 strong, which policed the city, and was the Emperor's deputy there.

THE EQUESTRIAN CURSUS

C. Gracchus[1] in 122 had first given the equestrian order a political significance, but no use was made of it in administration under the Republic, Julius Caesar preferring to increase the membership of the senate and the number of senatorial magistracies (he doubled the number of praetors and quaestors) to provide fresh man-power for the Civil Service. Augustus, however, realized the advantage of calling upon the *equites* as a body to provide men for completely new posts, so giving them a stake in the government of the country and utilizing their business experience.

Qualifications for the *cursus* were the possession of 400,000 sesterces, free birth and inclusion on the list of *equites* (this corresponded to the grant of the *latus clavu* in the case of the senatorial *cursus* and gave the *princep* a means of rejecting unsuitable candidates). Before passing on to a procuratorship in one of the imperial provinces, an *eques* had to serve in the army, generally a commander (*praefectus*) of an auxiliary cohort (infantry or *ala* (cavalry), or as tribune of a legion. *Equite* wishing to continue their military career might then hol

[1] See pages 48 and 150–1.

a tribunate in the *vigiles, cohortes urbanae* or praetorian guard.

The higher posts in the *cursus* were not at first graded in strict order of seniority, but the two most important were the governorship of Egypt, which no senator was allowed to enter because of its strategic importance, and the command of the nine cohorts of the praetorian guard. The *praefectus praetorio* (there were sometimes two) became a higher official than the *praefectus Aegypti* in Tiberius' reign owing to the prestige of Sejanus.[1] The *praefectus annonae*, with assistants in Rome and in the chief corn-producing countries, controlled the corn-supply of the city from A.D. 8 onwards. The *praefectus vigilum* dated from the creation of seven cohorts of *vigiles*, each 500 strong, in A.D. 6, to act as a fire-brigade, while the *praefecti classis*, stationed at Misenum and Ravenna, came into being when Augustus constituted permanent fleets based on these ports.

The distinguishing mark of an *eques* was the *angustus clavus*, or narrow purple stripe, worn on the *tunica.*

[1] See page 193.

CHAPTER VII

THE DEVELOPMENT OF THE PRINCIPATE
A.D. 14–96

THE JULIO-CLAUDIAN HOUSE

Tiberius	A.D. 14–37	Stepson of Augustus.
Gaius Caligula	37–41	Son of Germanicus and grandson of Drusus, Tiberius' younger brother.
Claudius	41–54	Younger brother of Germanicus and son of Drusus.
Nero	54–68	Stepson of Claudius and son of Agrippina, daughter of Germanicus.

TIBERIUS 14–37

AUGUSTUS had been repeatedly disappointed in his endeavours to choose a successor. He had no son ; and his nephew, Marcellus, his friend and lieutenant, Agrippa, and C. and L. Caesar, Agrippa's sons by Augustus' only daughter, Julia, all died young. The ageing emperor was, therefore, compelled to fall back on his elder stepson, Tiberius, whom he disliked. In A.D. 13 Tiberius was granted the *imperium proconsulare*, and when Augustus died in the following year, the senate accepted him as the new *princeps*. He was in no sense a loyable man, and his cold, reserved diffidence had been accentuated by the treatment he had received at Augustus' hands ; but he was a man with a very strong sense of duty, and in the early years of his reign he gave the Empire a thoroughly economical, sound, and efficient administration on the lines laid down by Augustus. Under him the Principate really settled down, but because Tiberius' work of consolidation was necessarily humdrum and inglorious we hear little of it.

More than any other emperor's, Tiberius' reputation has suffered undeservedly at the hands of the ancient authorities. The reason for this is not far to seek. Tiberius, for all his desire to follow in Augustus' footsteps, was completely lacking in the tact which had sweetened his predecessor's relations with the senate, and men could no longer delude themselves with the thought that the Principate was merely a form of republican government. It was not that Tiberius did not try to placate conservative sentiment : he tried too hard. In the early years of his reign he consulted the senate on important questions, even on military affairs, but he proved, as Augustus had foreseen, constitutionally incapable of leaving any decision entirely in the senate's hands. The increasing impotence of the popular assemblies in the government of Rome was formally recognized as early as A.D. 14 by the transference from them to the senate of the election of magistrates and by the rarity with which they were asked to legislate. These changes, coupled with its increased use as a court of justice, enhanced the senate's share in the actual business of government but did not make it any the more ready to like Tiberius.

It was with a heavy heart that he had taken the burden of an office for which he felt himself unfitted, and in A.D. 26 when he believed he had discovered a minister whom he could trust to carry on for him in Rome, he retired to the island of Capri, never to return. Like many naturally suspicious men, Tiberius, when he did give his confidence, gave it completely and gave it to an eminently unsuitable person. Sejanus, the commander of the praetorian guard, was Tiberius' evil genius and embittered still further his relations not only with the senate but with his own family. But in A.D. 31 Tiberius' eyes were at last opened to Sejanus' schemes for his own advancement. Secretly he secured the loyalty of the praetorian guard, whose concentration in a single camp just outside the city in A.D. 23 by Sejanus had increased the importance of gaining their support for any intended coup, and then denounced Sejanus in a long letter to the senate, which promptly passed sentence of execution.

Tiberius' disillusionment was complete. He felt even less able than before to trust anyone, and allowed his reign to end in an orgy of judicial murders. Informers saw their opportunity and, eager for the statutory reward of one-quarter of the condemned man's estate, brought case after case of *maiestas*, or high treason, before the senate. Although he sometimes intervened to secure an acquittal, Tiberius did not stamp on the practice as he should have done, and the hatred aroused by his failure to do so was largely responsible for the *damnatio memoriae* which he suffered.

GAIUS CALIGULA[1] 37–41

Tiberius had named as joint heirs in his will his grandson, Tiberius Gemellus, and his great-nephew, Gaius, who had already procured the favour of Macro, the prefect of the praetorian guard. Without demur the senate accepted Macro's nomination of Gaius, and thus the effect on the succession of Sejanus' massing of the praetorian guard was revealed the first time the succession was in doubt. Gaius' accession was hailed in Rome as a relief from the suspicions which had clouded Tiberius' last years, but in a few months his popularity, which his extravagant shows and apparent clemency had at first enhanced, began to wane, as it became clear that the throne was now occupied by a vain and imperious young man, undisciplined by experience, prodigal and funda-

[1] i.e. ' little boots ', a nickname given by the soldiers of his father, Germanicus.

nentally ruthless. Conspiracy followed conspiracy until n 41 the emperor was stabbed to death in the palace by a ribune of his own praetorian guard, named Cassius Chaerea. He left no permanent mark on the administraion except for the transference in 38 of the command of he African legion from the proconsul to a *legatus* directly esponsible, like all other military commanders, to the emperor.

CLAUDIUS 41–54

Far different was the legacy of his uncle and successor Claudius, Germanicus' younger brother, whose administration in the early years of his reign recalled in many ways the broad imperial outlook of Julius Caesar. Claudius' physical defects and mental instability had caused Augustus and Tiberius to ignore him as a possible occupant of the throne, and he had lived in retirement among his books and papers until Gaius dragged him into the limelight as a kind of court buffoon. After his nephew's murder, Claudius was discovered by the praetorian guard hiding behind a curtain and must have been intensely surprised when they saluted him as *imperator*. No less surprised was the senate, which had forgotten him altogether and was endeavouring to choose a new emperor from among its own members, after deciding against the restoration of the Republic. It was, however, compelled to accept the praetorians' choice, and Claudius soon proved that though he might be a fool, he was, like James I, a fool not unendowed with wisdom. That unprepossessing and slobbering exterior concealed besides much stupidity and pedantry a certain shrewd common-sense, allied with an imagination that neither Augustus nor Tiberius possessed. It is true that Claudius' mind was apt to wander while he was conducting public

business and that he often went to sleep at inopportune
moments, and in the second half of his reign these undesirable tendencies were accentuated ; yet, apart altogether from the conquest of South Britain and the forming
of the Mauretanias and Thrace into provinces, this curious
man influenced imperial policy more than any other of
the Julio-Claudians.

Unfortunately both his consorts, Valeria Messalina
and his niece, Agrippina, daughter of Germanicus, were
immoral and unprincipled women, who played un-
scrupulously on the emperor's weaknesses and so alarmed
him that in the end men of high rank felt even less secure
than they had done at the end of Tiberius' reign. The
influence of these two bad women did not, however,
affect the government of the Empire as a whole, and was
somewhat counteracted by the influence of the three principal freedmen of the imperial household, Narcissus, the
secretary *ab epistulis*, who dealt with the emperor's official
correspondence, Pallas, *a rationibus*, who kept his accounts,
and Callistus, *a libellis*, who dealt with petitions and
appeals from private individuals. Although they lined
their own pockets by a shameless sale of privileges and
their influence was deeply resented by the aristocracy,
who thought that such upstarts should be kept in the
background in accordance with the practice of Augustus,
these three advisers probably gave Claudius much shrewd
counsel.

In 47 Claudius' antiquarian leanings caused him to
revive the obsolete office of censor, and in that capacity
he admitted to the senate certain men who had held no
magistracy, including the chiefs of the Gallic tribe of
the Aedui. His imperial outlook is evinced by his grant
of *civitas* also (e.g. to Verulamium (St. Albans) in Britain
and Volubilis in Mauretania), but he was not at all lavish
as his enemies in the senate made him out to be, except

in comparison with Augustus and Tiberius. Among a considerable number of colonies founded by him overseas were Camulodunum (Colchester) and Cologne.

Of his public works the making of a harbour at Ostia, the draining of the *Lacus Fucinus*, and the opening of the *Via Claudia Augusta* over the Brenner Pass and of another road over the Great St. Bernard to the Rhône valley, were the most important.

NERO 54–68

When Claudius died suddenly at a banquet—whether as a result of overeating or from poison administered by the orders of his wife no one will ever know—Agrippina had already come to an arrangement with Burrus, the praetorian prefect, for Nero, her son by her first husband, to succeed to the throne in preference to Britannicus, Claudius' own son by Messalina. Nero was a mere pleasure-seeker. The duties of his position irked him, and if people started to be a nuisance or he was in need of money, any belief he may have had in the sanctity of human life immediately went by the board. The first years of his reign saw a struggle for power between Burrus and Nero's tutor, Seneca the Stoic philosopher, on the one hand and Agrippina on the other. Agrippina was at a disadvantage, partly because Nero soon began to regard her as tiresome whereas he had no quarrel with Seneca and Burrus, who were prepared to govern the Empire for him, and partly because Burrus was prefect of the praetorian guard. By 59 Nero, who had already had Britannicus murdered, could stomach her no longer, and she was stabbed to death after the failure of an attempt to drown her by sinking the boat in which she was crossing the bay of Naples. The death of Burrus in 62, followed by the retirement of Seneca, removed an influence that had somewhat checked the emperor's recklessness, and the range of his murders was considerably extended by the advent to power of Tigellinus, the new praetorian prefect. Under his influence there was a recrudescence of the *maiestas* trials in the senate which had sullied the last years of Tiberius' reign,[1] and sometimes people who had become ' tiresome ' were not tried at all but merely quietly removed or ordered to commit suicide.

Nero's love of display, rivalled only by his love of horse-racing and of appearing in person on the concert platform, combined with his utter disregard for human life, led men, when a great conflagration suddenly burst out in 64, to accuse him of setting fire to the city in order to see what the bonfire looked like. Even Nero is hardly likely to have been so silly and indeed is known to have been absent from Rome at the time, but while he adopted strong measures to alleviate distress, he took full advantage of the devastation by annexing some of the land for the building of a new palace, called the *Domus Aurea*, and the laying-out of gardens for his own enjoyment. So fierce did the public outcry become that Nero was compelled to find scapegoats. The Christians were eminently suited to his purpose ; they were extremely unpopular and they spoke freely of the impending destruction of the world by fire. People suspected of practising Christianity were accordingly arrested, and if they confessed to this, were held to have confessed to arson and burnt alive—the old punishment for arson within the city walls.

Even so Nero did not quench the public outcry against himself, and in 65 the strength of feeling against him among the senators, *equites* and army officers was evinced by the conspiracy of Piso, which might well have succeeded, had it been directed with a little more drive.

[1] See page 194.

THE YEAR OF ANARCHY, 68–69

Galba	A.D. 68–9	Governor of Hispania Tarraconensis.
Otho	69	Ex-governor of Lusitania and nominee of the praetorian guard.
Vitellius	69	Governor of Lower Germany.

In March 68 the standard of revolt against Nero was raised by Vindex, governor of Gallia Lugdunensis, who invited the support of Galba, the neighbouring governor of Hispania Tarraconensis. Galba had no love for Nero but hesitated to commit himself. While he dallied the initiative was taken by Verginius Rufus, commander of Upper Germany, in the belief that Vindex, who was of Gallic descent, was using the deposition of Nero merely as a pretext for a movement which really aimed at the independence of Gaul. The purity of Rufus' motive cannot be questioned, as he steadfastly refused after quelling the outbreak to allow himself to be proclaimed in Nero's place. In the meantime the praetorian guard saluted Galba as emperor, and the senate immediately passed sentence of death on Nero, who escaped execution only by taking his own life.

GALBA made the fatal mistake of refusing to pay the praetorian guards the donative they had been promised, and they were therefore ready to desert him as soon as they received another offer. They had not long to wait. OTHO, who had been governor of Lusitania when Galba was proclaimed emperor and had accompanied him to Rome, felt slighted when he appointed someone else as his successor and promptly secured for himself the allegiance of the guards, who proceeded to murder Galba and his associates in January, 69.

Even before Otho's accession the armies of the Rhine, no longer restrained by Rufus whom Galba had recalled

to Rome, had determined to have their own emperor, and
had proclaimed the sluggish and gluttonous VITELLIUS
governor of Upper Germany, as Galba's successor
When the flower of these armies marched into Italy
Otho's obvious strategy was to play a waiting game until
the arrival of the main body of the Danube legions should
give him a numerical superiority. But he was too
impatient to reach a decision to listen to the counsel of
his military advisers, and lost his only chance of success
by crossing the Po to give battle. His army was defeated
and as it had been deprived of any possibility of retreating
compelled to surrender. Otho himself committed suicide
without waiting to see whether the arrival of the Danube
armies would turn the scale in his favour.

On the 1st of July a fourth claimant to Nero's throne
was saluted emperor in Alexandria and quickly obtained
the support of all the forces in the East and of those on
the Danube, who were ready to fight for anyone who
opposed Vitellius. He was VESPASIAN, commander of the
troops engaged in quelling the revolt in Judaea,[1] and
significantly enough a *novus homo*. Although he could
not, like Galba, trace his family back to the old republican
nobility, nor even, like Otho and Vitellius, to the new
aristocracy of office, he was the only man of the four
capable of inspiring any feelings of real respect, and as
such he deserved to succeed where they had failed. But
for his victory in the field he was no more responsible
than they had been for theirs.

While he remained in Egypt with the object of cutting
Rome off from its corn supply and Mucianus, the governor
of Syria, proceeded from Asia into Europe with some
20,000 men at a leisurely pace, the Danube armies, under
the leadership of Antonius Primus, commander of *legio
VII Galbiana* stationed in Pannonia, took matters into

[1] See page 118.

their own hands.   Advancing rapidly into Italy without
waiting for Mucianus, they defeated the Vitellianist
legions between Bedriacum and Cremona at the end of
October, stormed their camp and sacked Cremona itself.
The Vitellianists were superior in numbers, but their
discipline had been undermined during the months they
had spent in the capital, and Primus' victory really
decided the issue.

The presence of so many troops in Italy had left the
frontiers dangerously under-protected, and already a
revolt had broken out among the Batavians on the lower
Rhine, led by Civilis.[1] Though it was put down without
great difficulty, it was an indication of the insecurity
which must inevitably arise if the armies of the Empire
should again forsake their proper business for the more
attractive task of emperor-making.   This ill-fated year
had made it clear, says Tacitus, that emperors could be
created elsewhere than in Rome.   He might have added
that it proved the Principate no better a form of government for preventing civil war between rival commanders
than the Republic—despite all Augustus' care—unless a
strong man happened to sit on the throne.

The Flavians 69–96

Vespasian	A.D.	69–79	Commander of the army in Judaea.
Titus		79–81	Elder son of Vespasian.
Domitian		81–96	Younger son of Vespasian.

As *novi homines* of middle-class Italian stock, the
Flavians brought to the task of government the same
lack of imagination and the same kind of shrewd common-
sense which had characterized Augustus, and under them
the administration of the Empire was conducted with a

[1] See page 112.

greater measure of efficiency than ever before. Domitian, in particular, demanded from officials both in Rome and in the provinces a high standard of industry and honesty, while Vespasian's careful economy, supplemented by the raising of the tribute and the imposition of new taxes, was so successful in repairing the ravages made in the finances of the state by Nero's extravagance and the succession of civil wars, that Domitian was able not only to engage in several campaigns on the Danube and Rhine frontiers and increase the legionaries' pay, but also to carry through a lavish building programme without curtailing the costly spectacles the *plebs* demanded.

As the founder of a new dynasty VESPASIAN felt it necessary to increase the dignity of his house by holding the consulship nearly every year, as Augustus had done at the outset of his reign, though only for the first four or six months. But he had a homely sense of humour which prevented him from mistaking ostentation for dignity or arrogance for firmness, and he earned the respect and even liking of the senate, while TITUS possessed considerable personal charm.

DOMITIAN's efficiency, on the other hand, was relieved by no really amiable traits. He treated the senate with studied contempt and summoned it only to issue orders or impart information. He had never been his father's favourite, and his character was soured by the same kind of treatment as Tiberius had suffered, though it made him in no sense unsure of himself. On the contrary Domitian was more of an autocrat than any *princeps* since Julius Caesar, and his attitude was symbolized by the triumphal robe which he habitually wore in the senate and by his predilection for the high-sounding title ' *dominus et deus* '. As a result he earned the dislike not only of the republican Stoics, who disapproved of the Flavians mainly because they wished to maintain the principle of heredity in the Principate, but of most of the senators, whose pride he had hurt. Several conspiracies took place, including the rebellion in 88 of Saturninus, governor of Upper Germany, and Domitian was eventually driven to allow the revival of *maiestas* charges in fear for his own security. In the end his own wife Domitia, whom he had divorced and remarried, succeeded where others had failed, and Domitian's murder was greeted with great rejoicing among the aristocracy.

He had no children, and for the first time in the history of the Principate the senate was in practice as well as in theory to choose the new emperor. Their choice of the jurist Nerva (96–98) inaugurated a succession of good emperors, Trajan (98–117), Hadrian (117–138), Antoninus Pius (138–161) and Marcus Aurelius (161–180). These were not related to one another by blood, but each of them in turn was adopted by the previous emperor as the most suitable man to succeed to the onerous task of governing the state. Under them men were able to live with far more sense of security than they had enjoyed since the reign of Augustus. The policy of making the senate more representative of the whole Empire and of making liberal grants of the *civitas* to the provinces, the policy which Julius Caesar had begun and Claudius and Vespasian (who had given *Latinitas* to the whole of Spain) had continued, was carried a stage nearer its goal. The extravagant and dangerous whimsies of the Julio-Claudians gave place to an almost Victorian respectability, and the Empire enjoyed a period of prosperity greater than it had yet known.

TABLE OF THE PRINCIPAL DATES MENTIONED IN PART III

PART IV

LATIN LITERATURE

LATIN LITERATURE

THE literature of Ancient Rome can be divided into four periods, the pre-Ciceronian or Early Age, down to 80 B.C. the Ciceronian Age, 80–40 B.C., the Augustan or Golden Age, 40 B.C.–A.D. 14, and the Post-Augustan or Silver Age, A.D. 14–A.D. 117.

THE EARLY AGE, TO 80 B.C.

We know the names of several writers of epic (i.e. narrative) poetry and of tragedies and comedies, all imitated from the Greek, such as Līvius Andronīcus, *c.* 284–204 Naevius, *c.* 260, and Pācuvius, 220–130, but the first author whose works survive is *T. Maccius Plautus*, 254–184 B.C. writer of comedies taken directly from the Athenian stage though he also introduced some Roman elements into his plays. Plautus was of humble birth and worked as an artisan until his plays made him independent. He is said to have written 130 plays, of which 20 are extant the better-known ones being *Captīvi*, *Trinummus*, *Mīles Glōriōsus*, *Rudens*, and *Amphitruo*. About one-third of each comedy is dialogue, generally in iambics, the rest being sung to music. His humour, shrewdness and vivacity made him very popular with his audiences.

Quintus Ennius, 239–169, also wrote for the stage, but his fame rests chiefly on his *Annāles*, an epic hexameter poem describing the history of Rome from the earliest days, of which a certain amount still survives.

P. Terentius Āfer (Terence), 185–159, the other great
author of comedies, was born at Carthage and was brought
to Rome as a slave. After obtaining his freedom he wrote
six comedies, *Andria, Hecyra, Heauton Tīmorūmenos,
Eunūchus, Phormio,* and *Adelphi,* in which, like Plautus,
he copied the Athenian ' New Comedy ', but he was a far
greater artist and wrote for his literary patrons rather
than for the crowd. He does not introduce Roman
scenes at all, and his characters are more lifelike and less
farcical than those of Plautus. His language is pure,
simple and refined, and he had a great influence on Latin
literature and on the development of European comedy.

The prose writers of this period were few, and only
fragments of their work survive.

THE CICERONIAN AGE, 80–40 B.C.

Marcus Tullius Cicero,[1] 106–43 B.C., who gives his name
to this period, was the greatest Roman orator, a statesman
of some importance, and the author of philosophical works
and of letters of great historical value. He was born at
Arpinum, the son of a Roman *eques,* and after studying at
Rome and finishing his education at Athens and Rhodes
he entered politics, becoming consul in 63, when he
suppressed the conspiracy of Catiline. In 51 he was
governor of Cilicia, which he administered honestly and
well. In the Civil War he supported Pompey, but was
reconciled to Caesar in 47. After Caesar's death he
opposed the Second Triumvirate and was murdered by
Antony's orders in 43. His most famous political
speeches were the Catilinarian and the Philippic Orations,
in which he attacked Catiline and Antony respectively,
and his best-known speeches in court were the Verrine
Orations, impeaching the extortionate governor of Sicily,

[1] See pages 162–6 and 172–4.

Verres, and the *Pro Milōne* (which was written but never delivered), a defence of Milo for killing his rival mob-leader Clodius. Besides composing a large number of speeches, Cicero wrote over 800 letters to his friends and relations, which reveal his character plainly and throw valuable light on the life and history of his times, and he also wrote several books on oratory and philosophy, such as *Dē Ōrātōre, De Fīnibus,* and *De Senectūte.* Ciceronian Latin is considered to be the highest development of Latin prose.

Contemporary with Cicero was *Gāius Iūlius Caesar,*[1] c. 100–44 B.C. He was an aristocrat by birth but he joined the popular party and became consul in 59, after forming the First Triumvirate with Pompey and Crassus. For the next ten years he was fighting his famous campaigns in Gaul, and when at last he returned to Italy, Pompey had joined the Senatorial party and so the Civil War broke out. In 48 he defeated Pompey at Pharsālus and after finishing off the war he became the undisputed ruler of the Roman world and carried out many excellent reforms, but Cassius and Brutus conspired against him and murdered him on March 15, 44. Caesar was not only one of the greatest generals and political reformers in the history of the world, but also author of the two celebrated histories of his own campaigns, the ' Gallic War ' in seven books and the ' Civil War ' in three, which are a combination of military despatches written by a commander in the field and a justification of his own actions ; his Latin is pure and straightforward, and the history is for the most part an accurate and unbiased account of his military achievements.

C. Sallustius Crispus (Sallust), 86–35 B.C., was born in the Sabine hills and after a chequered political career became governor of Numidia, where he acquired great

[1] See pages 164–171.

wealth, so that he was able to devote the rest of his life to literature. He wrote a history of the years 78–67, which has been lost, and monographs on the Conspiracy of Catiline and the War with Jugurtha, which are in some respects a critical study of history, written in a style marked by brevity and Graecisms.

Cornēlius Nepos, c. 100–c. 24 B.C., wrote several historical works, of which there survive only the Lives of twenty-two foreign (mostly Greek) celebrities, of Cicero's friend Atticus, and of the elder Cato. Nepos is not an accurate or critical historian, but he sketches clearly the character and main events in the lives of his subjects.

We now come to the two great poets of the Ciceronian Age. *Titus Lucrētius Cārus*, c. 98–54 B.C., was a philosophical poet, about whose life little is known; he dedicated his *Dē Rērum Nātūrā*, a poem in six books, to Memmius, pro-praetor of Bithynia. Lucretius was sceptical of the recognized religion and believed in the philosophy of Epicurus, which he conveyed to his readers in hexameter verses of rugged grandeur. He taught that the soul was doomed to perish and that the gods were indifferent to the fate of man, so that all human efforts were in vain and that all that was worth doing was to study the remarkable facts of the universe. He overcame the technical difficulties of expounding science and philosophy in verse with great skill, and wrote many passages of remarkable beauty and interest.

Gaius Valerius Catullus, 87–54 B.C., was the first Roman lyric poet. Lyric poetry in Greek literature was originally poetry sung to the lyre, but it soon came to include all light poems, whatever the metre, love poetry being a favourite kind of lyric. Catullus was born at Verona and lived at Rome or at his beloved Sirmio on Lake Garda. He was in love with Clodia, the sister of Cicero's enemy Clodius, whom he addressed in several poems as

' Lesbia '. Catullus died quite young, though not before producing many exquisite lyrics and fiery epigrams, written in several metres, including many in ' hendeca-syllables ' and in hexameters and elegiacs. His poems are mostly short pieces addressed to Lesbia, or to his friends or enemies, together with several longer poems, including some splendid weddings songs. As a lyric poet Catullus is inferior to Horace in polish and art, but he reveals a depth of genuine passion and love which is unique in Latin literature.

THE AUGUSTAN OR GOLDEN AGE, 40 B.C.–A.D. 14

This is the period of the highest development of Latin poetry. The end of the Civil Wars and the beginning of a settled form of government gave a fresh impetus to literature, which was encouraged by Augustus himself and by his chief adviser, Maecēnas, the patron of several poets of this era.

Publius Vergilius Maro (Virgil), 70–19 B.C., was born at Andes near Mantua in Cisalpine Gaul, the son of a farmer. After receiving a good education he lived at Rome until 42, when his father was compelled to give up his farm to soldiers discharged after Philippi, but Virgil obtained an introduction to Octavian (Augustus) and recovered the property. He then joined Maecenas' literary circle, and later became a friend of Augustus, with whom he was travelling home from Greece when he died. He was unmarried, and was a close friend of the poet Horace. Virgil's first work was the *Eclogues*, or *Bucolics*, written before 37, ten short poems in hexameters in the ' pastoral ' style of the Greek poet Theocritus. He spent the next seven years in perfecting the *Georgics*, a poem in four books dedicated to Maecenas, the first dealing with Agriculture, the second with Trees, mainly ines and olives, the third with Cattle and Horses, and the fourth with Bee-keeping. This was perhaps his most artistic work, written in exquisite poetry and combining practical advice on each subject with splendid descriptions of Italy and allusions to the great days of Roman history. Augustus then asked him to produce a national epic, and he wrote the *Aeneid*, in twelve books, modelled on Homer's *Odyssey* and *Iliad* ; this was the story of the fall of Troy and the wanderings of the Trojan prince Aeneas (see page 261), who settled in Italy and became the legendary ancestor of the family of Augustus. Aeneas is not the ideal epic hero, but the *Aeneid* is a magnificent poem, and together with the *Georgics* it sets Virgil by himself as the greatest Roman poet. Tennyson calls him " wielder of the stateliest measure ever moulded by the lips of man ", for his handling of the varying rhythms of the hexameter is unsurpassed, and his language throughout the poems is majestic. He was deeply religious, and a true patriot and lover of the countryside.

Quintus Horātius Flaccus (Horace), 65–8 B.C., was born near Venusia, the son of a freedman, and was educated at Rome and Athens. After serving as military tribune under Brutus at Philippi in 42 he lost his property and was glad to become a treasury clerk, until his poems brought him an introduction to Maecenas, who made him financially independent. Horace's first works were the two books of Satires, called *Sermōnes*, and the Epodes, all written between 35 and 30. ' Satire ' was a purely Roman invention, and meant originally a medley of prose and verse dealing with a variety of subjects. Early satirists were Lucilius, 180–102, and Varro, 116–27, and Horace followed Lucilius in attacking the vices and follies of his day, though in far less bitter language. His Satires are written in an easy form of hexameters and throw much light on the poet's life and on everyday affairs at Rome.

The Epodes are not of much importance except that they
led up to the publication of the first three books of the
famous Odes, between 30 and 23, which were followed in
17 by the *Carmen Saeculāre*, and in 13 by the fourth book
of Odes.   These were indeed what the poet calls *monumentum aere perennius*, " a memorial more lasting than
bronze ", for he introduced the Greek lyric to Rome in a
form never approached by any other Latin poet.   His
' national ' odes on Rome and her greatness reach a high
level of sonorous verse, while his other poems are of a more
personal character, dealing with his own life, his friends,
his loves, and so on, and though his work does not reach
the depth of feeling shown by Catullus at his best, it is
all delightful and quite perfect within its own range.
Alcaics and Sapphics are among the many lyric metres
used.   In the interval between the third and fourth book
of Odes Horace returned to his earlier style and published
the first book of *Epistulae* in 20, which express his mature
views on life and philosophy, and he spent his later years
on the second book of Epistles and the *Ars Poetica*, which
are mainly literary criticism ; all these are in hexameters
and like the Satires contain many passages of great
interest.   Horace's two styles of poetry are quite different
but the essential qualities of both are their gracefulness,
urbanity and art.   He was a man of great charm of
character and made many friends ; he was unmarried.

Next follows a group of Elegiac poets.   Elegy (perhaps
derived from the Greek ἒ λέγειν, ' to cry alas ') was at first
the medium for poems of mourning and epigram, but it was
later used mainly for love poetry.   The first writer in
this style was *Cornēlius Gallus*, 67–25 B.C., who became
Prefect of Egypt but was forced to commit suicide for
offending Augustus.   He wrote four books of successful
verse, though none of it has survived.

Albius Tibullus, c. 65–19 B.C., was an *eques*, whose

literary patron was Messalla. He wrote two books, called *Dēlia* and *Nemesis* after the ladies addressed in them, and a third which was published after his death, containing also poems by *Lygdamus* and by a niece of Messalla's called *Sulpicia*. Tibullus' elegies are full of a quiet charm and a love of the countryside, and though his love poems are not so genuine as those of Propertius, they have a sweet and delicate note that is well suited to their theme.

Sextus Propertius, *c.* 50–*c.* 16 B.C., was born in Umbria and lost his property in 40 ; he joined the literary circle of Maecenas. The first three of his four books of poems describe his ill-starred love for Cynthia (perhaps in real life Hostia), which lasted for five years, and they are full of passionate poetry, with wild alternations of love and hate. The fourth book was published after its author's death, and contained letters to friends and various other poems.

Publius Ovidius Naso (Ovid), 43 B.C.–A.D. 18, was born at Sulmo, the son of an *eques*, and was educated at Rome and Athens to be a lawyer, but he could not refrain from writing poetry. He married three times and had a daughter, and lived a fashionable life at Rome until A.D. 8, when Augustus suddenly banished him to Tomi on the Black Sea, where he spent the rest of his life, in spite of many appeals for permission to return. The cause of his exile remains to some extent a mystery. His poems were : 1. The *Amōres*, a series of short poems on subjects connected with love. 2. The *Hērōides*, imaginary letters from heroines of Greek legends to husbands or lovers who had deserted them. 3. The *Ars Amātōria*, or Art of Love. 4. The *Metamorphōses*, fifteen books, in hexameters, describing the miraculous transformations of mythology. 5. The *Fasti*, or Roman Calendar, of which only six months were finished, describing the events of Roman history and legend that occurred on each day of the year. These last two are the most solid and

H

important of Ovid's works. 6. The *Tristia*, or Sorrows of his exile. 7. *Ibis*, an attack on a false friend. 8. *Epistulae ex Ponto*, letters from exile, generally asking various friends to appeal to the emperor's mercy. He also wrote a tragedy, *Mēdēa*, which has not survived. Ovid's verse is admirably smooth and polished, and he is a gifted story-teller, though sometimes he writes at too great a length. He is the acknowledged master of the elegiac couplet which he reduced to a strict form, though his hexameters in the Metamorphoses cannot compare with Virgil's for vigour and variety. His poems on mythological subjects are interesting and contain many good stories.

Almost the only prose-writer of the Augustan Age was *Titus Līvius* (Livy), 59 B.C.–A.D. 17, who was born and educated at Patavium (Padua), and came to Rome in about 30. Practically nothing is known about his life except that he was married and that his fame was so high that a traveller came from Spain merely to see him and then returned home at once. Livy wrote a history of Rome from its foundation to the death of Drusus in 9 B.C., which was published at intervals and contained 142 books, of which only 35 survive. Although he is not a scientific historian or a military expert he has great powers of vivid description which make his work very readable, and his characters are excellently drawn. His style, which is developed from Cicero's, is rich, varied and poetical, and in spite of his lack of the critical faculty, his books contain many passages of great interest, and he is rightly placed in the front rank of descriptive historians.

THE POST-AUGUSTAN OR SILVER AGE, A.D. 14–117

This is the period when Latin literature began to decline from the high level of the Augustan Age, and much of it

s spoiled by dullness, redundancy, and attempts to make
pigrams or to score rhetorical ' points ' ; this was largely
lue to the lack of enterprise almost inevitable under the
Empire and to the narrow rhetorical training of Roman
ducation, which aimed mainly at producing clever
rators.

Of the poets, a Thracian freedman called *Phaedrus*
ublished between A.D. 20 and 40 five books of ' Fables ',
nainly based on those of Aesop, which are written in
ambic verse in excellent Latin. Next comes a group of
pic poets, of whom the best is *M. Annaeus Lūcānus*,
9–65, a nephew of Seneca and of the Gallio of Acts xviii.
Ie was a Spaniard, and wrote a hexameter poem on the
Civil War between Caesar and Pompey, called *Pharsāliā*,
vhich has a few brilliant passages but is monotonous and
s spoilt by the rhetorical love of effect. Nero was jealous
f Lucan's poetry and forbade him to publish any more,
o he joined in the conspiracy of Piso [1] and was forced to
ommit suicide. *Valerius Flaccus*, died *c.* 90, wrote an
ccount of Jason's quest for the Golden Fleece called
Argonautica, which has some excellent character sketches
nd is more poetical than the work of most Silver Latin
uthors. *P. Papinius Stātius*, *c.* 40–96, composed two
pics, the *Thēbais* and the *Achillēis*, which are on the
vhole dull, with a few originalities of treatment, and he
lso wrote five books of *Silvae*, poems mostly in hexameters
vith some in lyric metres dealing with his own and his
riend's affairs. *Sīlius Italicus*, 25–101, a man of high
ank, wrote a description of the Second Punic War in
7 books, called *Pūnica*, which is generally dreary and
noriginal.

We now come to a poet of much higher merit, *M.
Valerius Martiālis* (Martial), *c.* A.D. 40–104, who was born
t Bilbilis in Spain and came to Rome, where he lived

[1] See page 198.

for 34 years, at first in poverty but later in comparativ
wealth, until he returned to Spain in about 98. Beside
minor works he wrote twelve books of ' Epigrams ', th
first being published in 85 and the last after his return t
Spain. Epigrams among the Greeks were originall
inscriptions in elegiac couplets, written for dedicatior
or tombstones, but they were extended to express an
subject, especially love and satire, in brief and pointe
form. Catullus wrote several epigrams, but the chi
Latin epigrammatic poet is Martial, whose poems a
written mostly in elegiacs or ' hendecasyllables ' an
generally consist of an introduction and a descriptio
followed by the ' point ', usually contained in the last lin
Some are genuine epitaphs, others are brief tales, c
appeals to friends for assistance, or satirical descriptio
of contemporary characters or events, and the whole co
lection paints a very graphic picture of everyday life i
Rome. Martial's verse is vigorous, polished and varie
and can express satire, pathos and humour equally well.

The last two poets of this era are satirists. Satire h
been mentioned under *Horace* (page 211), and a poet wh
followed Horace closely in style was *Persius*, 34–62, auth
of six books of satires written in hexameters, which a
mainly Stoic homilies, very obscure in expression. Senec
and Petronius wrote satirical prose works, which will l
described later. The last and greatest satirist w
D. Iūnius Iuvenālis, (Juvenal), *c.* 65–*c.* 130, who was bor
at Aquinum and practised rhetoric ; he may have serve
in the army in Britain and Egypt, but he lived mostly i
Rome, at first in poverty but later owning some propert
He was writing poetry between 100 and 130, in a sty
similar to that of Lucilius and Horace, though he has nor
of the humanity of Horace and is unrelievedly censoriot
in the bitterest language, attacking the vices of the wor
age in Roman society during the First Century A.D. H

exameters are powerful though rather monotonous,
xpressed in ironically epigrammatic and rhetorical
anguage, and his poems, like Martial's, give a most vivid
picture of life at Rome. He is a master of the biting,
incisive phrase. He wrote 16 satires, of which the third
is a famous account of the life of the poor at Rome, the
ixth is a bitter attack on women, and the tenth a homily
n the vanity of human wishes.

Next come the prose authors of the Silver Age. *L.
Annaeus Seneca*, ' the philosopher ', *c.* 4 B.C.–A.D. 65, was
born at Corduba in Spain and became the tutor of the
young emperor Nero, whom he managed to restrain from
viciousness for the first few years of his reign, but in
65 he was forced to commit suicide for taking part in the
conspiracy of Piso ; in spite of his philosophical ideals
he had become enormously wealthy at the dissolute court
f Nero. He wrote several tragedies in iambic verse, of
which nine survive ; they are all on Greek subjects, such
s ' Oedipus ', and were popular in their time. He also
wrote the *Apocolocyntōsis*, or ' Pumpkinification ' of
Claudius, a satirical description of the emperor's deifica-
ion, in a mixture of prose and verse. The most impor-
ant of his many philosophical works are the twenty books
f *Epistulae Mōrāles*, Stoic moral essays on various
ubjects, written in the typically epigrammatic style of
he age.

Contemporary with Seneca was *C. Petrōnius*, a man
f high rank who was *elegantiae arbiter*, or ' arbiter of
aste ', at Nero's court, but who fell into disfavour and
ad to commit suicide *c.* A.D. 66. He wrote a book
alled *Satyricon*, in prose interspersed with some longish
poems, which is of great interest and is the forerunner of
he modern novel. It describes the adventures of two
people in the cities of south Italy, in one of which the
amous ' Dinner of Trimalchio ' takes place.

C. Plīnius Secundus (Pliny the Elder), *c.* A.D. 23-79 held high equestrian rank under his friend the emperor Vespasian and was killed in the eruption of Vesuvius. He was a man of untiring industry and wrote a large number of books of which only 37 volumes of his ' Natural History' survive. This is a work on the geography, science, medical knowledge, and art of his day, and contains a good deal of interesting information.

Fābius Quintiliānus, A.D. 35-95, a Spaniard who was appointed official teacher of rhetoric by Vespasian, was the tutor of several men of high rank. He wrote twelve books called *Institūtio Ōrātōria*, ' the Education of an Orator ', of which the tenth contains a valuable discussion on the merits of Greek and Roman writers in every branch of literature.

Pliny the Younger, *c.* A.D. 61-113, whose full name when he succeeded to his uncle the elder Pliny's estate in 79 was C. Plīnius Caecilius Secundus, was born at Novum Comum in N. Italy and eventually became governor of Bithynia in 111. He had a large practice at the bar, but his only extant speech, the ' Panegyric of Trajan ', is of inferior quality. His literary fame rest on his ' Letters ', nine books of which he published himself, while the tenth, his correspondence with Trajan on provincial administration, including the treatment of the Christians in Bithynia, was published after his death. The letters are on a variety of subjects, such as the eruption of Vesuvius in 79, ghost stories, descriptions of his seaside villas, and points of literary interest, and they give many interesting facts about the life of that time, written in a blend of Ciceronian and Silver Latin.

Publius (?) *Cornēlius Tacitus*, *c.* A.D. 54-117, married the daughter of Agricola,[1] later governor of Britain, and became a leading barrister and in 112 governor of Asia

---

[1] See pages 109-10.

His first work was a ' Dialogue on Oratory ', written in Ciceronian prose, probably in 81, but his other books are very different in style. In 98 he published a Life of his father-in-law Agricola and a monograph on Germany, and between 104 and 109 the ' Histories ' of the years A.D. 69–96, in about twelve books, of which only four and a half survive. Between 115 and 117 he produced the Annals ', which covered the years 14–69, but about a quarter of the sixteen or eighteen books has been lost. Tacitus is a stern moralist who paints the dark era from Tiberius to Nero in even darker colours than is warranted, but he is an expert in the art of narrative and character-study and has a unique ability to coin a telling phrase in a few words. His style is modelled on that of Sallust, with brevity and variety as its chief features.

C. *Suetonius Tranquillus, c.* A.D. 70–160, was one of Trajan's secretaries and thus obtained access to the imperial archives. His only extant works are the *Dē Vītā Caesarum*, biographies of the first twelve emperors from Iulius Caesar to Domitian, and some Lives of Roman men of letters. His work is by no means a critical history but merely a collection of gossipy facts about his subjects, containing interesting information about their virtues, vices and follies, much of it probably untrue.

METRE

(1) The earliest Latin poetry, for example that of Livius Andronicus and Naevius, was written in an accented verse called ' Saturnian ', the arrangement of which seems to have been

immortáles mortáles | sí forét fas flére ;

this is not unlike our nursery rhyme

Thé queen wás in the párlour eáting breád and
hóney.

(2) The dramatists Plautus and Terence copied th
Iambic and Trochaic metres of the Greek tragedians
An 'iambic senarius' contains six 'iambi' (◡ _) such as

ăprīs | rĕlī | quĭt ēt | răpāc | ĭbūs | lŭpīs,

but 'tribrachs' (◡ ◡ ◡) were allowed in the first fou
'feet', 'spondees' (_ _) in the 1st, 3rd and 5th, 'ana
paests' (◡ ◡ _) in the 1st and 3rd, and 'dactyls' (_ ◡ ◡
in the 1st. A 'trochaic septenarius' consists of seve
'trochees' (_ ◡) with a final half-foot, which is the sam
as the iambic line with an additional _ ◡ _ at the begin
ning. These Latin writers allowed themselves muc
greater licence in their verses than their Greek original
did, and made a compromise between accent and quan
tity ; they also used other metres, especially in thei
songs, *cantica*.

(3) Later Roman poets used strictly quantitative metres
First came the 'Hexameter' imitated from Homer b
Ennius, perfected by Virgil and standardized by Ovid
It contained six feet, consisting of dactyls (_ ◡ ◡) o
spondees (_ _), though the fifth foot must be a dacty
and the sixth a spondee (or a trochee, _ ◡). A pure dacty
line is

ātquĕ lĕ | vēm stĭpŭ | lām crĕpĭ | tāntĭbŭs | ūrĕrĕ | flāmmī

and a spondaic line is

īntēn | dūnt, scān | dīt fā | tālĭs | māchĭnă | mūrōs

but the poets used a skilful combination of dactyls an
spondees and obtained great variety in their rhythms

There is always a ' caesura ', or break between two words, in the third and/or the fourth foot.

(4) The ' Elegiac Couplet ' is used especially by Tibullus, Propertius and Ovid. It consists of a Hexameter followed by a five-foot ' Pentameter ' in two parts, each half containing two and a half feet ; the first two are dactyls or spondees, then comes a single long syllable followed by a ' caesura ', then two dactyls and another long (or ' open ') syllable, like

$$\bar{\text{da}} \,\, \bar{\text{pla}}\breve{\text{ci}} \mid \bar{\text{dam}} \,\, \bar{\text{fess}} \mid \bar{\text{o}}, \parallel \bar{\text{lect}}\breve{\text{or}} \,\, \bar{\text{a}} \mid \bar{\text{mi}}\breve{\text{ce}}, \,\, \text{m}\breve{\text{a}} \mid \bar{\text{num}}.$$

Tennyson imitates an elegiac couplet in his

These lame hexameters the strong-winged music

of Homer !

No—but a most burlesque barbarous experiment,

but the English accented verse is far removed from Latin quantitative elegiacs.

Next come many ' lyric ' metres, of which the following are the best known.

(5) ' Alcaics ', a favourite metre of Horace, in which each stanza contains two long lines of a similar metre, followed by two shorter lines, each in a different metre, like

$$\bar{\text{cae}} \mid \bar{\text{lo}} \,\, \bar{\text{ton}} \mid \bar{\text{an}}\bar{\text{tem}} \mid \bar{\text{cre}}\bar{\text{di}}\bar{\text{di}} \mid \bar{\text{mus}} \,\, \bar{\text{Iov}} \mid \bar{\text{em}}$$

$$\bar{\text{reg}} \mid \bar{\text{nare:}} \mid \bar{\text{prae}}\bar{\text{sens}} \mid \bar{\text{di}}\bar{\text{vus}} \,\, \text{h}\breve{\text{ab}} \mid \bar{\text{e}}\bar{\text{bi}} \mid \bar{\text{tur}}$$

$$\bar{\text{Au}} \mid \bar{\text{gus}}\bar{\text{tus}} \mid \bar{\text{a}}\bar{\text{diec}} \mid \bar{\text{tis}} \,\, \text{Bri} \mid \bar{\text{tan}}\bar{\text{nis}}$$

$$\bar{\text{im}}\bar{\text{peri}} \mid \bar{\text{o}} \,\, \bar{\text{gra}}\breve{\text{vi}} \mid \bar{\text{bus}}\bar{\text{que}} \mid \bar{\text{Per}}\bar{\text{sis}}.$$

(6) ' Sapphics ', used by Catullus and Horace, in which each stanza consists of three long lines in a similar metre

followed by a shorter line.   The last two lines of a stanza
are

$$\text{mĭtte} \mid \text{sēctā} \mid \text{rī, rŏsā} \mid \text{quŏ lŏc} \mid \text{ōrum}$$

$$\text{sērā mŏ} \mid \text{rētur.}$$

(7) ' Hendecasyllables ', a line of eleven syllables, used
largely by Catullus and Martial, like

$$\text{cŭi dō} \mid \text{nō lĕpĭ} \mid \text{dūm nŏ} \mid \text{vŭm lĭ} \mid \text{bēllŭm.}$$

The last syllable of all the lines in the metres given
above can be either long or short.

Among the many RULES FOR SCANSION, i.e.
dividing a line into feet with the long and short syllables
marked, the six following are the easiest and the most
important.   They apply to all Latin verses, though the
metres which you will probably have to scan most often
are Hexameters and Elegiacs.

1. A word ending in a vowel or -*m* when followed by a
word beginning with a vowel (or *h*) has its last syllable
cut off or ' elided ', so that it does not count at all in
scansion, e.g.

$$\text{dēfēss(i)} \mid \text{āspĭcĭ} \mid \text{mūs, quāe} \mid \text{cāus(a) īn} \mid \text{dĭgnă sēr} \mid \text{ēnos.}$$

2. All diphthongs, i.e. combinations of two vowels, like
the -*ae* of *mensae* are long.

3. A vowel before two consonants, either in the same
word or with one at the end of one word and another at
the beginning of the next, forms a long syllable.   If *r* or *l*
is the second consonant in the same word the syllable can
sometimes be long or short, e.g. *patrem* can have its first
syllable either long or short.   *x* and *z* count as double
consonants, and *h* does not count at all.

4. A vowel before another vowel in the same word is
usually short, e.g. *rĕi*.

5. The final -*a* of the 1st declension ablative singular is long ; most other final -*a*'s are short.

6. Final -*i*, -*o* and -*u* are usually long.

When you start scanning a Hexameter, first look for any 'elisions' according to rule 1. Then mark off the last five syllables, which are always _ ∪ ∪ | _ ≌, like 'bláckberry púdding'. Next, count up the remaining syllables ; if there are 12, there will be 4 dactyls ; if 11, 3 dactyls and 1 spondee ; if 10, 2 dactyls and 2 spondees ; if 9, 3 spondees and 1 dactyl ; if 8, 4 spondees. Then mark off all the syllables which you know from the other rules, remembering that a syllable between two longs must itself be long. Your pronunciation of the line may help with some of the syllables which you do not know for certain. You should also mark the 'caesura' in the 3rd or 4th foot with a thin wavy line.

The Pentameter is much easier to scan, because the last 8 syllables are always the same, _ || _ ∪ ∪ | _ ∪ ∪ | ≌, and can be marked off at once, the last 7 sounding like 'bláckberry ráspberry píe'. There is always a break in the middle of the line, to be marked with two downward strokes, between the first of these 2 dactyls and the preceding single long syllable. This leaves only the first two feet, which will contain either 6 syllables (i.e. 2 dactyls), 5 (1 dactyl and 1 spondee), or 4 (2 spondees), so you will have little difficulty in scanning them.

PART V

MYTHOLOGY

LEGENDS OF GODS AND HEROES

GREEK mythology contains many stories about the gods, demi-gods, and heroes of the legendary age. As Greek influences spread to Rome the Romans identified many of their native Italian gods with Greek gods, although in most cases the attributes of the Greek gods were quite unsuitable, and Latin authors generally refer to these deities by their Latin names. Since this is a book about Roman life and literature we also shall call the gods by their Roman names, but you must remember that this is not really correct and that the Roman gods are usually quite different from their Greek counterparts, whose names will be added when each deity is first mentioned. The legends of the heroic age were generally adopted by Roman poets without much alteration.

STORIES OF THE GODS

The Origin of the Gods

Ŭrănus, Heaven, and Gē or Gaia, Earth, had six sons and six daughters, called Titans, whom their father banished to Tartarus in the Underworld as soon as they were born. One of them, Crŏnus, afterwards identified with the Italian god of agriculture, Sātūrnus, led a rebellion against Uranus and became king ; from the blood of the wounded Uranus sprang the race of giants.

Saturn had six children, but he had been warned that one of them would overthrow him, so he swallowed each one as it was born. Their mother, however, substituted a stone for Jūpiter (in Greek Zeus), and conveyed the infant to Crete, where he was brought up in safety. When he grew up Jupiter compelled Saturn to disgorge the other gods, deposed him, and divided the universe between himself and his brothers.

THE SIX OLDER GODS, CHILDREN OF SATURN

The birth of Jupiter has just been described. He became the king of heaven and was supreme among the gods, who were supposed by the Greeks to live on the summit of Mount Olympus in Thessaly, and he was also the dispenser of good and evil to men, and the defender of their rights. He married his sister Jūno (Hēra), who had three children, Mars, Vulcan and Hēbē, and he had many other children also by other goddesses or by mortal women. Among the Romans Jupiter was called *Optimus Maximus*, ' Best and Greatest,' and had a temple on the Capitol which he shared with Juno and Minerva.

Neptūnus, in Greek Poseidon, was the lord of the sea, and is usually represented carrying a trident. He married a sea-nymph called Amphitrītē, and their children were the giant Cȳclōpes, who had one eye in the middle of their foreheads and forged thunderbolts in Sicily for Jupiter.

Plūto or Dis, in Greek Hādēs, ruled over the Underworld, the rivers of which are included in a hexameter line

Styx, Acheron, Lethe, Phlegethon, Cocytus, Avernus.

The souls of the dead were ferried across the Styx by Charon, the grim old boatman who would take them only if they had a coin in their mouths as his fee ; otherwise they had to wander up and down the bank for a hundred years. After crossing the Styx the dead came before the judge of the Underworld, Mīnŏs, who was guarded by the three-headed dog Cerberus. The righteous were sent to the happy fields of Elysium, where flowed the river of oblivion, Lēthē, but the wicked were doomed to endless torments in Tartarus, the depths below Erebus. Here Tantalus was punished with a dreadful thirst, which he could never quench although he stood up to his neck in water with bunches of grapes hanging near his mouth, for the water and the grapes both receded whenever he tried to reach them; Sīsyphus was doomed to roll up a steep hill a stone which continually rolled down again; Ixīon was bound to an ever-revolving wheel; and the daughters of Dănăus had to fill with water a vessel full of holes. Pluto's wife was Proserpine, whose story will be told under *Ceres*.

Vesta, in Greek Hestia, was the goddess of the domestic hearth, in whose circular temple at Rome a fire was always kept burning by the Vestal Virgins.

Cĕrēs, in Greek Dēmētēr, was the goddess of corn and agriculture. By her brother Jupiter she had a daughter Proserpĭna, in Greek Persĕphŏnē, who was gathering flowers near Enna in Sicily when she was carried off by her uncle, Pluto, to be queen of the Underworld. Ceres searched for her everywhere, and in her wanderings failed to look after the crops, which thus became barren, so eventually Pluto agreed to give up his wife if she did not eat any food in Erebus. In her joy at returning to her mother Proserpine forgot the condition and ate some seeds of pomegranate, so that she had to go back to Pluto, but Jupiter persuaded him to allow her to spend six months on earth and six months in the Underworld.

Jūno, in Greek Hēra, married her brother Jupiter and became the queen of the gods. She was the goddess of marriage and womanhood, and presided over child-birth under the title of Lūcīna.

GODS AND GODDESSES WHO WERE THE CHILDREN OF JUPITER

Minerva, in Greek Pallas Athēna, was the daughter of Jupiter and a sea-nymph called Mētis. Jupiter swallowed Metis whole to prevent her from bearing a son who, according to a prophecy, might depose him, and some time later had a severe headache, which he asked Vulcan to relieve by striking his head with an axe ; Vulcan did so, and Minerva sprang fully armed from her father's head. She was the virgin goddess of wisdom, war, and the arts, and was the patron deity of Athens. At Rome she was worshipped on the Capitol with Jupiter and Juno.

Vĕnus, in Greek Aphrodītē, the daughter of Jupiter and Diōnē, was said to have been born in the foam of the sea off Cyprus, and was the goddess of beauty and love. She married Vulcan, but she also loved Mars and a mortal called Anchīses, to whom she bore Aenēas, the Trojan hero who became ancestor of the Roman race. She fell in love with a beautiful youth called Adōnis, but he was killed by a boar while hunting, and she mourned bitterly for him. Her son Cupīdo, in Greek Ērōs, was the god of love, a winged boy who used to cause gods and men to fall in love by striking them at random with his arrows.

Phoebus Apollo, son of Jupiter and Lātōna, and twin-brother of Diana, was born at Dēlos and was the god of medicine, prophecy, music and light, being often identified with the sun. He wooed a nymph called Daphnē who fled from him and was turned into a laurel-bush, the leaves of which were afterwards sacred to Apollo. He also loved Cassandra, daughter of Priam of Troy, but when she rejected him he ordained that no one should ever believe the prophecies which he enabled her to make. Apollo was condemned by Jupiter to serve a mortal man for nine years because he had killed the Cyclōpes, the makers of the thunderbolt with which his son Aesculāpius, the god of healing, was slain, so he became the shepherd of Admētus and obtained for him escape from death if one of his family would die for him. Only his wife Alcestis was willing to do so, but Hercules wrestled with Death and restored her to life. Pan once challenged Apollo to a musical contest, which Apollo won, though Mĭdas, king of Phrygia, voted for Pan. As a penalty Apollo gave Midas ass's ears, which he concealed by letting his hair grow long, but his barber saw the deformity and being unable to keep the secret whispered it into a hole in the ground. Reeds later sprang up from the place and whispered as they moved in the wind " Midas the king has ass's ears." This Midas was given the power of turning into gold everything he touched because he had befriended Sīlēnus, the attendant of Bacchus, but being unable to eat or drink he prayed to be relieved of his ' golden touch ' and lost it in the waters of the Pactōlus, whose sands were henceforth rich in gold. In historical times Apollo had a famous oracle at Delphi, where his priestess, called the Pythoness, sat on a tripod over a cleft in the rock from which issued a vapour, and gave responses which the priests interpreted to those who consulted the god. The advice was often ambiguous but sometimes good and had some influence on politics.

Diāna, in Greek Artemis, the twin-sister of Apollo, was the virgin-goddess of hunting, chastity, child-birth, and the moon. She was sometimes identified with Hĕcătē, a goddess of the Underworld and of magic, and among the Romans she was called Trivia and was worshipped at cross-roads. The hunter Actaeon once saw her bathing in a forest-pool, and as a punishment was turned into a stag and killed by his own hounds. Nĭŏbē, daughter of Tantalus and wife of Amphīon of Thebes, boasted that she had seven sons and seven daughters while Latona had only Apollo and Diana, so the two deities punished her by shooting all her children with arrows. Niobe wept for them so long that she was turned into a stone on Mt. Sipylus in Lydia, which always ran with her tears.

Bacchus, in Greek Dionȳsus, was the son of Jupiter and Sĕmĕlē, who perished in flames when Jupiter visited her in his full glory. Jupiter snatched the infant from the fire and kept him sewn up in his thigh until he could be brought up in safety by the nymphs on Mt. Nysa. Bacchus was the god of vegetation and especially of wine, and the inspirer of tragedy and comedy; the Romans identified him with their wine-god Līber. He was usually attended by his drunken old tutor Sīlēnus and by female worshippers called Bacchantes; also by fauns and satyrs, half-men and half-goats, and by other followers, who carried the thyrsus, or Bacchic staff. He rode in a car drawn by leopards or tigers, and spread his worship far into the East, though he was attacked by unbelievers such as Pentheūs, king of Thebes, who was torn to pieces by his own mother and sisters in a Bacchic frenzy. Bacchus found Ariadne deserted by Theseus on Naxos and married her and raised her to heaven as a constellation.

Mars, in Greek Ărēs, the son of Jupiter and Juno, was the god of war. His savage nature, which delighted in bloodshed and ruin, made him hated by the other gods except Venus. The Romans regarded him as the father of Romulus and founder of their race.

Vulcānus, in Greek Hēphaestus, the son of Jupiter and Juno, was the god of fire and all mechanical arts. One story says that he was born lame and was thrown out of heaven by his mother out of shame for his deformity, another says that Jupiter threw him out because he supported Juno in a quarrel with Jupiter; he fell for nine days and nights, and landed in Lemnos with a broken leg. He lived in volcanic islands like Sicily, and with the help of the Cyclōpes made thunderbolts in his forges. He married Venus, but was jealous of her love for Mars, and his lameness made the gods laugh at him, though he built them palaces in heaven and did much skilled work for them.

Mercurius, in Greek Hermes, the son of Jupiter and Maia, was the messenger of the gods, the god of eloquence, dreams, gain and luck, and the conductor of the souls of the dead to Hades. On the day of his birth on Mt. Cyllēnē in Arcadia he invented the lyre, which he made from a tortoise shell, and he also stole the cattle of Admētus, which his brother Apollo was guarding, but he placated Apollo with the gift of the lyre and henceforth became the god of herdsmen while Apollo became the god of music. As messenger of the gods Mercury wore a winged cap and winged sandals, and carried a *cadūceus*, a herald's gold staff surmounted with wings and intertwined with snakes.

Hēbē, in Latin sometimes called Iuventas, the daughter of Jupiter and Juno, was the goddess of youth and the handmaiden of the gods; she married Hercules when he was admitted to Olympus.

The Nine Muses, daughters of Jupiter and Mnēmŏsȳnē,[1] were goddesses of art and literature and lived in Pieria in Thessaly or on Mt. Helicon in Boeotia. Their names were Clio (history), Euterpē (lyric poetry), Thalīa (comedy), Melpŏmĕnē (tragedy), Terpsĭchŏrē (dancing), Erato (love poetry), Polyhymnia (sacred music), Urania (astronomy), and Callĭŏpē (epic poetry). The Romans also called them Camēnae, identifying them with native Italian water-nymphs of that name.

[1] The Greek goddess of Memory.

OTHER DEITIES

Hēlios, the sun-god, was the son of the Titan Hyperīon. His son Phǎëthon asked to be allowed to drive the sun-chariot across the sky, to which Helios unwillingly agreed, but Phaethon could not control the horses, which ran too near the earth and scorched it, so Jupiter killed him with a thunderbolt. His sisters became poplars and continued to weep for him, their tears turning into amber. Helios' sister was Aurōra, the rosy-fingered goddess of dawn. She loved Tīthōnus, son of Laomedon of Troy, and obtained immortality for him, but she forgot to ask that he should remain young, so that he became very old and shrivelled. At last he was turned into a grasshopper at Aurora's request.

Pan, the son of Mercury and a wood-nymph, was half-man, half-goat, and guarded the crops and countryside. He loved a nymph called Syrinx, who shrank from his ugly appearance and begged the gods to save her from him, so she was changed into a reed by the river ; Pan made the pan-pipes from seven reeds of diminishing length, which he called the Syrinx. He was said to inspire anyone he met in the fields with 'panic' fear, and the Romans identified him with their own country god, Faunus, whose followers, also half-men, half-goats, were called Fauns.

Jānus, an old Roman god who became the god of beginnings, had two faces, one looking inwards, one outwards, from the gate, *iānua*. January was named after him, and he had a temple near the Roman Forum, with doors that were opened in time of war, perhaps showing that he had gone out to battle, and shut in time of peace.

The Fates, in Greek Moirae, in Latin Fāta or Parcae, were the daughters of Night or of Jupiter, and were called Clōtho, Lachesis and Atropos. They were said to spin

the thread of human life, breaking it off when a man'
life was ended.

The Furies, in Greek Erīnÿes or Eumenides (' th
kindly ones '), in Latin Furiae or Dīrae, were winge
maidens with snakes in their hair, who avenged crim
especially murder and sins against parents like the slayin
of his mother Clytemnestra by Orestes. Their name
were Tīsïphŏnē, Allecto and Megaera.

The Graces, in Greek Charites, in Latin Grātiae, wer
the personifications of grace and beauty and were usuall
in attendance on the gods or the muses. Their name
were Euphrŏsÿnē, Aglaia and Thalïa.

Iris was the rainbow goddess and the messenger of th
gods, and Ganymēdēs, son of Tros, was carried off by a
eagle to be the cup-bearer of Jupiter.

The Nymphs were personifications of nature in variou
forms, and were divided into sea-nymphs, called Oceanid
or Nēreids (daughters of Oceanus or Nēreūs, both sea
gods), water-nymphs, called Naiads, mountain-nymph
called Oreads, and tree-nymphs, Dryads. They wer
beautiful maidens, not immortal, and usually endowe
with prophetic powers.

THE ORIGIN OF MAN

Promētheūs (Forethought), one of the Titans, moulde
man out of clay, and Minerva breathed life into hin
Prometheus taught mankind many arts, like astronomy
mathematics, divination and medicine, and when Jupite
in anger deprived men of fire he climbed to heaven an
stole fire from the sun-chariot, bringing it down to eart
in a hollow reed. To avenge this theft Jupiter tol
Vulcan to make from clay a beautiful woman, on who
each god bestowed some gift, so that she was calle
Pandōra (all gifts), and gave her to Epimētheūs (Afte

hought), who married her in spite of his brother Pro-
netheus' warnings. She brought with her a chest or
ar, which when opened sent out all the miseries and
iseases that trouble mankind, while only Hope remained
t the bottom of the chest to comfort them.

Prometheus refused to reveal a secret concerning a
on of Jupiter who should be stronger than his father,
o to punish his obstinacy and his championship of
nan Jupiter had him chained to a lonely rock in the
Caucasus, where an eagle came every day and ate his
ver, which was restored at night, so that the torture
ever ceased. At last Jupiter relented and allowed
Hercules to shoot the eagle, whereupon Prometheus
old Jupiter that the son who should overthrow him
vould be a child of the sea-nymph Thetis; she was
herefore married to a mortal, Pēleūs, so that her son,
Achilles, might also be a mortal and thus be unable to
njure Jupiter.

The first age of man was called the Golden Age, when
nder the rule of Saturn war was unknown and nature
roduced everything without cultivation. This was
ollowed by the Silver Age, the Bronze Age and the Iron
Age, each one worse than the one before, when men were
ruel and warlike and had to work hard to obtain the
ruits of the earth. Finally Themis, Justice, departed,
nd nothing could save men from the very depths of sin,
o Jupiter sent a great flood, which destroyed all living
reatures except a son of Prometheus, called Deucălion,
nd his wife Pyrrha. These two floated about in a boat
or nine days until the flood subsided and left them on the
op of Mount Parnassus. They asked the oracle of
Themis how to restore human life to earth, and were told
o cover their heads and throw the bones of their mother
ehind them, which they concluded were the bones of
nother earth, so they threw stones over their shoulders.

Deucalion's stones became men, Pyrrha's women, an
thus the world was populated again.

STORIES OF DEMIGODS AND HEROES

PERSEUS

Persēus was the son of Jupiter and Dănāē, daughter o
Acrisius, king of Argos. An oracle had said that Danae'
son would kill Acrisius, so he kept her shut up in a towe
of brass, but Jupiter visited her in a shower of gold an
Perseus was born. Acrisius then set them both adri
in the sea in a chest, but Jupiter brought them safely t
the island of Serīphus, where they were treated kindly b
King Polydectes, who later wanted to marry Danae. H
therefore persuaded Perseus, now grown up, to try to ki
the Gorgon Medūsa, a terrible winged monster wit
serpents in her hair, whose face turned all who saw it int
stone. Pluto lent Perseus a helmet of invisibility
Mercury a pair of winged sandals and a magic sickle, an
Minerva a polished shield to use as a mirror so that h
should not have to look at the Gorgon.

Only the three aged Graiae knew where the Gorgon
lived, and Perseus compelled them to tell him the wa
by stealing the one eye and tooth which they share
among them. When he reached his goal he manage
to kill Medusa with the help of the gifts of the gods, an
cut off her head, which he put in a magic wallet. Th
giant Atlas, who supported the heavens on his shoulder
refused to receive Perseus in his kingdom, so Perse
turned Medusa's head towards him and made him into
mountain. He then flew on towards the land of th
Ethiopians, where he found a beautiful girl called Andr
meda bound to a rock and about to be devoured by

ea-monster. Her mother Cassiopeia had boasted that
he herself was more beautiful than the Nereids, the sea-
ymphs, so Neptune punished her by sending the sea-
monster, which could be placated only by the sacrifice
f her daughter. Perseus turned the monster into a rock
nd rescued Andromeda, whom he then wanted to marry,
ut at the wedding-banquet he was attacked by a rival
over, Phīneūs, the Ethiopian king's brother, and overcame
im by using the Gorgon's head once more.

Perseus then took his bride home to Seriphus, where he
ound Polydectes trying to compel Danae to marry him.
He petrified him with the Gorgon's head, which he there-
pon presented to Minerva as a decoration for the centre
f her shield, and returned their gifts to the gods who had
elped him. At some funeral games at Larisa he acci-
entally killed his grandfather Acrisius with a discus,
nd thus the oracle was fulfilled. Perseus afterwards
ounded Mycēnae, and one of his descendants was
Hercules.

HERCULES

Hercules, in Greek Hēraclēs, was the son of Jupiter
nd Alcmēna, the grand-daughter of Perseus and Andro-
eda. He was brought up at Thebes by his step-father,
mphitryon, son of Alcēūs, and is often called Alcīdes,
descendant of Alceus.' While still an infant he was
ttacked by two snakes sent by Juno, who was jealous
f him all his life, but with supernatural strength he was
ble to strangle them. After being educated by the
entaur Chīron, a famous tutor of heroes, and by Linus,
he son of Apollo, whom he killed with his own lyre for
orrecting him too sharply, he married Megara, daughter
f King Creon of Thebes, but Juno afflicted him with
adness and he killed his own children, a crime which
e had to expiate by serving Eurystheus, king of Mycēnae,

also a son of Jupiter, for twelve years. Eurystheu
imposed the following twelve labours upon him.

1. The Nemean Lion, which could not be killed by an
human weapon. Hercules strangled it and wore its ski
on his head and shoulders. 2. The Lernean Hydra,
water-snake with nine heads, each one of which grew int
two more when it was cut off. His nephew Iolāus pre
vented the growth of more heads by searing with
burning torch the place where they had been cut off, an
Hercules thus managed to kill the monster and dipped hi
arrows in its poisonous blood. 3. The Arcadian Stag
with golden antlers and brazen hoofs, which he caugh
after a year's chase. 4. The Erymanthian Boar, whic
he caught by tiring it out in a snowdrift. 5. The Augea
Stables, belonging to King Augēas of Elis, from whic
Hercules had to cleanse the dirt of years in one day. H
did so by making the rivers Alphēus and Pēnēus flo
through the stables. 6. The Stymphalian Birds, which b
roused with a brazen rattle and then shot down with hi
arrows. 7. The Cretan Bull, which had been sen
by Neptune for Mīnos to sacrifice. Hercules brough
it to Eurystheus, and it was allowed to settle at Mara
thon, where Thēseūs captured it later. 8. The Thracia
Mares of Diomēdēs, which lived on human flesh. Her
cules tamed them by giving them their master to eat
After this labour Hercules went on the Argonauti
expedition, which will be described later.[1] 9. The Gird
of Hippŏlўtē, queen of the Amazons, which he obtaine
for the daughter of Eurystheus by defeating the Amazon
in battle. 10. The Oxen of Gērўŏnes, a three-heade
giant living in the far west where Hercules set up th
' Pillars of Hercules ' at the Straits of Gibraltar. H
killed the giant and drove his cattle back to Greece
on his way through Italy killing another giant, Cācu

[1] See pages 238–240.

who attempted to steal the oxen. 11. The Golden Apples of the Hesperides. After defeating the Libyan giant Antaēus in a wrestling match and killing the cruel king Būsīris, who used to sacrifice all strangers, and shooting the eagle that tormented Prometheus, Hercules persuaded Atlas to go and fetch the apples while he supported the heavens instead, but when Atlas obtained the apples he refused to take up his burden again, until he was induced to do so by a trick. 12. Cerberus, the three-headed dog of the Underworld, which Hercules succeeded in dragging up to Eurystheus, on his way releasing Theseus from Hades. Eurystheus in terror returned the dog to Hell and set Hercules free from his bondage.

Returning to Thebes at last Hercules wrestled with Death and restored to life the faithful Alcestis, the only one who was willing to die for her husband Admētus. In a fit of madness he then killed Iphitus, brother of Iŏlē, princess of Oechalia, whom he wished to marry, and to expiate the crime had to serve Omphălē, queen of Lydia, for three years; she wore his lion's skin while he spun wool, dressed as a woman. At about this time he took part in the famous Calydonian Boar-hunt, and also killed Laomedon, king of Troy, for his treachery.[1]

He then wooed and married Dēïănīra, after defeating his rival the river-god Achelōus in single combat, and set out to revenge himself on Oechalia for the loss of Iole; he sacked the town and carried off the princess, stopping at Trāchis on the way back to make a sacrifice to Jupiter, for which he asked Deianira to send him a sacrificial robe. Fearing that he was in love with Iole, his wife first steeped the robe in the blood of the centaur Nessus, who had attempted to abduct her while carrying her across a river some time before. Hercules had shot him with his arrows and Nessus treacherously told Deianira that she

[1] See page 250.

should keep his blood to use as a love-charm if ever she
lost her husband's love, but it proved to be a terrible poison
which burnt and tortured his whole body. Realizing what
she had done Deianira killed herself, and Hercules mounted
a funeral pyre on Mount Oeta, which he begged his friends
to kindle and thus put him out of his agony. Only
Philoctētēs ventured to do so, and was given as a
reward the bow and arrows of Hercules, which played
an important part in the fall of Troy. After his death
Hercules was carried off to Olympus and was reconciled
to Juno, marrying her daughter Hēbē, the goddess of
youth.

JASON AND THE ARGONAUTS

Aeson, king of Iolcus in Thessaly, was expelled from the
throne by his brother Pelias, and sent his son Jāson to
be educated by the centaur Chīron. When he grew up,
Jason decided to recover his father's kingdom, and on
his way to Iolcus came to a river in full flood, over which
an old woman asked him to carry her. He took her
across, and she turned into a beautiful woman, who said
that she was the goddess Juno and that she would always
help him. He had lost a shoe in the river, which reminded
Pelias of an oracle that he would lose his kingdom to a
man wearing only one sandal, but he received his visitor
kindly and when Jason revealed his name Pelias promised
to resign the kingdom to him if he would first fetch the
Golden Fleece, the story of which was as follows.

Athamas, king of Thebes, had two children, Phrixus
and Hellē, who had to escape from their wicked step-
mother on the back of a winged ram with a golden fleece.
In their flight Helle fell into the sea which was called the
Hellespont after her, but Phrixus was brought safely to
Colchis, on the eastern shores of the Black Sea, where
King Aeētes received him hospitably. The ram was

acrificed to Jupiter, and its fleece was hung up in a grove
of trees at Colchis, where it was guarded by a sleepless
dragon. Jason willingly undertook the dangerous quest
and invited all the leading heroes of Greece to accompany
him, including Hercules, Pēleūs, Telamon, Castor and
Pollux, Admētus, Meleāger, Orpheūs, Thēseūs and
Pīrithŏus. With the help of Minerva, the craftsman
Argus built a fifty-oared vessel, the first ship that ever
sailed the seas, which was called the Argo after its
builder, and its crew were called the Argonauts.

The expedition set sail, and after a year's stay at Lemnos
with Queen Hypsĭpўlē lost the great warrior Hercules,
for his page, the beautiful Hylas, was drawn down into
a pool in Mysia by the water-nymphs, who fell in love
with him; Hercules searched everywhere for him, and
the Argo had to sail without either of them. Zētēs and
Cǎlǎis, winged sons of Boreas, drove off the Harpies, birds
with the faces of women who swooped down and defiled
the food of Phīneūs, a blind prophet; in gratitude
Phineus warned the Argonauts that the worst danger
that threatened them was the passage of the Symplē-
gades, two rocks at the entrance to the Bosporus that
clashed together and crushed ships passing between them.
They sent a dove to fly ahead of them, and when the
rocks came together and caught the tail-feathers of the
bird they sped the Argo through the passage as fast as
wind and oars could drive it while the rocks were re-
bounding from the shock. The rocks then became
anchored permanently to the bottom.

At last the Argonauts reached Colchis and were entertained by Aeetes, who was willing to surrender the
Golden Fleece if Jason would perform certain tasks.
These were to yoke two brazen-footed, fire-breathing
bulls, plough the field of Mars, and sow it with a dragon's
teeth, from which armed men would spring up to attack

the sower. Jason could never have done this alone, but Mēdēa, the king's daughter and a witch, had fallen in love with him and gave him a magic ointment to protect him against the fire, so that he managed to plough the field with the fiery bulls and sow the dragon's teeth. He threw a stone among the armed men who sprang up from the ground, whereupon they fought one another until all were killed. Medea then led Jason by night to the grove and put the dragon to sleep with an enchanted potion, while her lover removed the Golden Fleece in safety. She thereupon sailed away in the Argo with Jason and her brother Absyrtus.

Aeetes at once set off in pursuit, but delayed to pick up the limbs of Absyrtus, who (by Medea's advice) had been murdered, cut up and thrown overboard to achieve this object. The Argonauts thus escaped and came first to the island of the enchantress Circē and then to the sweet-singing Sirens, who lured passing sailors to ship-wreck, but Orpheus played a magic song on his lute and brought them past safely. They made their way between the sea-monster Scylla and the whirlpool Charybdis, in the Straits of Messina, and were driven by a storm to the coast of Libya, where they had to carry the Argo through the desert on their shoulders for twelve days, but at last they returned to Iolcus after many other adven-tures, bringing the Golden Fleece with them.

Pelias refused to resign the throne to Jason, so Medea, who had restored Aeson to youth by her magic art by boiling him in a cauldron, induced Pelias' daughters to treat their father in the same way so that he too could become young again, but she had changed the ingredients of the magic brew and Pelias perished. She and Jason had to flee to Corinth, where they lived happily until Jason wanted to divorce Medea and marry Glaucē, daughter of King Creon. Medea pretended to agree, and sent Glauce a wedding garment, but it was steeped in poison, which killed her in great agony. Medea then slew her own children before their father's eyes, and escaped to Athens in a chariot drawn by winged dragons ; Jason died soon afterwards. At Athens Medea married King Aegeūs, but when she tried to poison his son, Theseus, who had just arrived home from Troezen, the king expelled her and she returned to Colchis, where she was reconciled to her family and eventually died without doing any more mischief.

THESEUS

Aegeūs, king of Athens, married Aethra, daughter of Pittheūs, king of Troezen, but he had to leave her behind when he went home, first placing his sword and sandals under a large rock and telling his wife that if a son should be born to them he was to lift the rock as soon as he grew old enough and bring what he found under it as a token to his father at Athens. Thēseūs was born, and lived at Troezen till he was about sixteen, when he rolled away the rock and took possession of his father's sword and sandals. He then set out to find Aegeus at Athens.

On his way he had many adventures. At the Isthmus of Corinth he killed Sinis, who used to capture travellers, bend down two pine trees and tie his victims to the tree-tops, so that they were torn to pieces when the trees straightened up again. At Megara he overcame the robber Scīron, who compelled passers-by to wash his feet and while they were doing so would kick them over a cliff into the sea ; Theseus treated him in the same way. Finally he freed the country from the brigand Procrustes, who used to lay his victims on a bed, cutting off their feet if they were too long for it, and stretching them on a rack if they were too short ; he was made to fit his own bed and was then killed. When Theseus reached Athens he found that Aegeus had married the witch Medea after she had left Jason at Corinth. She prepared a cup of poison for her step-son, but Aegeus recognised Theseus by the sword which he had found under the rock and banished Medea and accepted Theseus as his son and heir. Theseus then did Athens a great service by ridding the land of the fierce Bull of Marathon, which Hercules had brought from Crete. His next exploit was the slaying of the Minotaur.

Many years before, Jupiter had fallen in love with Europa, princess of Tyre, and came to her in the shape of a bull, on whose back she ventured to climb. The bull swam off with her to Crete, where she became the mother of Mīnōs, who after his death was one of the judges in the Underworld. His grandson, also called Minos, a famous king of Crete, married Pasïphäē and had two daughters, Ariadne and Phaedra. Pasiphae fell in love with a bull sent out of the sea by Neptune and gave birth to the Mīnotaur, a monster half-man, half-bull, which Minos kept in a labyrinth constructed by a skilful Athenian craftsman called Daedalus ; this man had murdered his nephew out of jealousy for his having invented the saw and compasses, and had fled to Crete to escape punishment. The Athenians treacherously killed Minos' son Androgeos, and Minos compelled them to send an annual tribute of seven youths and seven maidens to the Minotaur. Theseus resolved to slay the monster and free Athens from this tribute.

He volunteered to be one of the fourteen victims and set off for Crete, promising to hoist white sails on his return as a signal of success instead of the black sails generally used on this voyage. Minos' daughter Ariadne fell in love with him and gave him a sword and a clue of thread to help him find his way out of the labyrinth, and with this assistance he killed the Minotaur, escaped from the maze and eloped with Ariadne, but he cruelly abandoned her on the island of Naxos and returned to Athens without her. The god Bacchus found Ariadne on Naxos, married her, and raised her to the sky as the constellation of the ' Cretan Crown '.

After the death of the Minotaur Daedalus was forbidden by Minos to leave Crete, so he made wings for himself and his son Ícarus, fastening them on with wax. They flew away, but Icarus forgot his father's warning and went too near the sun, so the wax melted, his wings fell off, and he was plunged into the sea and drowned.

Another incident in Minos' life took place when he was besieging Megara. King Nīsus had a purple lock of hair on which his life depended, and his daughter Scylla, who had fallen in love with Minos, cut off her father's lock, thus causing his death and the fall of the city. Minos despised such treachery and dragged Scylla through the sea tied to the stern of his ship. She was turned into a sea-bird called Ciris and was constantly pursued by Nisus in the form of an eagle.

When Theseus returned home from Naxos he forgot to hoist the white sails, and Aegeus thought that he was dead and threw himself into the sea. Theseus thus became king of Athens and married the Amazon Hippŏ̆ytē; their son was Hippolytus. Soon afterwards Theseus took part in the Argonautic expedition and the Calydonian Boar-hunt, and when Hippolyte died he married Phaedra, sister of Ariadne. His son Hippolytus was now grown up and Phaedra fell in love with him, but he refused to return her love and in her shame and despair she hanged herself, leaving a letter saying that Hippolytus was the cause of her death. Theseus thought that his son was guilty and called upon Neptune to destroy him, which the sea-god did by sending a sea-

monster to frighten Hippolytus' horses as he was driving
along the shore.   He was thrown out and killed, learning
just before his death that Theseus had discovered his
innocence.

Theseus' great friend Pīrĭthŏus, at whose wedding-feast
a great battle had been fought in defence of the bride by
his people, the Lapithae, against the Centaurs, had also
lost his wife, and they both determined to marry a
daughter of Jupiter.   Theseus carried off Helen, daughter
of Lēda, from Sparta, although she was only nine years
old, but her brothers Castor and Pollux rescued her.
Pirithous more ambitiously wanted to capture Pro
serpine[1], wife of Pluto, king of the Underworld.   The
two friends descended to Hell and attacked Proserpine,
but they were seized by Pluto and tied to a rock.
While he was fetching the dog Cerberus Hercules released
Theseus, but the more guilty Pirithous had to stay there
for ever.   During Theseus' absence from Athens a rebellion
took place and he had to take refuge in Scȳros, where he
was eventually killed by king Lycomēdēs.   In historical
times the 'bones of Theseus' were brought back from
Scyros by Cimon, father of Miltiades, and placed in
temple called the Thesēum in Athens.

THE CALYDONIAN BOAR-HUNT

Althaea, wife of Oēnēus, king of Calydon, had a son
called Meleāger, at whose birth the Fates appeared and
said that the new-born child would live until a brand
then burning on the hearth was consumed.   His mother
snatched up the brand, extinguished it, and kept it
carefully hidden in a chest.

When Meleager was grown up, Diana sent a boar to
ravage the countryside, because she had not received

[1] See page 226.

acrifice from Oeneus. Meleager had just returned from
he Argonautic expedition and collected many of the
eroes who had taken part in it to join in the boar-hunt.
he hunters included Jason, Theseus, Pirithous, Castor
nd Pollux, Admetus, Pēleūs and Telamon, Laertes, and
he maiden Atalanta, daughter of Schoēneūs, who was
amed for her beauty, chastity, and skill in the chase.
wo of the heroes were killed by the boar, but Atalanta
as the first to wound it, and when Meleager eventually
illed it he gave a trophy of the head and hide to Atalanta,
ith whom he was in love. His mother's brothers pro-
ested so strongly against his giving her the prize that he
illed them both in a fit of anger. His mother Althaea
as torn between love for her brothers and love for her
on, but at last sisterly love won the day and she threw
nto the fire the brand on which Meleager's life depended.
s soon as it was consumed he died, and Althaea in
emorse committed suicide.

After this Atalanta was still unwilling to marry, but
er father persuaded her to agree to marry the first man
ho could defeat her in a race. She defeated many
hallengers, all of whom had to pay the penalty of death
or their failure. At last Hippŏmĕnēs (or by another
ory, Mīlănĭon) entered for the race and by the advice
f Venus carried three of the golden apples of the Hes-
erides, one of which he threw down before Atalanta
henever she began to draw ahead. Each time she
opped to pick it up, and thus Hippomenes won the race
nd his bride.

CASTOR AND POLLUX

Also known as the Dioscūri, 'sons of Zeus', and
emini, 'the Twins', these were the twin sons of Jupiter
nd the Spartan girl Lēda, whom Jupiter visited in the

form of a swan ; Castor was a famous horseman and
charioteer, and Pollux a great boxer. They took part
in the Argonautic expedition and the Calydonian boar
hunt, and rescued their sister Helen when she was carried
off by Theseus. In a quarrel with the brothers Idas and
Lynceūs, Castor, who was mortal, was killed, and Pollux
asked to be permitted to give up his immortality for his
brother, but Jupiter allowed them instead to spend alter
nate days in Olympus and Hades. They were regarded as
the protectors of sailors, to whom they appeared as ' St
Elmo's fire', and they became the constellation Gemini
They were said by the Romans to have assisted them
against the Latins at the battle of Lake Regillus in 496 B.C

ORPHEUS AND EURYDICE

Orpheūs, son of Apollo and the muse Calliŏpē, was such
a skilful musician that when he sang and played his lyre
he could make rivers stand still, mountains and tree
follow him, and the wild beasts gather round to listen
He went on the Argonautic expedition and saved his
companions from shipwreck and death by drowning with
his music the magic song of the Sirens. He married
the beautiful nymph Eurўdĭcē, and lived happily with
her until she was bitten by a snake concealed in the gras
while she was fleeing from a shepherd called Aristaeus
and died. Orpheus was heart-broken and at last wa
allowed to bring her back from Hades (where his song
enthralled the guilty even in the midst of their torments)
provided that he did not look back at her until he reached
the world above, but he forgot the condition imposed by
Proserpine, looked round, and lost Eurydice for ever
He mourned her in solitude for many months, and refused
to join in the rites of the Bacchantes, female worshipper
of Bacchus, in Thrace, so they tore him to pieces and

hrew his head into the river Hebrus. It floated down
tream and across the sea to Lesbos, while the lifeless
ongue still continued to lament for Eurydice.

ARION, AND OTHER STORIES

Arīon was a poet of Lesbos who while returning from
taly to Corinth was thrown overboard by the sailors for
he sake of the money which he had with him. A
olphin, enchanted by the song which he asked to be
llowed to sing before being thrown into the sea, carried
im safely to land on its back.

Bellerophon of Corinth refused to accept the love of
ntēa, queen of Argos, who accused him to her husband
f having attacked her. The king sent Bellerophon with
letter to his father-in-law Iŏbătēs, asking him that the
earer should be killed, so Iobates sent him to fight the
himēra, a fire-breathing monster, part lion, part goat,
art dragon, which Bellerophon overcame with the help
f his winged horse Pēgasus.

Hero and Leander were a pair of lovers who lived on
pposite sides of the Hellespont. Leander used to swim
cross every night from Abȳdos to meet his love at Ses-
os, but one stormy night he was drowned and Hero in
er despair drowned herself too.

Philomēla and Procnē were daughters of Pandīon of
thens. Procne married Tērēus, who wronged Philomela
nd cut out her tongue to ensure her silence, but she
mbroidered the tale of her sufferings in needlework and
ent it to her sister. Procne in revenge killed her own
on Itys and served up his flesh to his father Tereus, who
ursued the sisters, but he was changed into a hoopoe,
hilomela into a nightingale, and Procne into a swallow.

Pȳramus and Thisbē were lovers who used to speak to
ch other through the wall that separated their houses

I 2

in Babylon, for their parents forbade them to meet
They agreed to meet one night at Nīnus' tomb outsid
the city, but Thisbe arrived first and fled from a lion
leaving her cloak, which the lion tore with his blood
jaws. Pyramus found the cloak and thought tha
Thisbe was dead, so he killed himself, and Thisbe on he
return found his body and killed herself too. The whit
mulberry tree under which the lovers stabbed themselve
afterwards bore red fruit because of their blood.

OEDIPUS AND HIS CHILDREN

Lāius, king of Thebes, married Jocasta, sister of Creo
but an oracle had said that he would die at the hands of
his son, so as soon as a child was born he bound its fee
together, transfixed them with a spike, and exposed i
on Mt. Cithaeron to die. A shepherd brought the infar
to King Polybus of Corinth, who adopted it as his ow
son, calling him Oedipus, or 'Swell-foot', from the swellin
caused by the spike. When he grew up Oedipus was tol
by the Delphic oracle that he would kill his father an
marry his mother, so he left Corinth at once to avoid a
risk of doing such a wrong to his supposed parents. A
some crossroads on his journey he quarrelled with
stranger over the right of way and killed him in a scuffle
the dead man was Laius, and thus part of the oracle wa
fulfilled, though Oedipus did not know whom he ha
killed.

Thebes was being plagued by the Sphinx, a monster wit
a woman's head and a winged lion's body, which sat on
rock outside the city and asked passers-by a riddl
tearing them to pieces if they could not answer it. Creo
brother-in-law of Laius, offered the kingdom and h
sister in marriage to anyone who could destroy th
monster, an offer which Oedipus accepted. The ridd

vas "What creature has four feet in the morning, two
at noon, and three in the evening?", and Oedipus gave
the correct answer, "A man, who crawls on all fours when
an infant, walks upright in the prime of life, and hobbles
with a stick in old age." The Sphinx in rage hurled
herself over the cliff, and Oedipus became king and
married his own mother Jocasta.

They lived happily together for many years and had
our children, Ětĕoclēs, Polynīcēs, Antĭgŏnē and Ismēnē,
but at last a pestilence attacked the country, which could
only be stopped, according to an oracle, if the slayer of
Laius was expelled. On learning from the blind prophet
Tiresias that he himself was the guilty man, Oedipus
blinded himself and Jocasta committed suicide ; Oedipus
then went into exile as an outcast and a beggar, accompanied only by the faithful Antigone, and at last reached
sanctuary at Colōnus, near Athens, where he died in
peace.

His two sons meanwhile became kings of Thebes, each
agreeing to reign for a year. Eteocles refused to resign the
throne at the end of the first year, so Polynices obtained
help from Adrastus, king of Argos, whose daughter he had
married. Adrastus led an army to expel Eteocles, and
each of the seven gates of the city was defended by a
champion and attacked by one of the famous ' Seven
against Thebes', seven warriors who included Adrastus
and Polynices. The two brothers killed each other in
single combat, and the invaders were driven off with the
loss of all the seven except Adrastus himself. Creon became king and refused to allow the body of the rebellious
Polynices to be buried, but Antigone could not let her
brother be deprived of the funeral rites without which
his spirit could not rest, and in spite of the strict pro-
hibition against it she gave his remains ritual burial with
three handfuls of dust. Creon ordered her to be buried

alive in a cave, where she hanged herself, and her be
trothed, Haemon, son of Creon, stabbed himself when h
found her dead body. Creon received the final punish
ment for his brutality by learning that his wife had als
committed suicide on hearing of Haemon's death.

LEGENDS OF TROY

The Foundation of the City

Dardanus, son of Jupiter, settled on the Asiatic shore
of the Hellespont and married the daughter of Teucer
Their grandson was Trōs, and his son was Īlus, th
founder of the city of Troy, or Īlium, whose inhabitant
were called Trojans, Teucri, or Dardanidae. Laomedon
son of Ilus, asked the gods Apollo and Neptune to buil
the walls of the city, but refused them their promise
reward on the completion of the work. Neptune therefor
sent a sea-monster against Troy. Laomedon's daughter
Hēsĭŏnē, was going to be sacrificed to the monster, bu
Hercules killed it on condition that he should receive th
famous horses of Tros as a reward. Laomedon agai
withheld the prize, so Hercules later killed him and gav
Hesione in marriage to Telamon, king of Salamis, whos
son was the great hero Ajax.

The Origin of the Trojan War

Laomedon's son, Priam, then became king, marrie
Hecuba, and had many children, of whom the best know
were the brave warrior Hector, the prophetess Cassandra
and Paris, the cause of the war. Before Paris was bor
Hecuba dreamed that she had given birth to a flamin
torch, which was interpreted to mean that her son woul

uin his country, so he was left on Mount Ida to die ; but
ie was brought up by shepherds and married a mountain
nymph called Oĕnōnē, with whom he lived happily until
he ' Judgment of Paris ' took place. At the marriage
f Pēleūs and Thĕtis, Eris, the goddess of discord, was not
invited, and in anger she threw down on the table a golden
apple inscribed ' For the fairest '. The goddesses Juno,
Minerva and Venus all claimed the prize and the decision
was referred to Paris, to whom Juno offered power and
wealth, Minerva wisdom and success in war, and Venus
the loveliest woman in Greece as his wife ; he gave the
prize to Venus.

Soon after this Paris was acknowledged by Priam and
Hecuba as their son, and was sent on a visit to Greece,
where he was entertained by Menelāus, king of Sparta,
and his wife, the beautiful Helen, the daughter of Jupiter
and Lēda, and the sister of Clytemnestra and Castor and
Pollux. She had been wooed by all the heroes of Greece,
who on the suggestion of Ulysses swore to abide by her
choice and defend her and her husband after she was
married. She chose Menelaus, and bore him a daughter
called Hermĭŏnē. Paris and Helen fell in love with each
other and eloped to Troy, and thus the promise of Venus
was fulfilled ; this also caused the Trojan War, because
in accordance with their oath all Helen's former suitors
were bound to help her husband to recover her.

PREPARATIONS FOR THE WAR

Agamemnon, king of Mycēnae, began to collect a force
f Greeks to attack Troy with his brother Menelaus ; the
two were known as the Atrīdae, or sons of Atreus. Most
f the chiefs came willingly, but the crafty Ulysses, son of
āertes, did not want to leave his wife Pēnĕlŏpē and his
young son Tēlemachus, and pretended to be mad; the

trick was exposed by Palamēdēs, who placed Telemachus on the ground in front of a moving plough, whereupon Ulysses showed his sanity by saving his son ; he afterwards had his revenge on Palamedes. The greatest warrior of the Greeks, Achilles, son of Pēleūs, was kept back by his mother, the sea-nymph Thetis, who disguised him as a girl at the court of Lycomēdēs of Scȳros, but when Ulysses set weapons before him he could not refrain from grasping them and so revealed himself and went willingly with his friend Patroclus to Troy.

After ten years' preparation a fleet of a thousand ships and a host of a hundred thousand men assembled at Aulis under the command of Agamemnon, who in ignorance killed a hind sacred to the goddess Diana. As a punishment she sent a calm to prevent the fleet from sailing and the prophet Calchas declared that only the sacrifice of Agamemnon's daughter Īphĭgĕnīa would appease the angry goddess, so the king had to send for his daughter under pretence of wishing to marry her to Achilles, and was about to sacrifice her when Diana relented and substituted a deer ; Iphigenia was carried off to be the priestess of Diana in the land of the Tauri (the Crimea) from which her brother Orestes afterwards rescued her. The Greek fleet thus obtained a fair wind and set sail, but on the way Philoctetes, who now had the bow and arrows of Hercules, had to be marooned on Lemnos because he had been bitten in the foot by a serpent and the smell of the poisoned wound and his cries of pain were intolerable to his companions.

THE WAR

Whoever landed first at Troy was fated to die, but Protesilāus bravely leaped ashore and was killed by Hector. The gods allowed him to return for three hours to his mourning wife Laodamīa, who on his departure

:illed herself. The Greeks attempted to storm the city
at once, but were repulsed and settled down to a ten
years' siege, though many skirmishes were fought on the
plain between Troy and the sea. Agamemnon received
among the plunder of a neighbouring city a girl called
Chrȳsēïs, daughter of a priest of Apollo, and Achilles
received one called Brīsēïs, whom he was forced to hand
over to Agamemnon because Apollo sent a plague that
could only be stopped by the return of Chryseis to her
father. Achilles was so vexed at this that he withdrew
from the fighting and sulked in his tent.

During his absence the Greeks were driven back and
begged Achilles to help them, which he refused to do,
though he lent his armour to his friend Patroclus and let
him lead his followers, the Myrmidons, against the enemy.
Despite Achilles' warnings he advanced too far and was
killed by Hector and stripped of the armour. Achilles
lamented his friend bitterly and swore to kill Hector in
revenge, and after his mother Thetis had asked Vulcan
to forge new armour for him he drove the Trojans into
the city, chasing Hector three times round the walls and
finally killing him at the Scaean gate ; as he died, Hector
prophesied that Achilles himself would perish there.
Achilles then bound the corpse to his chariot and dragged
it thrice round the walls of Troy before the eyes of his
parents and his faithful wife Andrŏmăchē, but he gener-
ously returned the body to Priam, who came himself to
ask for his son's corpse.

Penthesilēa, a daughter of Mars, now led an army of
Amazons against the Greeks, and Achilles unwillingly
killed her after a brave struggle. He also fought Memnon,
the Ethiopian son of Tithōnus and Aurōra, the dawn
goddess. Aurora and Thetis each begged Jupiter to aid
her own son ; Jupiter placed the fates of the two heroes,
who both had divine armour made by Vulcan, in his

golden balance, and Memnon's weighed down the scal
and so he was killed. Achilles finally attacked Troy
itself, but as he fought at the Scaean gate Apollo directed
an arrow shot by Paris at his heel, the only place in which
he was vulnerable, for Thetis had dipped him in the Styx
as an infant to protect him against all wounds, holding
him by the right heel as she did so, so that he was un
protected in that spot alone. Achilles was thus slain, and
his body was recovered by Ajax and Ulysses ; after his
funeral his arms were to be awarded to the hero who had
fought most bravely. The decision went to Ulysses, and
Ajax in his anger lost his reason, killed some sheep which
in his madness he thought were the Greek leaders, and
then committed suicide.

THE FALL OF TROY

The Greeks had lost their best and bravest warrior in
Achilles, and guile now had to take the place of force
Ulysses learnt from Helenus, a son of Priam who had the
gift of prophecy, that the Greeks would take Troy only
if (i) the son of Achilles fought for them, (ii) the arrow
of Hercules were used against the city, and (iii) the
Palladium, an image of Minerva in Troy, fell into their
hands. The son of Achilles, Neoptolemus or Pyrrhus
willingly came from Scyros, and he (or Diomēdēs) and
Ulysses eventually persuaded Philoctetes, who was still
marooned at Lemnos, bitterly resentful against the
Greeks for leaving him there, to bring the arrows of
Hercules to Troy, where the wound in his foot was cured
by Machāon, son of Aesculapius the god of healing
Philoctetes then joined in the fighting and mortally
wounded Paris, who remembered a prophecy that only
his deserted wife Oenone could cure his wounds and
begged her to heal him. At first she refused, but she soon

epented and went down to Troy, only to find Paris
already dead, so she killed herself beside his funeral pyre.
Ulysses and Diomedes then managed to remove the
Palladium, the position of which Ulysses had discovered
previously by entering the city disguised as a beggar, when
Helen had recognized him but had not betrayed him.
All was now ready for the final stratagem.

A craftsman called Epēus made a huge Wooden Horse,
in which many heroes concealed themselves, while the
rest of the host set fire to the camp and sailed away,
though only as far as the island of Tenedos.   The Trojans
flocked out of the city to examine the horse, and Lāŏcŏōn,
a priest of Apollo, begged them not to touch the ' Greek
gift ', even hurling a spear at it, but while he and his two
sons were sacrificing to Neptune, two sea-serpents came
out of the sea and killed all three of them ; this convinced
the Trojans that Laocoon had been impious in attacking
the horse.   Besides this, a pretended Greek deserter
called Sinon persuaded them that the Greeks had gone
home, leaving the horse as a tribute to placate Minerva,
who was vexed at the theft of her image.   In spite of the
protests of King Priam's daughter Cassandra, to whom
Apollo had given the gift of prophecy that no-one should
ever believe, because she had rejected his love, the Trojans
dragged the horse inside the city amid great rejoicing.

That night Sinon released the warriors from inside the
horse and signalled to the Greek fleet to return from
Tenedos.   Attacked from within and without, the Trojans
fought bravely but in vain, and the city was captured and
burnt.   Neoptolemus killed one of Priam's sons before
his own eyes, in spite of the old king's appeal to him to
remember his chivalrous father Achilles, and then killed
Priam himself ; Menelaus found Helen as beautiful as
ever, and took her back to Sparta, where they lived
happily for many years ; Cassandra was given to Aga-

memnon ; and the only Trojan hero who escaped was
Aenēas, whose adventures will be described later.[1]

THE FAMILY OF AGAMEMNON AND HIS FATE

The family of King Agamemnon was under a curse, which
originated in the following way. His great-grandfather,
Tantalus, a son of Jupiter, had served the flesh of his own
son Pelops to the gods at a banquet, but only Cĕrēs, who
was still mourning for Proserpine, failed to recognize the
human flesh and ate one shoulder. Pelops was restored
to life and the missing shoulder was replaced by an ivory
one. Tantalus was punished by being made to stand in
a lake in Hades with bunches of grapes hanging close to
his mouth, but whenever he tried to satisfy his raging
thirst the water and the fruit receded from his lips
Pelops grew up and won a chariot race against Oenŏmăus,
king of Ēlis and Pisa, the prize for which was the king's
daughter Hippŏdămīa, but he had bribed the charioteer,
Myrtilus, to remove the linch-pins of the king's chariot,
so that Oenomaus was thrown out and killed. Pelops
refused to pay the promised reward and flung Myrtilus
into the sea ; Myrtilus' last words were a terrible curse
on the whole house of Pelops.

The two sons of Pelops, Atreūs and Thyestes, killed
their half-brother and had to flee to Mycēnae, of which
Atreus became king. Thyestes fell in love with Atreus'
wife, and was punished by having his own children served
up to him by Atreus at a banquet. Thyestes cursed his
brother, and afterwards became the father of Aegisthus,
who was adopted by Atreus, and when Atreus sent
Aegisthus to kill Thyestes, father and son recognized
each other and Aegisthus killed his uncle Atreus instead
Atreus' two sons were Agamemnon and Menelāus.

[1] See pages 261-263.

After the fall of Troy Agamemnon returned home with Cassandra as his captive ; she prophesied misfortune for him, but he did not believe her warnings. His wife Clytemnestra had never forgiven him for being willing to sacrifice Iphigenia at Aulis, and in his absence at Troy she had fallen in love with his cousin Aegisthus. Together they plotted Agamemnon's death and killed him as soon as he returned home, while he was having a bath ; Aegisthus then became king instead. Agamemnon's brave daughter Ēlectra had conveyed her young brother Orestes to a place of safety, and when he grew up he sent the false news that he had been killed in a chariot race ; he then came to Mycenae to avenge his father and killed both his mother Clytemnestra and Aegisthus.

For this crime of matricide Orestes was relentlessly pursued by the avenging Furies, until he appealed to Apollo and was told to bring back the statue of Diana from the land of the Tauri (the Crimea). His sister Iphigenia had been brought to this place by Diana from Aulis and was now the priestess whose duty was to sacrifice all strangers to the goddess. She was about to sacrifice Orestes and his friend Pÿlădes when she recognized her brother, and all three managed to escape with the image of Diana. Being still pursued by the Furies, Orestes appealed to Minerva at Athens and was tried by the court of the Areopagus. The votes for and against were equal, but Minerva gave her casting vote in his favour and he was acquitted, afterwards marrying Hermione, daughter of Menelaus and Helen, and settling down as king of Mycenae.

THE ADVENTURES OF ULYSSES

After the ten year's siege of Troy the brave and crafty Ulysses (in Greek Odyssēus) had to wander for ten more

years before reaching his home in Ithaca. He and hi
companions were first driven to the land of the Lotus
eaters, where all who ate the plant forgot their homes and
wished to stay for ever. They then reached Sicily, the
home of the Cyclōpes, giants with only one eye in the
middle of their foreheads. Ulysses and twelve others
were shut up in the cave of the Cyclops Polyphēmus
who ate two of his prisoners at every meal, but he drank
deeply of some wine that Ulysses had brought with him
and fell into a drunken slumber, after blocking the mouth
of the cave with a huge stone. The Greeks then heated
the giant's staff in the fire and blinded him by thrusting
it into his single eye. When he cried for help his fellow
Cyclopes came but went away again on being told that
' No-man ' was hurting him, for Ulysses had said that his
name was ' No-man '. Ulysses tied each of his companions under the bellies of three sheep linked together,
he himself clinging to the wool of the ram, and thus they
escaped from the cave, though Polyphemus nearly sank
their departing ships with huge rocks.

After Aeolus, king of the winds, had given him a bag
with all the contrary winds tied up in it, Ulysses
reached Ithaca safely, but his comrades in curiosity
opened the bag and the winds rushed out and drove the
fleet away to the land of the cannibal Laestrygonians,
who sank all but one of the twelve ships. This last ship
reached Aeaea, the island of the enchantress Circē,
daughter of the sun-god, who turned half its crew into
swine with a magic potion. Eurylochus refused the
drink and told Ulysses what had happened ; Ulysses was
given a herb called ' moly ' by Mercury, which had the
power of counteracting the potion, and he changed his
friends back into human shape, but afterwards was
persuaded by Circe to stay with her for a year.

On Circe's advice Ulysses then visited the entrance of

Hades in the land of the Cimmerians. He dug a trench and made a sacrifice to the powers of darkness, whereupon the spirits of the dead came flocking up to drink the blood and recover their strength. He allowed the prophet Tīresias to approach first, and was warned by him how to escape his future dangers, and after conversing with many of his friends among the dead he continued on his voyage. He sailed safely past the sweet-singing but treacherous Sirens, who lured sailors to their doom, by filling the ears of his crew with wax, so that they should not hear the music, and by having himself bound to the mast, after giving strict orders to his comrades not to loose him in spite of all his entreaties. The next danger was the passage of the Straits of Messina, with the sea-monster Scylla on one side and the whirlpool Charybdis on the other. Ulysses got past with the loss of six men, and reached Trinacria (Sicily), where the Sun-god pastured his herds. Although they had sworn an oath not to touch them Ulysses' companions killed and ate some of the oxen, and to appease the angry god Jupiter destroyed the last ship and all its crew in a storm. Only Ulysses escaped, clinging to the mast for nine days, and reached Ogygia, the island of the nymph Calypso, with whom he had to stay for seven years, for the anger of Neptune still pursued him for having blinded the sea-god's son, Polyphemus. Finally he was allowed to depart on a raft and arrived at Scheria, the land of the Phaeacians, where he was entertained hospitably by King Alcinŏus, whose daughter, the beautiful Nausicăa, had found him asleep near the shore. He was given a ship and landed at last on Ithaca after twenty years' absence.

During this time his son Telemachus had grown up and had just gone off to look for him, and his wife Penelope was being wooed by many suitors, who believed him dead and were trying to make her marry one of them. She promised to do so after she had finished weaving a winding-sheet for Ulysses' old father, Laertes, but every night she unravelled what she had woven during the day ; the trick had now been discovered and the suitors demanded her immediate marriage. Minerva gave Ulysses the appearance of an old beggar, so that he should not be recognized, but he revealed himself to his faithful swine-herd Eumaeus and to Telemachus, who had just returned home, and they made a plan for revenge on the suitors. Telemachus with great difficulty persuaded his mother to agree to marry whoever could string the great bow of Ulysses, which he had left behind when he went to Troy, and Ulysses entered the house as a beggar. His faithful old dog Argus recognized him and died of joy, and his aged nurse Euryclea, while washing his feet, saw an old scar made by the tusks of a boar and knew that it was her master.

Next day after a great banquet Penelope invited the suitors to try to string Ulysses' bow and shoot an arrow through twelve axe-heads put side by side. None of them could even bend the bow, so among the jeers of the arrogant suitors the pretended beggar offered to try, and of course succeeded easily in performing both tasks. With the help of his son and Eumaeus he then killed all the suitors, and revealed himself in his right form to Penelope, who at first could not believe that it was her husband but finally acknowledged him with great joy. The story of Ulysses is told in Homer's *Odyssey* ; according to a later legend he placated the anger of Neptune and was eventually killed by Telegonus, his son by Circe, who came to Ithaca to find his father.

THE ADVENTURES OF AENEAS

Aenēas, the son of Anchīses and Venus, was a Trojan prince who fought bravely until Troy fell and then managed to escape with his son Iulus, or Ascanius, and his household gods, carrying on his shoulders his old father, but his wife Crĕūsa was lost in the burning city. He built a fleet and set out to find a new home in the land which first bore the Trojan race, the place where the Delian oracle declared he should live. After trying first to settle in Crete, Aeneas learnt in a dream that Italy was to be his future home, and on their way there the Trojans landed on the isle of the Harpies, birds with women's faces, who defiled their food and prophesied that they would never found a city until hunger forced them to eat their tables. The seer Helenus, a son of Priam, told Aeneas to visit the Sibyl, an old prophetess living at Cumae near Naples, and to settle in a place where he should see a white sow with a litter of thirty young.

They then touched at Sicily, where they rescued a Greek who had been left behind in Polyphemus' cave by Ulysses, and only just managed to escape from the angry giant. A storm drove them to North Africa, where Dīdo was building the walls of her newly-founded Carthage. She received them kindly and fell in love with Aeneas, but Jupiter ordered him to leave at once to follow his destiny, and in despair Dido cursed him and his descendants and stabbed herself on a funeral pyre as the ships sailed away.

Aeneas celebrated the anniversary of his father Anchises' death by holding sacrifices and games in Sicily, and visited the Sibyl at Cumae, who told him to pluck a Golden Bough which would enable him to visit the Underworld. Led by her he crossed the Styx and found his father among the dead; he saw all the future heroes of the Roman race, and also his old love Dido, who turned away from him in silence. The Trojans then landed at the mouth of the Tiber, where they consumed their ' tables ', which turned out to be the bread that they were using as plates. King Latīnus welcomed the strangers and promised his daughter Lavinia in marriage to Aeneas, but Juno, who was always hostile to the Trojans, roused Queen Amāta against them, and war broke out between them and the Latins under the leadership of Turnus, a Rutulian prince who had been betrothed to Lavinia. Aeneas sailed up the Tiber to get the help of the Arcadian Evander, and saw on the river bank a white sow with thirty young, as had been foretold by Helenus. Venus had meanwhile requested Vulcan to forge divine armour for her son, which she brought to him herself.

In Aeneas' absence Ascanius drove off an attack led by Turnus on the Trojan camp, and when Aeneas returned with Etruscan allies, Turnus killed Pallas, the son of Evander, and was rescued from meeting Aeneas only by the intervention of Juno. A single combat between the two leaders was agreed upon to settle the war, but fighting broke out again between the two armies until Aeneas and Turnus eventually met face to face. Aeneas wounded Turnus and would have spared him if he had not seen the spoils of Pallas which the Rutulian was wearing, and so he killed him in revenge. Virgil's great epic, the *Aeneid*,[1] ends at this point.

Aeneas married Lavinia and became king of the combined peoples ; one of his descendants was the Vestal Virgin Rhea Silvia, daughter of Numitor, the last king of Alba. She had two sons, Rōmulus and Rĕmus, by Mars, the god of war, but when their usurping uncle Amulius had them exposed on the banks of the Tiber they

[1] See page 211.

were saved by a she-wolf and brought up by a shepherd called Faustulus. They grew up and restored their grandfather Numitor to the throne, and decided to found a new city on the Tiber, agreeing to consult the omen of the flight of birds to see on which hill to build it. Romulus on the Palatine saw twelve vultures, while Remus on the Aventine saw only six, so Rome was founded on the Palatine, traditionally in 753 B.C. Remus despised the little walls of the new city and jumped over them, so he was killed, and Romulus ruled for 37 years and was eventually taken up to heaven during a thunderstorm, being afterwards worshipped as the god Quirīnus. Augustus and his family, which included Julius Caesar, claimed descent from Romulus and thus from Aeneas and Venus.

INDEX

PRINTED IN GREAT BRITAIN BY ROBERT MACLEHOSE AND CO. LTD.
THE UNIVERSITY PRESS, GLASGOW